CW01003666

Research Methods
Fundamental Principles

We work with leading authors to develop the strongest educational materials bringing cutting-edge thinking and best learning practice to a global market.

Under a range of well-known imprints, including Financial Times/Prentice Hall, Addison Wesley and Longman, we craft high quality print and electronic publications which help readers to understand and apply their content, whether studying or at work.

Pearson Custom Publishing enables our customers to access a wide and expanding range of market-leading content from world-renowned authors and develop their own tailor-made book. You choose the content that meets your needs and Pearson Custom Publishing produces a high-quality printed book.

To find out more about custom publishing, visit www.pearsoncustom.co.uk

A Pearson Custom Publication

Research Methods
Fundamental Principles

Compiled from:

Introduction to SPSS in Psychology:
For Version 16 and Earlier
Fourth Edition
by Dennis Howitt and Duncan Cramer

Introduction to Research Methods in Psychology
Second Edition
by Dennis Howitt and Duncan Cramer

Introduction to Statistics in Psychology
Fourth Edition
by Dennis Howitt and Duncan Cramer

Introduction to Research Methods and
Data Analysis in Psychology
Second Edition
by Darren Langdridge and Gareth Hagger-Johnson

Introduction to Research Methods and
Statistics in Psychology
by Ronald A. McQueen and Christina Knussen

Statistics without Maths for Psychology
Fourth Edition
by Christine P. Dancey and John Reidy

PEARSON
Custom
Publishing

Pearson Education Limited
Edinburgh Gate
Harlow
Essex CM20 2JE

And associated companies throughout the world

Visit us on the World Wide Web at:
www.pearsoned.co.uk

First published 2010
This Custom Book Edition © 2010 Published by Pearson Education Limited

Compiled from:

Introduction to SPSS in Psychology: For Version 16 and Earlier Fourth Edition
by Dennis Howitt and Duncan Cramer
ISBN 978 0 13 205164 4
Copyright © Prentice Hall Europe 1997
Copyright © Pearson Education Limited 2000, 2005, 2008

Introduction to Research Methods in Psychology Second Edition
by Dennis Howitt and Duncan Cramer
ISBN 978 0 13 205163 7
Copyright © Pearson Education Limited 2005, 2008

Introduction to Statistics in Psychology Fourth Edition
by Dennis Howitt and Duncan Cramer
ISBN 978 0 13 205161 3
Copyright © Prentice Hall Europe 1997
Copyright © Pearson Education Limited 2000, 2008

Introduction to Research Methods and Data Analysis in Psychology Second Edition
by Darren Langdridge and Gareth Hagger-Johnson
ISBN 978 0 13 198203 1
Copyright © Pearson Education Limited 2009

Introduction to Research Methods and Statistics in Psychology
by Ronald A. McQueen and Christina Knussen
ISBN 978 0 13 124940 0
Copyright © Pearson Education Limited 2006

Statistics without Maths for Psychology Fourth Edition
by Christine P. Dancey and John Reidy
ISBN 978 0 132 05160 6
Copyright © Pearson Education Limited 2007

All rights reserved. No part of this publication may be reproduced, stored in a
retrieval system, or transmitted in any form or by any means, electronic,
mechanical, photocopying, recording or otherwise, without either the prior
written permission of the publisher or a licence permitting restricted copying in
the United Kingdom issued by the Copyright Licensing Agency Ltd, Saffron House,
6–10 Kirby Street, London EC1N 8TS.

ISBN 978 1 84959 183 6

Printed and bound in Great Britain by 4edge, Hockley, www.4edge.co.uk "FSC Certified".

Contents

1 Basics of SPSS data entry and statistical analysis

Overview

■ This chapter gives the basics of operating SPSS on a personal computer. It includes data entry as well as saving files. There will be small variations in how SPSS is accessed from location to location. The basics are fairly obvious and quickly learnt. By following our instructions, you will quickly become familiar with the essential steps in conducting a statistical analysis.

■ Unfortunately, there is no gain without some effort in statistics. There are a number of statistical concepts that need to be understood in order to carry out a decent statistical analysis. Each of these is discussed and explained in this chapter. They include score variables versus nominal (category) variables, unrelated versus related designs, descriptive versus inferential statistics and significance testing.

■ The chapter provides detailed advice on how to select a statistical technique for the analysis of psychological data.

1.1 What is SPSS?

SPSS Releases 16, 15, 14, 13 and 12 are commonly available on university and college computers. Individuals may still be using earlier versions such as Releases 11 and 10. SPSS is by far the most widely used computer package for statistical analysis throughout the world. As such, learning to use SPSS is a transferable skill which is often a valuable asset in the job market. The program is used at all levels from students to specialist researchers, and in a great many academic fields and practical settings. One big advantage is that once the basics are learnt, SPSS is just as easy to use for simple analyses as for complex ones. The purpose of this introductory chapter is to enable beginners quickly to take advantage of the facilities of SPSS.

Most people nowadays are familiar with the basic operation of personal computers (PCs). The total novice though will not be at too much of a disadvantage since the elements of SPSS are quickly learnt. Users who have familiarity with, say, word processing will find much of this relevant to using SPSS – opening programs, opening files and saving files, for instance. Do not be afraid to experiment.

Since SPSS is commonly used in universities and colleges, many users will require a user name and a password that is obtained from their institution. Documentation is often available on registration at the college or university. If not, such documentation is usually easily available.

SPSS may be found as a shortcut among the on-screen icons or it may be found in the list of programs on Windows. Each institution has its own idiosyncracies as to where SPSS can be found.

This book is based on Release 16 of SPSS. Although it is slightly different from earlier releases, the users of earlier releases will probably not notice the differences as they follow the instructions given in this book.

1.2 To access SPSS

SPSS for Windows is generally accessed using buttons and menus in conjunction with clicks of the mouse. Consequently the quickest way of learning is simply to follow our steps and screenshots on a computer. The following sequence of screenshots is annotated with instructions labelled Step 1, Step 2, etc.

Step 1:

Double left click on the SPSS icon with the mouse if it appears anywhere in the window – otherwise click the Start button to find the list of programs, open the list of programs, and click on SPSS.

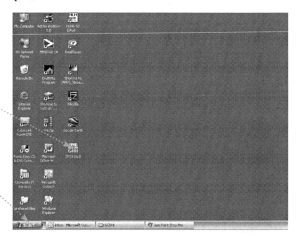

Step 2:

This screen eventually appears after a few moments. You could choose any of the options in the window. However, it is best to close down the superimposed menu by clicking on the close-down button. The superimposed menu may not appear as it can be permanently closed down.

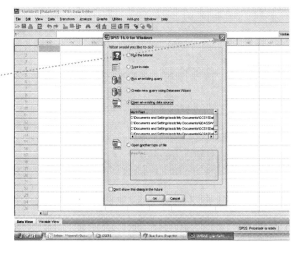

1.3 To enter data

Step 1:

The SPSS Data Editor can now be seen unobstructed by the menu. The Data Editor is a spreadsheet into which data are entered. The columns are used to represent different variables, the rows are the different cases (participants) for which you have data.

The columns are variables.

The rows are cases or individuals.

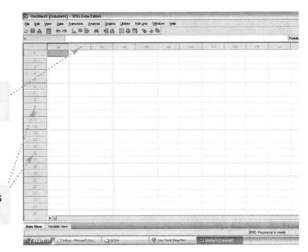

Step 2:

To enter data into SPSS simply highlight one of the cells by clicking on that cell – SPSS always has one cell highlighted.

Step 3:

Then type a number using the computer keyboard. On pressing return on the keyboard or selecting another cell with the mouse this number will be entered into the spreadsheet as shown here. The value 6.00 is the entry for the first row (first case) of the variable VAR00001.

Notice that the variable has been given a standard name automatically. It can be changed – just click on variable name which brings up 'Variable View' (see section 1.8) and make the change.

Step 4:

Correcting errors – simply highlight the cell where the error is using your mouse and type in the correction. On pressing return or moving to another cell, the correction will be entered.

1.4   Moving within a window with the mouse

One can move a row or column at a time by clicking on the arrow-headed buttons near the vertical and horizontal scroll bars.

For major movements, drag the vertical and horizontal scroll bars to move around the page.

The relative position of the scroll bar indicates the relative position in the file.

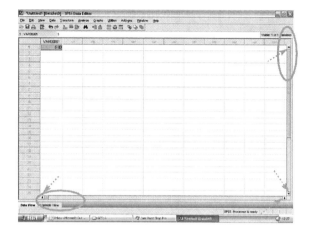

1.5   Moving within a window using the keyboard keys with the mouse

One can move one page up or down on the screen by pressing the Pg Up and Pg Dn keyboard keys.

The cursor keys on the keyboard move the cursor one space or character according to the direction of the arrow.

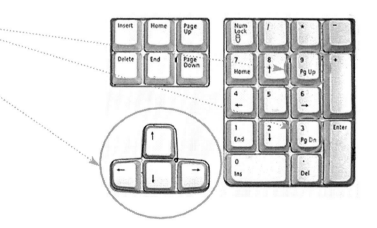

1.6 Saving data to disc

Step 1:

By selecting 'File' then 'Save As ...' it is possible to save the data as a file. The saved data file is automatically given the extension '.sav' by SPSS. A distinctive file name is helpful such as 'eg1' so that its contents will be clear.

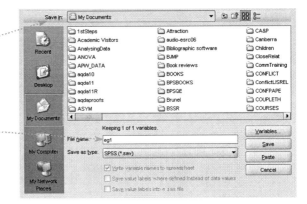

Step 2:

To choose the place where the data file will be saved, indicate this place in the 'Save in:' box. Use the arrow to browse to the selected location.

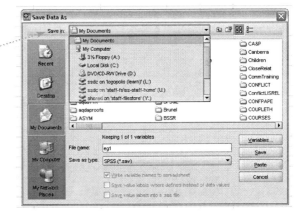

1.7   Opening up a data file

To open an existing file, click on
'File', 'Open', 'Data', 'Look in:' if the
file is not in the 'Open File' box
(which it will be if you have just
saved it), type in the file name
('eg1') and then 'Open'.

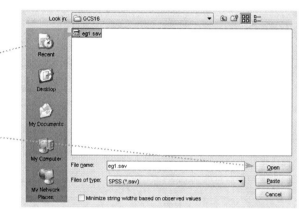

Step 2:

To open a new file click on 'File',
'New' and then 'Data'. This file can
be saved as in Step 1 in section 1.6.

1.8   Using Variable View to create and label variables

Step 1:

Clicking on the 'Variable View' tab
at the bottom changes the 'Data
View' (the data spreadsheet) screen
to one in which information about
your variables may be entered
conveniently.

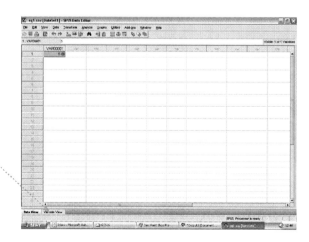

Step 2:

This is the 'Variable View' spreadsheet. In this case one variable is already listed. We entered it in Step 3 in section 1.3. But we can rename it and add extra variables quite simply by highlighting the appropriate cell and typing in a new or further variable names.

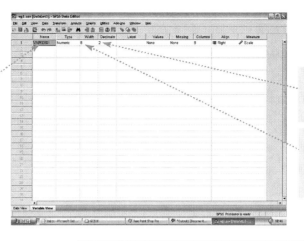

Change the number of decimals here.

Change the width of the data column here.

Step 3:

There is no practical limit to the length of variable names in Release 12 and later. Earlier releases were limited to 8 characters. Highlight one of the cells under 'Name' and type in a distinct variable name. The rest of the columns are given default values but may be changed. These renamed and newly defined variables will appear on the 'Data View' screen when this is selected. That is, new variables have been created and specified.

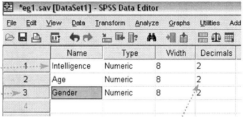

This is the number of decimals that will appear on screen – the calculation uses the actual decimal value.

Step 4:

It is important to note that other columns are easily changed too.

Missing values are dealt with in Chapter 34.

Label allows one to give the variable a longer name than is possible using the Variable name column. Simply type in a longer name in the cells. This is no longer so important now that Variable names can be much longer in Release 12 and later.

Values allows one to name the different categories or values of a nominal (category or categorical) variable such as gender. See Step 5 for details. It is recommended that 'Values' are given for all nominal variables.

Step 5:

This 'button' appears. Click on it.

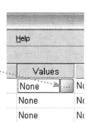

Step 6:

This small window appears. Follow the next few steps. They show how male and female would be entered using the codes 1 for male and 2 for female.

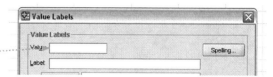

Step 7:

Type in 1 next to 'Value:' and male next to 'Value Label:'.

Then click 'Add'.

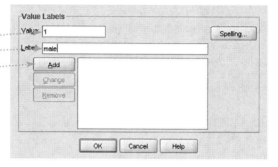

Step 8:

This transfers the information into the large box.

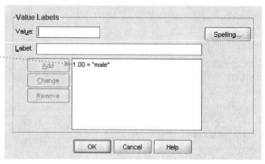

Step 9:

Now type in 2 next to 'Value:' and female next to 'Value Label:'.

Then click 'Add'.

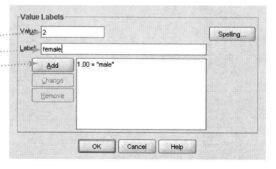

Step 10:

This transfers the information into the large box.

Click OK to close the window.

Note: It is bad practice NOT to label values in this way.

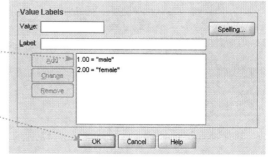

1.9   More on Data View

Step 1:

To return to 'Data View' click on
this tab at the bottom left of the
screen.

Step 2:

This is how 'Data View' looks now.
The data can be entered for all of
the variables and cases. Remember
that the value 5.00 was entered
earlier along with the variable
names. We can start entering the
data in full now.

To enter data, simply highlight a cell, enter
the number, then press return. You will be in
the next cell down which will be highlighted.

Step 3:

This shows how a typical data
spreadsheet appears. Notice how the
values for gender are coded as 1.00
and 2.00. It is possible to reveal
their value labels instead. Click on
'View' on the task bar at the top.

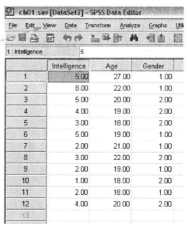

Step 4:

Then click on 'Value Labels'.

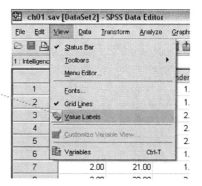

Step 5:

Now the values are given as male and female – just as we coded them in Steps 7 to 8 in section 1.8.

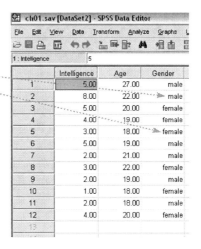

Step 6:

There are many options available to you – including statistical analyses. Some of these options are shown here.

Select 'Data' to insert extra variables, extra cases, select cases and other data manipulations.

Select 'Window' to switch between the data spreadsheet and any output calculated on the data.

Select 'Transform' for a range of things that can be done with the data – such as recoding the values and computing combinations of variables.

Select 'Analyze' to access the full range of statistical calculations that SPSS calculates.

Select 'Graphs' for bar charts, scatterplots and many other graphical representation methods.

1.10   A simple statistical calculation

Step 1:

To calculate the average (i.e. mean) age follow the following stages:

Click 'Analyze'.

Select 'Descriptive Statistics'.

Select 'Descriptives'.

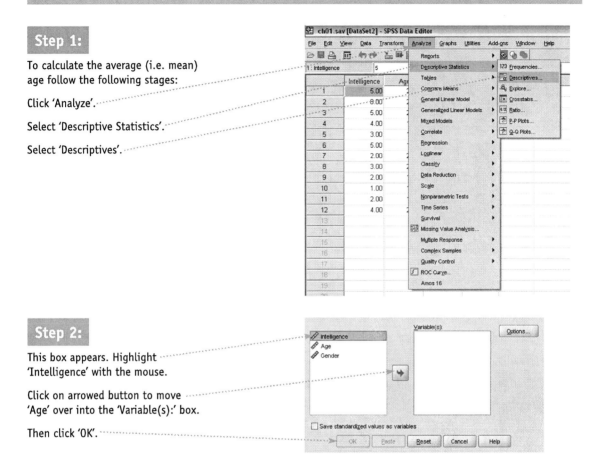

Step 2:

This box appears. Highlight 'Intelligence' with the mouse.

Click on arrowed button to move 'Age' over into the 'Variable(s):' box.

Then click 'OK'.

1.11   The SPSS output

The Data Editor window is replaced in view by the SPSS output.

The first part of output is a list of commands that can be used to run this procedure. These kinds of commands are discussed in Chapters 35–37.

The second part is a table of statistics.

The average (mean) intelligence score is circled here for clarity.

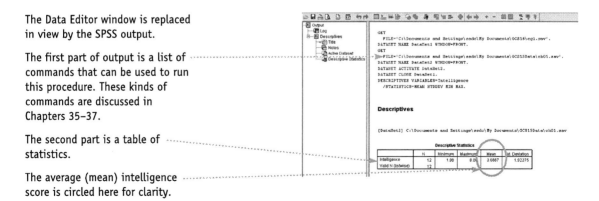

The good news is that anyone who can follow the above steps should have no difficulty in carrying out the vast majority of statistical analyses available on SPSS with the help of this book. It is worthwhile spending an hour or so simply practising with SPSS. You will find that this is the quickest way to learn.

1.12 Basic statistical concepts essential in SPSS analyses

The elements of statistics are quite simple. The problem is in putting the elements together. Nobody can become expert in statistical analysis overnight but, with a very small amount of knowledge, quite sophisticated analyses can be carried out by inexperienced researchers. Mathematical ability has very little role to play in data analysis.

There are just a few basic concepts that the researcher needs to understand before proceeding to SPSS analyses. These include:

■ *Variable*   A variable is any concept that can be measured and that varies. Variables are largely inventions of the researcher and they vary enormously from study to study. There are a few fairly standard variables, such as age and gender, that are very commonly measured. Typically, however, the variables used tend to be specific to particular topics of study. Variables appear in SPSS analyses as the columns of the data spreadsheet.

■ *Cases*   A case is simply a member of the sample. In psychology a case is usually a person (i.e. an individual participant in the research). Cases (normally) appear in SPSS analyses as the rows of the data spreadsheet.

■ *Types of variable*   For all practical purposes, variables can be classified as being of *two* types:

1. *Score variables*   Some variables are scores. A score is when a numerical value is given to a variable for each case in the sample. This numerical value indicates the quantity or amount of the characteristic (variable) in question. So age is a score variable since the numerical value indicates an increasing amount of the variable age. One could also describe this as quantitative.

2. *Nominal or category variables*   Some variables are measured by classifying cases into one of several named categories. These are also known as nominal, categorical or category variables. For example, gender has two named categories – male and female. Nationality is another example: English, Welsh, Irish and Scottish are the traditional nationalities of people of Britain. They have *no* numerical implications as such. To say that a person is Scottish is simply to put them into that named category. One could also describe this as qualitative. There is one risk of confusion – categories such as gender are entered into SPSS using different numbers to represent the different categories. For example, the variable gender has two categories – males could be represented by the number 1 and females by the number 2 (or vice versa). The numbers used are arbitrary. It is vital not to confuse these numbers, which merely represent different coding categories with scores. For this reason, it is important to label the different values of nominal variables in full in the SPSS data spreadsheet. This is easily done as was shown on pages 9–10.

■ *An alternative classification system:* Sometimes variables are classified as nominal, ordinal, interval and ratio. This is mainly of conceptual interest and of little practical significance in selecting appropriate statistics. Generally speaking, we would advise that this system is ignored because it does not correspond with modern practice. *Nominal* is exactly the same as our classification of nominal (category) data and is important. Of the other three, interval measurement is the most important. Interval measurement is where the steps on the scale of measurement are equal (just as centimetre steps on a rule are equal). Some psychologists are inclined to the view that this scale of measurement should reflect the underlying psychological variable being measured. Unfortunately, it is very difficult (near impossible) to identify whether a psychological measure has equal intervals but, nevertheless, it is a sort of holy grail to them. Others, us included, take the view that so long as the numerical scale on which variables are measured has equal intervals (which is always the case except for nominal (category) data, of course, from this perspective) then there is no problem as it is these numbers on which the statistical calculation is based. However, as a concession, we have mentioned equality of intervals as being desirable from time to time in the text though we (and no one else) can tell you how to establish this. *Ratio* measures have equal intervals and a zero point which means one can calculate ratios and make statements such as one score is twice as big as another score. Unfortunately, yet again, it is impossible to identify any psychological variables which are definitely measured on a ratio measurement scale. Finally, *ordinal* data are data that do not have equal intervals so that they only give the rank order of scores. Since the size of the intervals does not matter for ordinal data, then it is assumed that any psychological score data correspond to the ordinal measurement scale at a minimum. For this reason, some psychologists have advocated the use of non-parametric (distribution-free) statistics for the analysis of much psychological data. The problem is that these techniques are not so powerful or flexible as most statistics.

 You will find an extended discussion of ordinal, interval and ratio scales of measurement in Howitt, D. and Cramer, D. (2008) *Introduction to Research Methods in Psychology*. Harlow: Pearson.

■ *Importance of deciding the types of variable involved:* It is crucially important to decide for each of your variables whether it is a nominal (category) variable or a score variable. Write a list of your variables and classify each of them if you are a beginner. Eventually you will do it without much thought. The statistical techniques which are appropriate for score variables are often inappropriate for qualitative variables (and vice versa). So, for example, it is appropriate to calculate the mean (numerical average) of any variable which is a score (e.g. average age). On the other hand, it is totally inappropriate to calculate the mean (average) for variables which consist of categories. It would be nonsense to say that the average nationality is 1.7 since nationality is not a score. The problem is that SPSS works with the numbers in the data spreadsheet and does not know whether they are scores or numerical codes for different categories.

■ *The difference between descriptive and inferential statistics:* There are two main types of statistical techniques – *descriptive* and *inferential* statistics:

1. Descriptive statistics chiefly describe the main features of individual variables. So to calculate the average age of a sample of people is an example of descriptive statistics. Counting the number of English people would be another example of descriptive statistics. If one variable is considered at a time this is known as univariate statistics. Bivariate statistics are used when the relationship between two (or more) variables is being described.

2. Inferential statistics is a totally distinct aspect of statistics. It only addresses the question of whether one can rely on the findings based on a *sample* of cases rather than *all* cases. The use of samples is characteristic of nearly all modern research. The problem with samples is that some of them are not similar to the populations from which they are taken. The phrases 'statistically significant' and 'not statistically significant' simply indicate that any trends in the data can be accepted as substantial (i.e. statistically significant) or not substantial enough to rely on (i.e. not statistically significant). A statistically significant finding is one which is unlikely to be the result of chance factors determining the results in a particular sample.

See Box 1.1 or the authors' accompanying statistics text, *Introduction to Statistics in Psychology* (4th edition, 2008: Pearson Education), for a detailed discussion of the meaning of statistical significance since it is difficult to explain accurately in a few words.

Every descriptive statistic has a corresponding inferential statistic. For example, the correlation coefficient is a descriptive statistic indicating the direction and the strength of the relationship between two variables. Associated with it is the inferential statistic – the significance of the correlation coefficient. The descriptive statistic is important for understanding the trends in the data – the inferential statistic simply deals with the reliance that can be placed on the finding.

■ *Related versus unrelated designs:* Researchers should be aware also of *two* different types of research design – that which uses *related measures* and that which uses *unrelated measures*. Related measures may also be called correlated measures or paired measures. Unrelated measures may also be called uncorrelated measures or unpaired measures. The terms are mostly used when the mean or averages of scores are being compared for two or more samples of data:

–   Where the means of a single sample of individuals are compared on two (or more) measures of the same variable (e.g. taken at different points in time) then this is a related measures design.

–   Where the means of two quite different samples of participants are compared on a variable, this is an unrelated design.

–   Where two (or more) groups of participants have been carefully matched so that *sets* of participants in the two (or more) conditions are similar in some respects, then this is a related design too. In this case, members of each set are treated as if they were the same person. Normally, a researcher would know if the participants were matched in sets because it requires effort on the part of the researcher. For example, the researcher has to decide on what characteristics to match sets, then choose individuals for the sets on the basis of their similarity to these characteristics, and (often) has to allocate participants to the different samples (conditions), especially in experimental research.

The main point of using related designs is that variability due to sampling is reduced.

Almost without exception, the researcher will be using a variety of these techniques with the same data. Fortunately, once the data are entered, in many cases, data analysis may take just a minute or so.

Box 1.1   STATISTICAL SIGNIFICANCE

A crucial fact about research is that it is invariably carried out on samples of cases rather than all possible cases. The reasons for this are obvious – economies of time and money. Sometimes it is very difficult to specify what the population is in words (e.g. when one collects a sample of participants from a university restaurant). The realisation that research could be done on relatively small samples was the initial stimulus for many of the statistical techniques described in this book.

For many, statistics = tests of significance. This is a mistaken emphasis since, in terms of importance in any analysis, basic descriptive statistics are the key to understanding one's data. Statistical significance is about a very limited question – is it reasonably safe to generalise from my sample?

In order to do this, in statistics usually we take the information based on the sample(s) of data that we have collected and generalise to the population from which we might assume the sample is drawn. Sometimes one simply takes the sample characteristics and assumes that the population characteristics are the same. On other occasions the sample characteristics have to be slightly modified to obtain the best estimate of the population characteristics. Whichever applies, one then uses these estimated population characteristics to plot the distribution of the characteristics of random samples taken from the estimated population. The most important characteristic that is estimated from samples is the variation of scores in the data.

The distribution of these random samples forms a baseline against which the characteristic of our sample obtained in our research can be compared with what happens under conditions of randomness. If our actual sample characteristic is unlikely to have occurred as a consequence of randomness then we say that it is *statistically significant*. All that we mean is that it is at the extremes of the distribution of random samples. If our sample is very typical of what happens by random sampling, then we say that our sample characteristic is *not statistically significant*.

Often in psychology this is put in terms of accepting the null hypothesis or rejecting the null hypothesis. The null hypothesis is basically that there is no relationship or no difference in our data. Usually the population is specified in terms of the null hypothesis. That is, in our population there is no correlation or in our population there is no difference.

Statistical significance is often set at the 0.05 or 5% significance level. This is purely arbitrary and is not actually set in stone. Sometimes one would require a more stringent significance level (say 0.01 or 1%) and in some circumstances one could relax the criterion a little. However, unless you are very experienced you perhaps ought to stick with the 0.05 or 5% level of statistical significance. This level of significance simply means that there is a 1 in 20 chance of getting a result as extreme as ours by random sampling from the estimated population.

One-tailed significance testing is used when the direction of the trend in the data is predicted on the basis of strong theory or consistent previous research. The prediction is made prior to collecting the data. Such conditions are rarely met in student research and it is recommended that you stick to two-tailed testing.

Finally, notice that the precision of this approach is affected by how representative the sample characteristics are of the population characteristics. One cannot know this, of course. This may help you understand that despite the mathematical sophistication of statistics, in fact it should be used as a guide rather than a seal of approval.

■ *Succinct methods of reporting statistics:* You will probably be aware of the short (succinct) methods used to report statistical findings throughout psychological research reports. We have, of course, used these in this book where we describe how to report research findings. The system is quite simple though there is no universal standard and there will be some variation. Typical of the methods used would be the following:

The hypothesis that students who just work and have no play was supported ($t = 2.10$, $df = 22$, $p < .05$)

What the stuff in brackets says is that the statistical test used was the t-test, that the degrees of freedom are 22, and that the significance level is less than .05. In other words, our findings are statistically significant.

■ *Confidence intervals versus point statistics:* Traditionally, psychological statistics use point statistics. These are where the characteristics of the data are defined by a single measure such as the average (mean) score. It is often recommended that confidence intervals should be used instead. Usually in statistics we are trying to estimate the characteristics of the population of scores from a sample of scores. Obviously samples tend to vary from the population characteristics so there is some uncertainty about what the population characteristic will be. Confidence intervals give the most likely range of values in the population and not simply a single value. In this way, the variability of the data is better represented. Chapter 12 discusses confidence intervals in more detail.

1.13 Which test to use

One common heartfelt plea is the demand to know how to choose appropriate statistical techniques for data. Over the years, writers of statistics textbooks have laboured to simplify the process of choosing. This is done largely by producing spreadsheets or tables that indicate what sorts of statistics are appropriate for different sorts of data. If you want that sort of approach then there are a number of web sites that take you through the decision-making process:

http://www.wtc.edu/online/bcanada/choose2.htm
http://www.members.aol.com/statware/pubpage.htm
http://www.socialresearchmethods.net/selstat/ssstart.htm
http://www.graphpad.com/www/Book/Choose.htm
http://www.whichtest.info/

For basic statistics this is probably a useful approach. The difficulty increasingly is that research designs, even for student projects, are very varied and quite complex. Once psychology was almost a purely laboratory-based subject that concentrated on randomised experiments. Psychologists still use this sort of experimentation, but their methods have extended greatly, so extending the demands on their statistical knowledge. Therefore, there is a distinct limit to the extent to which a simple spreadsheet or flow diagram can help the researcher select appropriate statistical analyses.

One fundamental mistake that novice researchers make is to assume that data analysis is primarily driven by statistics. It is more accurate to regard statistics as being largely a tool that adds a little finesse to the basic task of research – to answer the researcher's research questions. Only the researcher can fully know what they want their research to achieve – what issues they want resolving through collecting research data and analysing it. Unless the researcher clearly understands what they want the research to achieve, statistics can be

Table 1.1 Major types of analysis and suggested SPSS procedures

Type/purpose of analysis	Suggested procedures	Chapter
All types of study	Descriptive statistics, tables and diagrams	2–6
Assessing the relationship between two variables	Correlation coefficient	7
	Regression	8
Comparing two sets of scores for differences	Unrelated *t*-test	11
	F-ratio test	16
	Related *t*-test	10
	Unrelated ANOVA	17
	Related ANOVA	18
	Mann–Whitney	14
	Wilcoxon matched pairs	14
Comparing the means of two or more sets of scores	Unrelated ANOVA	17
	Related ANOVA	18
	Multiple comparisons	20
Comparing the means of two or more sets of scores (ANOVAs) while controlling for spurious variables influencing the data	ANCOVA	22
Complex experiments, etc. with *two* or more unrelated independent variables and *one* dependent variable	Two (or more)-way ANOVA	19
■ if you have related *and* unrelated measures	Mixed-design ANOVA	21
■ if other variables may be affecting scores on dependent variable	Analysis of covariance	22
ANOVA designs with several conceptually-relevant dependent variables	MANOVA	23, 24
Eliminating third variables which may be affecting a correlation coefficient	Partial correlation	25
Finding predictors for a score variable	Simple regression	8
	Stepwise multiple regression	28
	Hierarchical multiple regression	29
	Log-linear analysis	30
Finding predictors for a category variable	Multinomial logistic regression	31
	Binomial logistic regression	32
Analysing a questionnaire	Factor analysis	26
	Alpha reliability	27
	Split-half reliability	27
	Recoding	35
	Computing new variables	35–37
Comparing frequency data	Chi-square	13
	Fisher exact test	13
	McNemar test	13
	Kruskal–Wallis	15
	Friedman	15
	Log-linear analysis	30
Coding open-ended data using raters	Kappa coefficient	27

of little help. Very often, when approached for statistical advice, we find that we have to clarify the objectives of the research first of all – and then try to unravel how the researcher thought that the data collected would help them. These are *not* statistical matters but issues to do with developing research ideas and planning appropriate data collection. So the first thing is to list the questions that the data were intended to answer. Too often sight of the purpose of the research is lost in the forest of the research practicalities. The following may help clarify the role of statistics in research:

■ Many of the most important aspects of data analysis need little other than an understanding of averages and frequency counts. These are common in SPSS output. Many research questions may be answered simply by examining differences in means between samples, cross-tabulation tables or scattergrams. It is useful to ask oneself how one could answer the research questions just using such basic approaches. Too often, the complexities of statistical output become the focus of attention, which can lead to confusion about how the data relate to the research question. It is not easy to focus on the research issues and avoid being drawn in unhelpful directions.

■ Statistical analyses are actively constructed by the researcher. There is usually no single correct statistical analysis for any data but probably a range of equally acceptable alternatives. The researcher may need to make many decisions in the process of carrying out data analysis – some of these may have to be carefully justified but others are fairly arbitrary. The researcher is in charge of the data analysis – statistics is the researcher's tool. The analysis should not be a statistical *tour de force*, but led by the questions that necessitated data collection in the first place. There is no excuse – if you collected the data then you ought to know why you collected them.

■ The more research you read in its entirety the better you will understand how statistics can be used in a particular field of research. Very little research is carried out which is not related to other research. What are the typical statistical methods used by researchers in your chosen field? Knowing what techniques are generally used is often the best guide to what ought to be considered.

Table 1.1 gives some insight into the styles of analysis that researchers may wish to apply to their data and what sections of this book describe these statistical techniques in detail.

For further resources including data sets and questions, please refer to the CD accompanying this book.

2 Describing variables
Tables and diagrams

Overview

■ Tables and diagrams should quickly and effectively communicate important features of one's data. Complexity, for its own sake, is not a helpful characteristic of good tables and diagrams.

■ Clear and meaningful tables and diagrams are crucial in statistical analysis and report writing. Virtually every analysis of data uses them in order to allow the distributions of variables to be examined. In this chapter we provide the basic computer techniques to allow the construction of tables and diagrams to describe the distributions of individual variables presented one at a time.

■ All tables and diagrams should be clearly titled and labelled. Depending on the table or diagram in question, horizontal and vertical axes should be labelled, bars identified, scales marked and so forth. Great care should be taken with this. Generally speaking, SPSS tables and diagrams require considerable work to make them optimally effective.

■ Frequency tables merely count the number of times the different values of the variable appear in the data. A simple example would be a count of the number of males and the number of females in the research. Tables need to be relatively simple and this usually requires that the variable only has a small number of values or, if not, that a number of different values of the variable are grouped together.

■ Pie diagrams are effective and simple ways of presenting frequency counts. However, they are only useful when the variable being illustrated has a small number of different values. Pie diagrams are relatively uncommon in publications because they consume space, although they are good for conference presentations and lectures.

■ A bar chart can be used in similar circumstances to a pie chart but can cope with a larger number of values of variables before becoming too cluttered. Frequencies of the different values of the variable are represented as physically separated bars of heights that vary according to the frequency in that category.

■ A histogram looks similar to a bar chart but is used for numerical scores rather than categories. Thus the bars in a histogram are presented in size order of the scores that they represent. The bars in histograms are *not* separated by spaces. Often a histogram will need the ranges of scores covered by each bar to be changed in order to maximise the usefulness and clarity of the diagram. This can be done by recoding variables (Chapter 35) but SPSS also allows this to be done in the 'Chart Editor'. Producing charts like these is one of the harder tasks on SPSS.

2.1 What are tables and diagrams?

Now this sounds like a really silly question because we all know what tables and diagrams are, don't we? But simply because we know about these things does not mean that we understand their importance in a good statististical analysis or what makes a good table or diagram. The bottom line is that unless you very carefully study each of your variables using the methods described in this and the next few chapter then you risk failing to identify problems that may undermine the validity of your analysis.

Tables in data analysis are almost always summary tables of key aspects of the data since rarely are the actual data tabulated and reported in statistical analyses – usually because this would be very cumbersome. Tables then report important features of the data such as: (1) frequencies (counts) or the number of participants in the research having a particular characteristic such as the number of males and the number of females in the study; and (2) the average score on a variable in different groups of participants such as the average (known as the mean in statistics) age of the male participants and the female participants in the research.

Diagrams in statistics do much the same sort of job as tables but, of course, they are intended to have greater visual impact. So you are almost certain to be familiar with diagrams that illustrate frequencies of things in data. Pie charts represent the proportion of cases in each category of a variable using proportionate slices of a circle (the pie) (see the examples on pages 32–35). Very much the same sort of thing can be illustrated using bar charts in which each category of a variable is represented by a bar and the frequencies by the heights of the relevant bar (see the examples on page 36). Neither is better than the other except a pie chart shows more quickly the proportions of each category compared to the total number of participants. Histograms are very similar in appearance to bar charts but are used when the categories are actually scores on a particular measure which are ordered from smallest to the largest. Examples of histograms are to be found on pages 37–38. Technically, a bar chart should have a gap between the bars but a histogram should not since it represents a dimension rather than a number of distinct categories.

Tables do much the same task as diagrams but usually in a more compact form so that more information can be put into the same physical space. They are much more common in professional publications than diagrams. There is probably an infinite variety of possible tables. Table 2.1 on page 26 is quite a simple example of a table. It gives a number of occupations together with the frequencies and percentage frequencies of participants in a study who have a particular type of job.

Although it may be tempting to think that diagrams are preferential to tables this is not the case. Complex data are often difficult to report in a simple diagram and possibly much easier to put into a table. Diagrams tend to be reserved for circumstances where the researcher is trying to communicate the findings of a study quickly and with impact. This is more likely to be the case with spoken presentations of research findings rather than written ones. So diagrams are often better as part of lectures than tables so long as the diagram does not get too complicated.

2.2 When to use tables and diagrams

Tables and diagrams are a vital part of the analysis of data as well as being used to present data. The examination of basic tables and diagrams that describe the data is an important aspect of understanding one's data and familiarising oneself with it. There is nothing unsophisticated in using them – quite the contrary since it is poor statisticians who fail to make good use of them. We will look at a number of circumstances where tables and diagrams can prevent us making basic mistakes.

In terms of practical reports and dissertations, you may well find that tables are generally more useful than diagrams because they can handle complexity better.

2.3 When not to use tables and diagrams

Never use tables and diagrams as a substitute for reporting your research findings in words in the body of a report. To do so is not good because it leaves the reader with the job of interpreting the tables and diagrams, which is really the task of the researcher.

2.4 Data requirements for tables and diagrams

Different sorts of tables and diagrams have different requirements in terms of the variables measured. Bar charts and pie charts are largely used for nominal (category) data that consist of named categories. Histograms are used for score data in which the scores are ordered from the smallest values to the largest on the horizontal axis of the chart.

2.5 Problems in using tables and diagrams

There are many problems, including the following:

- Remember to label clearly all of the important components of tables and diagrams. Not to do so is counterproductive.
- Problems can occur because of rounding errors for percentages such that the total of the percentages for parts of the table or diagram do not add up to 100%. Keep an eye open for this and make reference to it in your report if it risks confusing the reader.

- Technically, the bars of histograms should each have a width proportionate to the range of numbers covered by that bar. SPSS does not do this so the output can be misleading.

- You need to be very careful when a scale of frequencies on a bar chart or histogram does not start at zero. This is because if part of the scale is missing then the reader can get a very wrong impression of the relative frequencies as some bars can look several times taller than others whereas there is little difference in absolute terms. This is one of the 'mistakes' which has led to the suggestion that one can lie using statistics.

- We would recommend that you *never* use tables and diagrams directly copied and pasted from SPSS. For one thing, SPSS tables tend to contain more information than is appropriate to report. But the main reason is that often SPSS tables and diagrams are simply confusing and could be made much better with a little work and thought. Many SPSS diagrams can be modified on SPSS to improve their impact and clarity. For example, there is no point in using coloured slices in a pie chart if it is to be photocopied in black and white. Such a chart may be very confusing because the shades of gray cannot be deciphered easily.

You can find out more about tables and diagrams in Chapter 2 of Howitt, D. and Cramer, D. (2008) *Introduction to Statistics in Psychology*. Harlow: Pearson.

2.6 The data to be analysed

SPSS is generally used to summarise raw data but it can use data that have already been summarised such as those shown in Table 2.1 (*ISP*, Table 2.1).

In other words, since the data in Table 2.1 are based on 80 people, the data would occupy 80 cells of one column in the 'Data Editor' window and each occupation would be coded with a separate number, so that nuns might be coded 1, nursery teachers 2 and so on. Thus, one would need 17 rows containing 1 to represent nuns, 3 rows containing 2 to represent nursery teachers and so on. However, it is possible to carry out certain analyses on summarised data provided that we appropriately weight the categories by the number or frequency of cases in them.

Table 2.1   Occupational status of participants in the research expressed as frequencies and percentage frequencies

Occupation	Frequency	Percentage frequency
Nuns	17	21.25
Nursery teachers	3	3.75
Television presenters	23	28.75
Students	20	25.00
Other	17	21.25

2.7   Entering summarised categorical or frequency data by weighting

It seems better practice to define your variables in 'Variable View' of the 'Data Editor' before entering the data in 'Data View' because we can remove the decimal places where they are not necessary. So we always do this first. If you prefer to enter the data first then do so.

For this table we need two columns in 'Data View': one to say what the categories are; the other to give the frequencies for these categories. In 'Variable View' variables are presented as rows.

Step 1:

Select 'Variable View' in 'Data Editor'. Name the first 2 variables 'Occupation' and 'Freq'. Remove the 2 decimal places. Select the right side of the cell for the 'Values' of 'Occupation'.

Step 2:

Label the 5 'Values' of 'Occupation' as shown and as described in Steps 6–10 in section 1.8 in Chapter 1.

Select 'OK'.

Step 3:

Select 'Scale' for this variable and the downward arrow to give the drop-down menu.

Select 'Nominal'.

Step 4:

Select 'Data View'. Enter the data as shown.

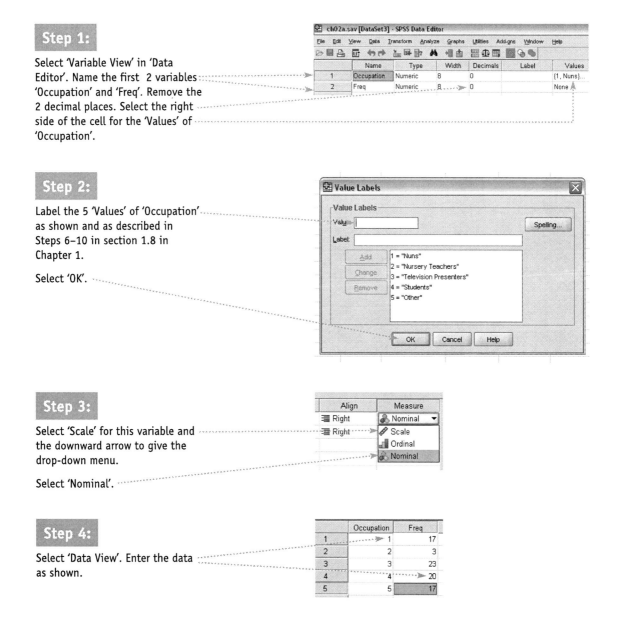

Step 5:

Select 'Data' and
'Weight Cases ... '.

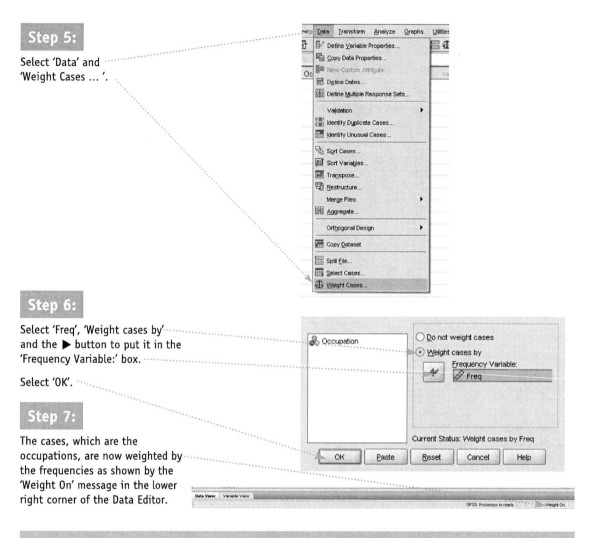

Step 6:

Select 'Freq', 'Weight cases by'
and the ▶ button to put it in the
'Frequency Variable:' box.

Select 'OK'.

Step 7:

The cases, which are the
occupations, are now weighted by
the frequencies as shown by the
'Weight On' message in the lower
right corner of the Data Editor.

2.8 Percentage frequencies

Step 1:

Select 'Analyze',
'Descriptive Statistics'
and 'Frequencies ...'.

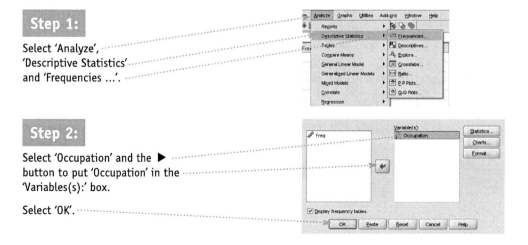

Step 2:

Select 'Occupation' and the ▶
button to put 'Occupation' in the
'Variables(s):' box.

Select 'OK'.

2.9 Interpreting the output

The first column of this table gives the value of the 5 categories. To change these to labels, which is more meaningful, carry out the following 3 steps and rerun the analysis as in the next section.

Occupation

		Frequency	Percent	Valid Percent	Cumulative Percent
Valid	1	17	21.3	21.3	21.3
	2	3	3.8	3.8	25.0
	3	23	28.8	28.8	53.8
	4	20	25.0	25.0	78.8
	5	17	21.3	21.3	100.0
	Total	80	100.0	100.0	

2.10 Labelling the values

Step 1:

Select 'Edit' and then 'Options ...'.

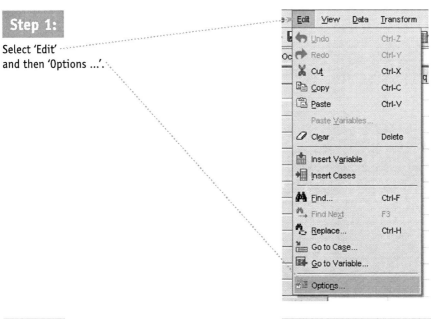

Step 2:

Select 'Output Labels'.

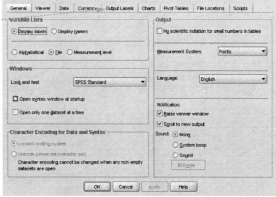

Step 3:

Select the ▼ button below 'Variable values in labels shown as:' and 'Labels' from the drop-down menu.

Select 'OK'.

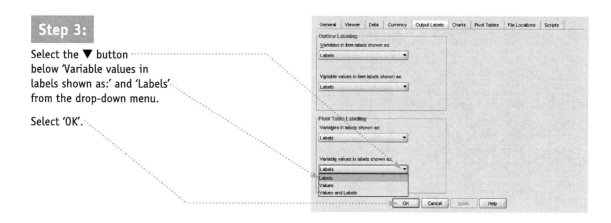

The fourth column adds the percentages down the table so 25.0 of the cases are nuns or nursery teachers.

The labels are now given.

The second column gives the percentage frequency for each category, including any missing values of which there are none.

So 17 is 21.3% of a total of 80.

Occupation

		Frequency	Percent	Valid Percent	Cumulative Percent
Valid	Nuns	17	21.3	21.3	21.3
	Nursery Teachers	3	3.8	3.8	25.0
	Television Presenters	23	28.8	28.8	53.8
	Students	20	25.0	25.0	78.8
	Other	17	21.3	21.3	100.0
	Total	80	100.0	100.0	

The third column gives the percentage frequency, excluding any missing values. As there are none, these percentages are the same as those in the second column.

Reporting the output

Only the category labels, the frequency and the percentage frequency need be reported, consequently you need to simplify this table if you are going to present it. If the occupation was missing for some of the cases you would need to decide whether you would present percentages including or excluding them. There is no need to present both sets of figures. Also omit the term 'Valid' in the first column as its meaning may only be familiar to SPSS users.

2.11 Pie diagram of category data

Step 1:

Select 'Graphs'
and 'Chart Builder ...'.

Step 2:

Select 'OK'.

If you have not defined 'Occupation'
as a nominal variable select 'Define
Variable Properties ...'.

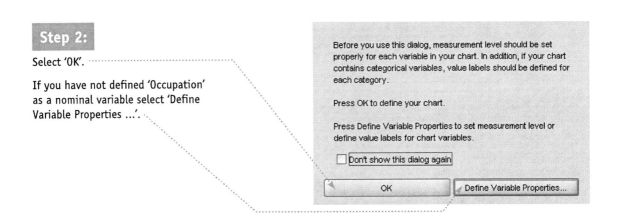

Step 3:

Drag the pie diagram into the box
above it.

Select 'OK'.

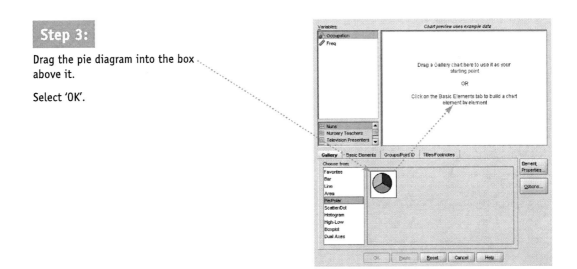

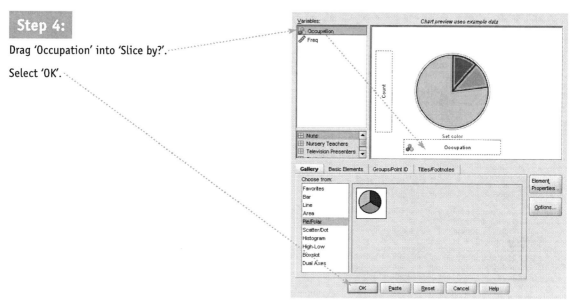

Step 4:

Drag 'Occupation' into 'Slice by?'.

Select 'OK'.

This is the way the pie diagram appears if the default options in SPSS have not been altered.

The slices are colour coded. The colours have not been reproduced here.

Features in this diagram may be altered with the 'Chart Editor'.

We will show how to label each slice (so that the reader does not have to refer to the colour code) and how to change the colours to monochrome patterns.

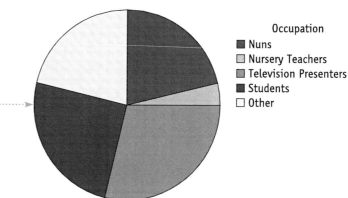

2.12   Adding labels to the pie diagram and removing the legend and label

Step 1:

Double click anywhere in the rectangle containing the diagram to select the 'Chart Editor'.

Select 'Elements' and 'Show Data Labels'.

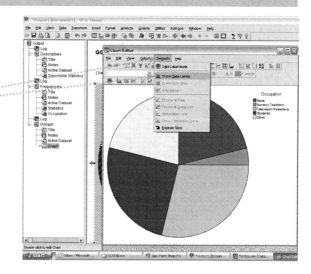

Step 2:

Select 'Percent' and the red 'X' to put it in the box below.

Select 'Occupation' and the curved upward green arrow to display the names of the occupations.

Do the same for 'Percent' to display the percentage of each occupation.

Select 'Apply' and 'Close' if you do not want to make further changes to the properties of the pie diagram.

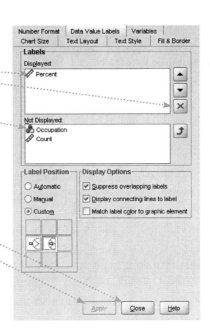

Step 3:

Select 'Text Style' if you want to change aspects of the text such as making it bold and increasing its font size.

To make it bold, select the ▼ button next to 'Style' and 'Bold' from the dropdown menu.

To increase the font size to 14, select the ▼ button next to 'Size' and '14' from the dropdown menu.

Note: Because of the small size of this slice, the font for Nursery Teachers will not be 14. To change this you need to click on the box for this group. If you do not want to make further changes, select 'Apply' and 'Close' ('Cancel' changes to 'Close').

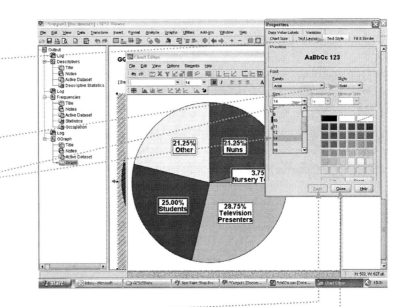

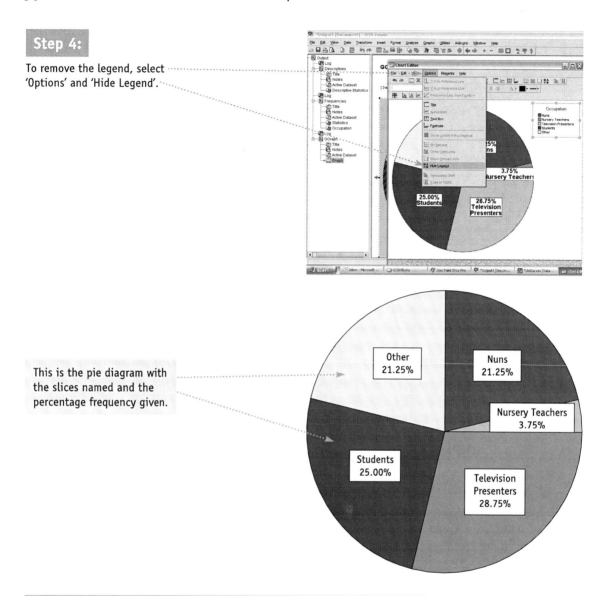

Step 4:

To remove the legend, select 'Options' and 'Hide Legend'.

This is the pie diagram with the slices named and the percentage frequency given.

| Other 21.25% | Nuns 21.25% |

Nursery Teachers 3.75%

Students 25.00%

Television Presenters 28.75%

2.13 Changing the colour of a pie diagram slice to a black and white pattern

Step 1:

In the 'Chart Editor', click on the slice you want to change and then click again when the border will have a double line.

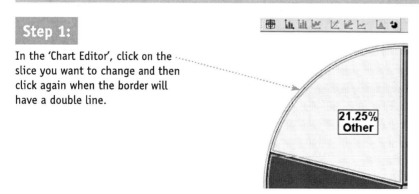

21.25% Other

Step 2:

Select 'Edit' and 'Properties'.

Select 'Fill' and the colour of white.

To add a black border, select 'Border' and the colour of black.

To add a pattern, select the ▼ button beside 'Pattern' and the pattern you want.

Select 'Apply' and then 'Close'. Apply this same procedure to the other 4 slices.

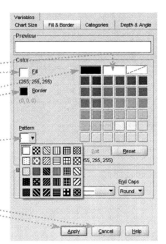

This is a pie diagram with black and white patterned slices.

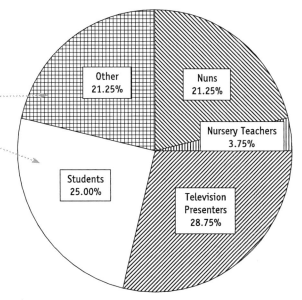

Other 21.25%

Nuns 21.25%

Nursery Teachers 3.75%

Students 25.00%

Television Presenters 28.75%

2.14 Bar chart of category data

Step 1:

Follow the first two steps for the pie diagram, selecting 'Graphs' and 'Chart Builder ...', and then 'OK' in the dialog box.

Select 'Bar' and then drag the 'Simple Bar' icon into the box above.

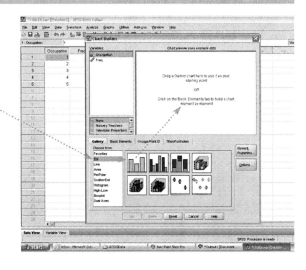

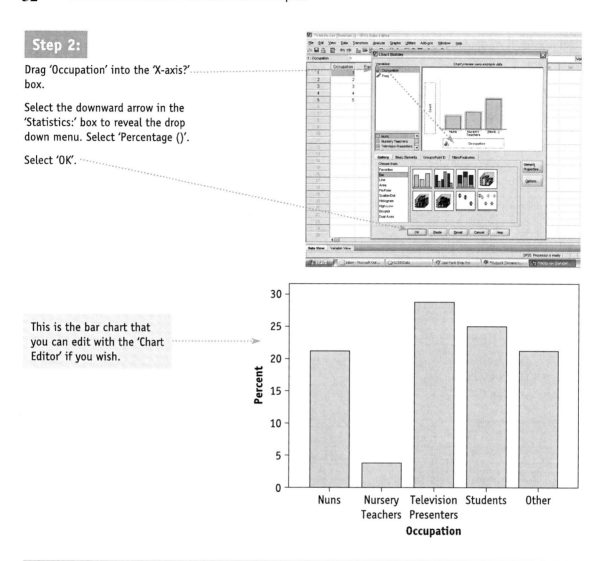

Step 2:

Drag 'Occupation' into the 'X-axis?' box.

Select the downward arrow in the 'Statistics:' box to reveal the drop down menu. Select 'Percentage ()'.

Select 'OK'.

This is the bar chart that you can edit with the 'Chart Editor' if you wish.

2.15   Histograms

We will illustrate the making of a histogram with the data in Table 2.2 which shows the distribution of students' attitudes towards statistics. We have labelled this variable 'Response'.

Table 2.2   Distribution of students' replies to the statement 'Statistics is my favourite university subject'

Response category	Value	Frequency
Strongly agree	1	17
Agree	2	14
Neither agree nor disagree	3	6
Disagree	4	2
Strongly disagree	5	1

Step 1:

In the 'Data Editor' enter the data, weight and label them as described at the beginning of this chapter.

	Response	Freq
1	1	17
2	2	14
3	3	6
4	4	2
5	5	1

Step 2:

Follow the first two steps for the pie diagram and bar chart, selecting 'Graphs' and 'Chart Builder ...', and then 'OK' in the dialog box.

Select 'Histogram' and then drag the 'Simple Histogram' icon into the box above.

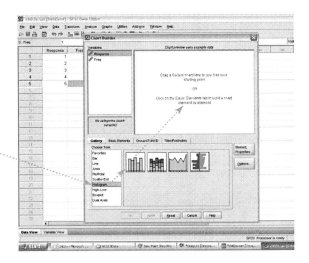

Step 3:

Drag 'Response' into the 'X-axis?' box.

Select 'OK'.

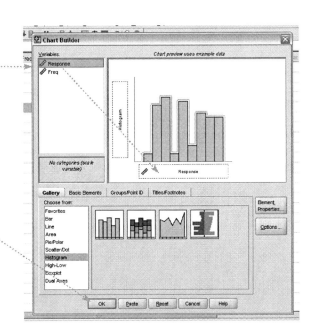

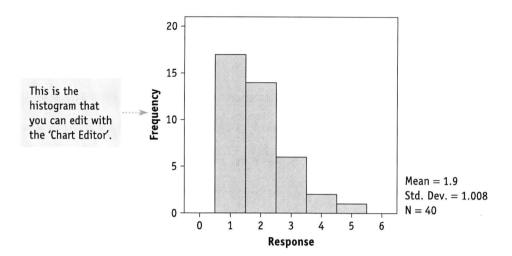

This is the
histogram that
you can edit with
the 'Chart Editor'.

Mean = 1.9
Std. Dev. = 1.008
N = 40

For further resources including data sets and questions, please refer to the CD
accompanying this book.

3 Describing variables numerically
Averages, variation and spread

Overview

■ The computation of a number of statistics that summarise and describe the essential characteristics of each important variable in a study is explained. The techniques presented in this chapter involve individual variables taken one at a time. In other words they are single variable or univariate statistical techniques.

■ Each technique generates a numerical index to describe an important characteristic of the data.

■ With the exception of the mode, which can be used for any type of data, all of the techniques are for data in the form of numerical scores.

■ The mean is the everyday or numerical average of a set of scores. It is obtained by summing the scores and dividing by the number of scores.

■ The mode is simply the most frequently occurring score. A set of scores can have more than one mode if two or more scores occur equally frequently. The mode is the value of the score occurring most frequently – it is *not* the frequency with which that score occurs.

■ The median is the score in the middle of the distribution if the scores are ordered in size from the smallest to the largest. For various reasons, sometimes the median is an estimate of the score in the middle – for example, where the number of scores is equal, and so that there is no exact middle.

■ The procedures described in this chapter can readily be modified to produce measures of variance, kurtosis and other descriptive statistics.

3.1 What are averages, variation and spread?

Most of us when we think of averages imagine what statisticians call the *mean*. This is the sum of a number of scores divided by the number of scores. So the mean of 5, 7 and 10 is 22/3 = 7.33. However, statisticians have other measures of the average or typical score or observation that are conceptually different from the mean. These include the median and mode. The *median* is obtained by ordering the scores from the smallest to the largest and the score that separates the first 50% of cases from the second 50% of cases is the median. If there is an even number of scores then there is no one score right in the middle and so a slight adjustment has to be made involving the mean of the score just below the middle and the score just above the middle. Sometimes even finer adjustments are made but SPSS will do the necessary calculation for you. The third measure of the average is called the *mode*. This is the most frequently occurring value in the data. This can be the most frequently occurring score if the data are score data or the most frequently occurring category if the data is nominal (category) data. The mode is the only measure of the average that can be used for nominal (category) data.

In statistics, rather than speak of average it is more usual to refer to measures of *central tendency*. The mean, median and mode are all measures of central tendency. They are all measures of the typical score in the set of scores.

If a frequency distribution of scores is symmetrical (such as in the case of the normal distribution discussed in Chapter 4), then the value of the mean, the median and the mode will be identical. But only in those circumstances. Where the frequency distribution of scores is not symmetrical then the mean, the median and the mode will have different values. Figure 3.1 contains an example of an asymmetrical frequency distribution – though it is only slightly so. There are a total of 151 participants. The mean in this case is 5.47, the median is 6.00, and the mode is also 6.00. It is easy to see that the mode is 6.00 as this is the most frequently appearing score (i.e. it has the highest bar). Since there are 151 cases then the median is the 76th score from the left-hand side of the bar chart.

The spread of the scores is another characteristic that can be seen in Figure 3.1. Quite clearly the scores vary: the largest is 10 and the smallest is 1. The difference between the largest score and the smallest score is known as the *range*, which in this case is 9. Sometimes the top and bottom quarter of scores are ignored to give the *interquartile range*,

Figure 3.1   A slightly asymmetrical frequency distribution

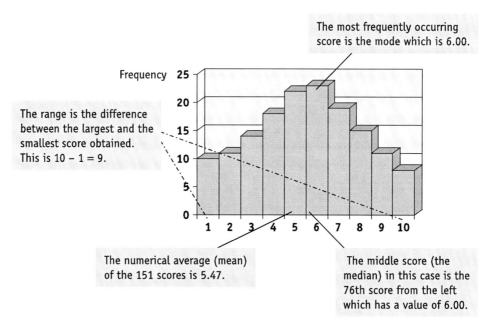

The most frequently occurring score is the mode which is 6.00.

The range is the difference between the largest and the smallest score obtained. This is 10 − 1 = 9.

The numerical average (mean) of the 151 scores is 5.47.

The middle score (the median) in this case is the 76th score from the left which has a value of 6.00.

which is less susceptible to the influence of unusual exceptionally large or small scores (outliers).

Variance is the most important measure of the spread of scores. It is based on the squared deviation (difference) between each score and the mean of the set of scores in the data. In fact it is the average squared deviation from the mean. SPSS calculates this to be 6.06 for these data. (Actually SPSS calculates the variance estimate and not the variance which is a little smaller than 6.06. This is no great problem as the variance estimate is generally more useful – it is an estimate of what the variance is in the population from which our sample came. The variance estimate is bigger than the variance since it is the sum of the squared deviations of each score from the mean score divided by the number of scores minus 1).

3.2 When to use averages, variation and spread

These should be routinely (always) calculated when dealing with score variables. However, many of these can be calculated using different analysis procedures on SPSS and there may be more convenient methods than the ones in this chapter in some circumstances. For example, you will find that SPSS will calculate means as part of many tests of significance such as the *t*-tests or ANOVA though they may have to be requested.

3.3 When not to use averages, variation and spread

Apart from when using nominal (category) data, all measures of average, variation and spread discussed in this chapter are useful when exploring one's data.

3.4 Data requirements for averages, variation and spread

All of the techniques described in this chapter require a variable which is in the form of scores. The only exception is the mode which can be calculated on any type of data.

3.5 Problems in the use of averages, variation and spread

The measures of central tendency (mean, median and mode) refer to quite different ideas and none of them is intrinsically better than the others. They each contain different information and each can be presented in any data analysis. There is, however, a tendency to ignore the median and mode, which is a mistake, for anything other than symmetrical distributions of scores (for which the three different measures of central tendency give the same value). Be careful when considering the mode since a distribution has more than one mode if it has more than one peak. SPSS will not warn you of this but a glance at the frequency distribution for the scores will also alert you to this 'bimodal' or 'multimodal' characteristic of the distribution.

The range is sometimes given in error as being from 1 to 10, for example. This is not the range as the range is a single number such as 9. The value 1 is the *lower bound* of the range and the value 10 is the *upper bound* of the range.

Initially when learning statistics, it is sometimes easy to understand a concept but difficult to see the importance or point of it. Variance is a good example of this since it is basically a very abstract notion (the average of the sum of squared differences between each score and the mean score). A particular value of variance is not intuitively meaningful since it does not refer to something that we regard as concrete such as, say, the mean score. Although variance is a fundamental statistical concept, it becomes meaningful only when we compare the variances of different variables or groups of participants. Nevertheless, it will rapidly become apparent that the concept of variance is involved in a great many different statistical techniques. Indeed, nearly all of the techniques in this book involve variance in some guise.

Be careful to note that variance as calculated by SPSS is really what is known technically as the variance estimate. It would be better to refer to it as the variance estimate but in this respect SPSS does not set a good example.

You can find out more about describing data numerically in Chapter 4 of Howitt, D. and Cramer, D. (2008) *Introduction to Statistics in Psychology*. Harlow: Pearson.

3.6 The data to be analysed

We will illustrate the computation of the mean, median and mode on the ages of university students – see Table 3.1 (*ISP*, Table 3.7).

Table 3.1   Ages of 12 students

18	21	23	18	19	19	19	33	18	19	19	20

3.7 Entering the data

Step 1:

In 'Variable View' of the 'Data Editor' name the 1st variable 'Age'.

Remove the 2 decimal places.

	Name	Type	Width	Decimals
1	Age	Numeric	8	0

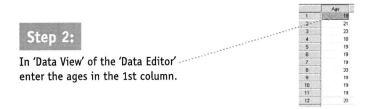

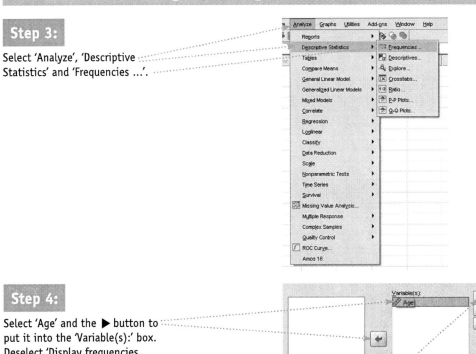

Step 2:

In 'Data View' of the 'Data Editor' enter the ages in the 1st column.

3.8 Conducting the analysis

Step 3:

Select 'Analyze', 'Descriptive Statistics' and 'Frequencies …'.

Step 4:

Select 'Age' and the ▶ button to put it into the 'Variable(s):' box. Deselect 'Display frequencies tables:'. Ignore the warning message.

Select 'Statistics …'.

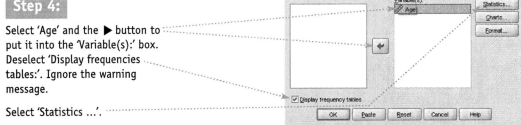

Step 5:

Select 'Mean', 'Median' and 'Mode'.

Select 'Continue'.

Select 'OK' (as in the above box).

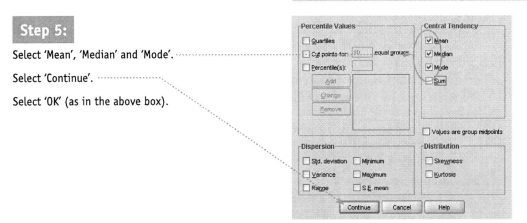

3.9 Interpreting the output

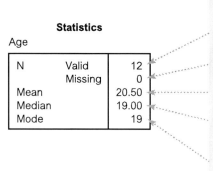

Statistics

Age

N	Valid	12
	Missing	0
Mean		20.50
Median		19.00
Mode		19

There are 12 cases with valid data on which the analysis is based.

There is no (0) missing data. See Chapter 34 on 'missing values' for a discussion.

The mean age (mathematical average) = 20.5 years.

The median age (the age of the person halfway up a list of ages from smallest to largest) is 19.00.

The modal (most common) age is 19. Check the next table on the output. This gives frequencies for each value. A variable may have more than one mode.

3.10 Other features

You will see from the dialogue box in Step 5 there are many additional statistical values that may be calculated. You should have little difficulty obtaining these by adapting the steps already described.

■ *Percentiles* – indicate the cutoff points for percentages of scores. Thus the 90th percentile is the score that cuts off the bottom 90% of scores in terms of size.

■ *Quartiles* – values of a distribution that indicate the cutoff points for the lowest 25%, lowest 50% and lowest 75% of scores.

■ *Sum* – the total of the scores on a variable.

■ *Skewness* – frequency distributions are not always symmetrical about the mean. Skewness is an index of the asymmetry or lop-sidedness of the distribution of scores on a variable. It takes a positive value if the values are skewed to the left and a negative value if they are skewed to the right.

■ *Kurtosis* – an index of how much steeper or flatter the distribution of scores on the variable is compared to the normal distribution. It takes a '+' sign for steep frequency curves and a '−' sign for flat curves.

■ *Standard deviation (estimate)* – this is a measure of the amount by which scores differ on average from the mean of the scores on a particular variable. Its method of calculation involves unusual ways of calculating the mean. In SPSS the standard deviation is calculated as an estimate of the population standard deviation. It is an index of the variability of scores around the mean of a variable. Some authors call this the sample standard deviation.

■ *Variance (estimate)* – this is a measure of the amount by which scores on average vary around the mean of the scores on that variable. It is the square of the standard deviation and is obviously therefore closely related to it. It is also always an estimate of the population variance in SPSS. Some authors call this the sample variance. Like standard deviation, it is an index of the variability of scores around the mean of a variable but also has other uses in statistics. In particular, it is the standard unit of measurement in statistics.

■ *Range* – the numerical difference between the largest and the smallest scores obtained on a variable. It is a single number.

■ *Minimum (score)* – the value of the lowest score in the data for a particular variable.

■ *Maximum (score)* – the value of the highest score in the data for a particular variable.

■ *Standard error (SE mean)* – the average amount by which the means of samples drawn from a population differ from the population mean. It is calculated in an unusual way. Standard error can be used much like standard deviation and variance as an index of how much variability there is in the scores on a variable.

Reporting the output

▨ The mean, median and mode can be presented in tabular form such as Table 3.2.

▨ Two decimal places are more than enough for most data. Most measurement is approximate, and the use of several decimal places tends to imply an unwarranted degree of precision.

▨ For the median, it is probably less confusing if you do not report values as 19.00 but as 19. However, if the decimal places were anything other than .00 then this should be reported since it indicates that the median is estimated and does not correspond to any actual scores for these particular data.

Table 3.2   Mean, median and mode of age

	Ages of students ($N = 12$)
Mean	20.50 years
Median	19 years
Mode	19 years

For further resources including data sets and questions, please refer to the CD accompanying this book.

4 Shapes of distributions of scores

Overview

- It is important to study the shape of the distribution of scores for each variable. Ideally for most statistical techniques, a distribution should be symmetrical and normally distributed (bell-shaped).

- Some statistical techniques are at their most powerful when the distributions of the variables involved are normally distributed. Major deviations from normality should be avoided but, for relatively small sample sizes, visual inspection of frequency diagrams is the only practical way to assess this. The effects of failure to meet this criterion can be overstated. Sometimes it is possible to transform one's scores statistically to approximate a normal distribution but this is largely a matter of trial and error, using, for example, logarithmic scales.

- Nevertheless, researchers should be wary of very asymmetrical (skewed) distributions and distributions that contain a few unusually high or low scores (outliers). Histograms, for example, can be used to help detect asymmetry and outliers.

- Consider combining ranges of scores together (as opposed to tabulating each individual possible score) in order to clarify the distribution of the data. Small sample sizes, typical of much work in psychology and other social sciences, can lead to a sparse figure or diagram in which trends are not clear.

4.1 What are the different shapes of scores?

The initial stages of data analysis involve calculating and plotting statistics that describe the shape of the distribution of scores on each variable. Knowing how your data are distributed is obviously an intrinsic part of any study though it is frequently by-passed by those who see the primary aim of research as checking for statistical significance rather than understanding the characteristics of the things they are investigating. But there are other reasons for examining the distributions of scores. Statistical techniques are developed based on certain working assumptions – a common one is that that scores on the variables follow the pattern of the bell-shaped curve or normal distribution (Figure 4.1). Since

Figure 4.1   The normal distribution

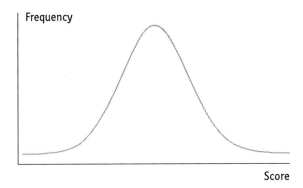

many statistical techniques are built on this assumption, if the data being analysed do not correspond to this ideal then one would expect, and it is the case, that the statistical techniques would work less than perfectly. Some departures from the 'ideal' bell-shaped curve can affect how powerful (capable of giving statistically significant results) the test is. Distributions which are heavily skewed to the left or to the right may have this effect. Figure 4.2 is an example of a distribution skewed to the left.

Apart from skewness in a distribution, some distributions depart from the ideal normal distribution by being relatively steep or relatively flat (Figures 4.3 and 4.4). The degree of flatness and steepness is known as kurtosis. Kurtosis compares the shape of a distribution with that of the normal distribution using a special formula but SPSS will calculate it for you (see Chapter 3). If the curve is steep then the kurtosis has a positive value, if the curve is flat then the kurtosis has a negative value.

We discussed histograms in Chapter 3. There is more to be said about them – in particular the concept of the frequency curve. A frequency curve is basically a smoothed-out line that joins the peaks of the various bars of the histogram. This smoothed-out line fits very uncomfortably if there are just a few different values of the scores obtained. It is not easy to fit a smooth curve to the histogram that appears at the end of Chapter 2 (p. 38). The more data points the better from this point of view. Figure 4.5 is a histogram with many

Figure 4.2   An example of a skewed distribution

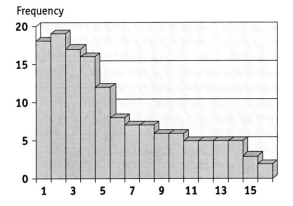

Figure 4.3   A flat frequency distribution

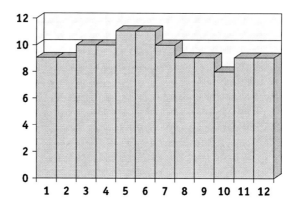

Figure 4.4   A steep frequency distribution

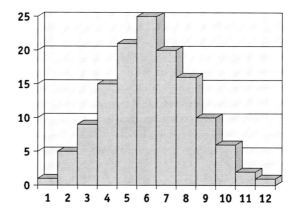

Figure 4.5   A histogram with more data points making frequency curve fitting a little easier

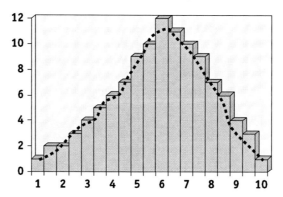

more data points – it is easier to fit a relatively smooth curve in this case as can be seen from the roughly drawn curve we have imposed on the figure.

As might be expected, and assuming that all other things are equal, the more data points the better the fit the data can be to the normal curve. For this reason, often continuous variables (those with an infinite variety of data points) are regarded as ideal. Few psychological measures meet this ideal. Most psychological measures yield relatively bumpy frequency curves. Again this means that the fit of the data to the normal distribution is not as good as it could be. The consequence is that the data depart somewhat from the assumptions on which many statistical tests are built. Again this will result in a degree of inaccuracy though psychologists happily tolerate this. Generally speaking, these inaccuracies will tend to make the statistical test less powerful (i.e. less capable of giving statistical significant outcomes). This is illustrated in Figure 4.6.

Of course, sometimes it may be preferable to use frequency tables to look at the way in which the scores on a variable are distributed. Naturally, this makes it more difficult to identify a normal distribution but it does make it easier to spot errors in data entry (e.g. scores out of the range).

Figure 4.6   The influence of distribution shapes on tests of significance

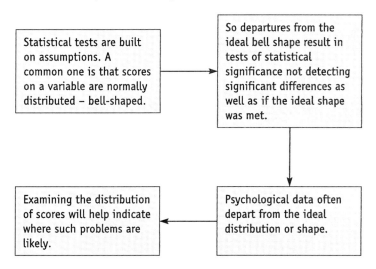

4.2   When to use histograms and frequency tables of scores

It is always highly desirable to obtain histograms and/or tables of frequencies of scores. This is an essential part of data analysis as conducted by a good researcher. Not to do so is basically incompetent as many important items of information are contained within these simple statistics. Authorities on statistics have often complained that psychologists fail to use simple statistical techniques to explore their data prior to more complex analyses. Too often this failing is encouraged by SPSS instruction manuals that hardly mention descriptive statistics.

4.3 When not to use histograms and frequency tables of scores

Use a histogram in favour of a frequency table when the frequency table would contain so many categories of scores that it would be unwieldy. Too large frequency tables can be problematic.

4.4 Data requirements for histograms and frequency tables of scores

Histograms require score variables. But frequency tables can also be computed for nominal (category) data.

4.5 Problems in using histograms and frequency tables of scores

The major problem occurs when frequency tables are computed without consideration of the number of scores or categories that it will produce. Any variable can be used to generate a frequency table on SPSS but it needs to be remembered that for every different score then a new category will be created in the table. So if you measured people's heights in millimetres the resulting frequency table would be horrendous. This is a common problem with SPSS – that it readily generates output whether or not the requested output is sensible. The adage 'junk in – junk out' is true but it is also true that thoughtless button pressing on SPSS means that a wheelbarrow may be needed to carry the printout home. Of course, it is possible to use SPSS procedures such as recode (see Chapter 35) to get output in a manageable and understandable form.

Be wary of the first charts and diagrams that SPSS produces. Often these need to be edited to produce something optimal.

Finally, it is common to find that student research is based on relatively few cases. This can result in somewhat difficult tables and diagrams unless some care is taken. It is very difficult to spot shapes of distributions if there are too many data points in the table or diagram. Consequently, sometimes it is better to use score ranges rather than the actual scores in order to generate good tables and diagrams. This will involve recoding your values (Chapter 35). Remember that in the worst cases SPSS will generate a different category for each different score to be found in your data. Recoding data would involve, for example, expressing age in ranges such as 15–19 years, 20–24 years, 25–39 years and so so. Some experimentation may be necessary to achieve the best tables and diagrams.

You can find out more about distributions of scores in Chapter 4 of Howitt, D. and Cramer, D. (2008) *Introduction to Statistics in Psychology*. Harlow: Pearson.

4.6 The data to be analysed

We will compute a frequency table and histogram of the extraversion scores of the 50 air-line pilots shown in Table 4.1 (*ISP*, Table 4.1).

Table 4.1 Extraversion scores of 50 airline pilots

3	5	5	4	4	5	5	3	5	2
1	2	5	3	2	1	2	3	3	3
4	2	5	5	4	2	4	5	1	5
5	3	3	4	1	4	2	5	1	2
3	2	5	4	2	1	2	3	4	1

4.7 Entering the data

Step 1:

In 'Variable View' of the 'Data Editor'
name the 1st variable 'Extrav'.
Remove the 2 decimal places.
Save this data as a file to use for
Chapter 9.

	Name	Type	Width	Decimals
1	Extrav	Numeric	8	0

Step 2:

In 'Data View' of the 'Data Editor'
enter the extraversion scores in the
1st column.

	Extrav
1	3
2	5
3	5
4	4
5	4

4.8 Frequency tables

Step 1:

Select 'Analyze',
'Descriptive Statistics' and
'Frequencies ...'.

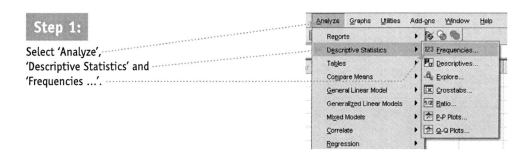

Step 2:

Select 'Extrav' and the ▶ button to put it in the 'Variable(s):' box.

Select 'OK'.

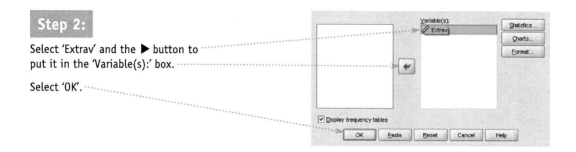

4.9 Interpreting the output

The 1st column shows the 5 values of extraversion which are 1 to 5.
The 2nd column shows the frequency of these values.
There are 7 cases with a value of 1.
The 3rd column expresses these frequencies as a percentage of the total number including missing data. Of all cases, 14% have a value of 1.

Extrav

		Frequency	Percent	Valid Percent	Cumulative Percent
Valid	1	7	14.0	14.0	14.0
	2	11	22.0	22.0	36.0
	3	10	20.0	20.0	56.0
	4	9	18.0	18.0	74.0
	5	13	26.0	26.0	100.0
	Total	50	100.0	100.0	

The 4th column expresses these frequencies as a percentage of the total number excluding missing data. As there are no missing cases the percentages are the same as in the 3rd column.

The 5th column adds these percentages together cumulatively down the table. So 56% of the cases have values of 3 or less.

Reporting the output

Notice that we omitted some of the confusion of detail in Table 4.2. Tables and diagrams need to clarify the results.

Table 4.2   One style of reporting output in Table 4.2

Extraversion score	Frequency	Percentage frequency	Cumulative percentage frequency
1	7	14.0	14.0
2	11	22.0	36.0
3	10	20.0	56.0
4	9	18.0	74.0
5	13	26.0	100.0

4.10   Histograms

Step 1:

Select 'Graphs',
'Legacy Dialogs' and
'Histogram ...'.

Step 2:

Select 'Extrav' and the ▶ button to
put it in the 'Variable:' box.

Select 'OK'.

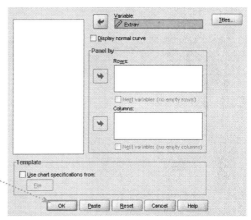

4.11   Interpreting the output

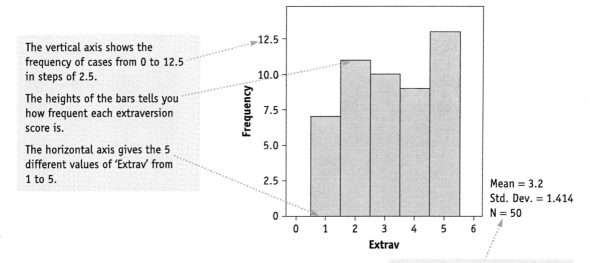

The vertical axis shows the
frequency of cases from 0 to 12.5
in steps of 2.5.

The heights of the bars tells you
how frequent each extraversion
score is.

The horizontal axis gives the 5
different values of 'Extrav' from
1 to 5.

Mean = 3.2
Std. Dev. = 1.414
N = 50

The mean extraversion score is 3.2.
The standard deviation is 1.414.
The number of cases is 50.

Reporting the output

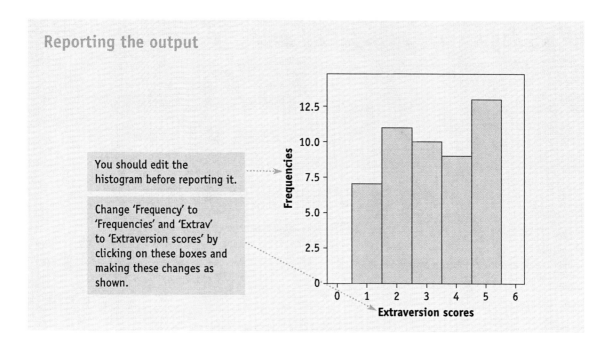

You should edit the histogram before reporting it.

Change 'Frequency' to 'Frequencies' and 'Extrav' to 'Extraversion scores' by clicking on these boxes and making these changes as shown.

For further resources including data sets and questions, please refer to the CD accompanying this book.

3 Variables, concepts and measures

Overview

- The variable is a key concept in psychological research. A variable is anything which varies and can be measured. There is a distinction between a concept and how it is measured.

- Despite the centrality and apparent ubiquity of the concept of variables, it was imported into psychology quite recently in the history of the discipline and largely from statistics. The dominance of 'variables' has been criticised because it tends to place emphasis on measurement rather than theoretical and other conceptual refinements of basic psychological concepts.

- In psychology, the distinction between independent and dependent variable is important. Generally, the independent variable is regarded as having an influence on the dependent variable. This is especially so in terms of experimental designs which seek to identify cause-and-effect sequences and the independent variable is the manipulated variable.

- Nominal variables are those which involve allocating cases to two or more categories. Binomial means that there are two categories, multinomial means that there are more than two categories. A quantitative variable is one in which a numerical value or score is assigned to indicate the amount of a characteristic an individual demonstrates.

- Stevens' theory of measurement suggests that variables can be measured on one of four different measurement scales – nominal, ordinal, interval and ratio. These have different implications as to the appropriate mathematical and statistical procedures which can be applied to them. However, generally in psychological research where data is collected in the form of numerical scores the analysis tends to assume the interval scale of measurement underlies the scores.

- Operational definitions of concepts define concepts in terms of the procedures or processes used to measure those concepts. It is an idea introduced by psychologists from the physical sciences which attempts to avoid a lack of clarity in the definition of concepts. There is a risk that this places too great an emphasis on measurement at the expense of careful understanding of concepts.

■ Mediator variables intervene between two variables and can be regarded as responsible for the relationship between those two variables. Moderator variables, on the other hand, simply show that the relationship between an independent and a dependent variable is not consistent but may be different at different levels of the moderator variable. For example, the relationship between age and income may be different for men and women. In this case, gender would be the moderator variable.

■ Hypothetical constructs are not variables but theoretical or conceptual inventions which explain what we can observe.

3.1 Introduction

Variables are what we create when we try to measure concepts. So far we have used the term variable without discussing the idea in any great detail. Yet variables are at the heart of much psychological research. Hypotheses are often stated using the names of variables involved closely followed by a statement of the relationship between the variables. So in this chapter we will explore the idea of variables in some depth. A variable is any characteristic or quality that has two or more categories or values. Of course, what that characteristic or quality is has to be defined in some way by the researcher. By saying that a variable has two or more categories or values simply reminds us that a variable must vary by definition. Otherwise we call it a *constant*. Researchers refer to a number of different types of variable which we will discuss in this chapter. Despite the apparent ubiquity of the idea of variables in psychology textbooks, the centrality of the concept of variables in much of modern psychology should be understood alongside the idea that a significant amount of psychology does not employ the concept. Furthermore, historically the concept of variable was a relatively modern introduction into the discipline largely from statistics.

Variables are the things that we measure, they are not exactly the same thing as the concepts that we use when trying to develop theories about something. In psychological theories we talk in terms of concepts: in Freudian psychology a key concept is the ego; in social psychology a key concept is social pressure, in biological psychology a key concept might be pheromones. None of these, in itself, constitutes a variable. Each of them is a concept which helps us understand things – they are not the same as the variables we measure. Of course, it is a major task in research to identify variables which help us measure concepts in some way. For example, if we wished to measure social influence we might do so in a number of different ways such as the number of people who disagree with a participant in a study.

3.2 The history of the variable in psychology

The concept of *variable* has an interesting history in that psychology existed almost with no reference to variables for the first fifty or so years of the discipline's modern existence.

Search through the work of early psychologists such as Freud and you find that they discuss psychological phenomena and not variables. The term 'independent variable', so familiar to all psychology students nowadays, was hardly mentioned at all in psychology publications before 1930. Most psychologists use the term without questioning the concept and it is probably one of the first pieces of psychological jargon that students come across. Psychology textbooks almost invariably discuss studies, especially laboratory experiments, in terms of *independent* and *dependent variables*; these terms are used instead of the names of the psychological phenomena that they are studying.

Variables, then, were latecomers in the history of psychology. It probably comes as no surprise to learn that the term 'variable' has its origins in nineteenth century mathematics especially the field of statistics. It was introduced into psychology in the work of Karl Pearson who originated the idea of the correlation coefficient. By the 1930s, psychologists were generally familiar with statistical ideas so familiarity with the term was common.

Edward Tolman, who is probably best remembered for his cognitive behavioural theory of learning and motivation, was the first to make extensive use of the word *variable* in the 1930s when he discussed *independent variables* and *dependent variables* together with his new idea of *intervening variables*. The significance of this can be understood better if one tries to discuss Freudian psychology, for example, in terms of these three types of variable. It is difficult to do so without losing the importance and nuances of Freudian ideas. In other words, these notions of variables tend to favour or facilitate certain ways of looking at the psychological world.

Danziger and Dzinas (1997) studied the prevalence of the term 'variables' in four major psychological journals published in 1938, 1949 and 1958. In the early journals there is some use of the term 'variable' in what Danziger and Dzinas describe as the 'softer' areas of psychology such as personality, abnormal and social psychology; surprisingly laboratory researchers were less likely to use the term. The increase in the use of the word 'variable' cannot be accounted for by an increase in the use of statistics in published articles since this was virtually universal in published research from the early part of the content analysis onwards. The possibility that the increase was due to a rapidly expanding use of the term 'intervening variable' can also be dismissed on the basis that these were rarely mentioned in the context of empirical research – it was a term confined almost exclusively to theoretical discussions.

The use of the concepts of independent variable and dependent variable was being encouraged by experimental psychologists to replace the terminology of stimulus-response. Robert Woodworth, a prominent and highly influential author of a dominant psychology textbook of the time, adopted the new terminology and others followed his lead. Perhaps influenced by this, there was a substantial increase in the use of the terms independent variable and dependent variable over the time period they studied.

Danziger and Dzinas argue that the term *variable* took prominence because psychologists reconstrued psychological phenomena in terms of the *variables* familiar from statistics. In this way, psychological phenomena became mathematical entities or, at least, the distinction between the two was obscured. Thus psychologists write of personality variables when discussing aspects of personality which have not yet even been measured as they would have to be to become statistical variables. This amounts to a 'prestructuring' of the psychological world in terms of variables and the consequent assumption that psychological research simply seeks to identify this structure of variables. Thus variables ceased to be merely a technical aspect of how psychological research is carried out but a statement or theory of the nature of psychological phenomena:

> *When some of the texts we have examined here proceeded as if everything that exists psychologically exists as a variable they were not only taking a metaphysical position, they were also foreclosing further discussion about the appropriateness of their procedures to the reality being investigated.*
>
> (Danziger and Dzinas, 1997, p. 47)

So are there any areas of psychology which do not use the concept of variable? Well it is very difficult to find any reference to variables in qualitative research, for example. Furthermore, it might be noted that facet theory (Canter, 1983; Shye and Elizur, 1994) regards the measures that we use in research simply as aspects of the world we are trying to understand. The analogy is with cutting precious stones. There are many different possible facets of a diamond depending on the way in which it is cut. Thus our measures simply reflect aspects of reality which are incomplete and less than the full picture of the psychological phenomena we are interested in. In other words, our measures are only a very limited sample of possible measures of whatever it is we are interested in theoretically. So the researcher should avoid confusing the definition of psychological concepts with how we measure them, but explore more deeply the definition of the concept at the theoretical level.

3.3   Types of variable

There are numerous different types of variable in psychology which may be indicative of the importance of the concept in psychology. Some of these are presented in Table 3.1 which indicates something of the relationship between the different types. However,

Table 3.1   Some of the main types of variable

Type of variable	Domain (Psychological or statistical)	Notes
Causal variable	Psychological	It is not possible to establish cause-and-effect sequences simply on the basis of statistics. Cause-and-effect can only be established by the use of appropriate research designs.
Hypothetical construct	Psychological	Not really a form of variable but an unobservable psychological structure or process which explains observable findings.
Independent variable	Both	The variation in the independent variable is assumed to account for all or some of the variation in the dependent variable. As a psychological concept, it tends to be assumed that the independent variable has a causal effect on the dependent variable. This is not the case when considered as a statistical concept.

→

Table 3.1   *continued*

Type of variable	Domain (Psychological or statistical)	Notes
Dependent variable	Both	See entry for independent variable.
Moderator variable	Statistical	A moderator variable is one which changes the character of the relationship between two variables.
Mediator variable	Primarily psychological but also statistical	A variable (concept) which is responsible for the influence of variable A on variable B. In other words it mediates the effect of variable A on variable B.
Intervening variable	Primarily psychological but also statistical	More or less the same as mediator variable. It is a variable (concept) which is responsible for the influence of variable A on variable B. In other words it intervenes between the effect of variable A on variable B.
Third variable	Statistical	A general term for variables which in some way influence the relationship between two variables of interest.
Confounding variable	Psychological	A general term for variables which cause confusion as to the interpretation of the relationship between two variables of interest.
Suppressor variable or masking variable	Statistical	A suppressor variable is a third variable which hides (reduces) the true relationship between two variables of interest.
Score variable	Statistical	Any variable which is measured using numbers which are indicative of the quantity of a particular characteristic.
Nominal (category or categorical) variable	Statistical	Any variable which is measured by allocating cases to named categories without any implications of quantity.
Ordinal variable	Statistical	A variable which is measured in a way which allows the researcher to order cases in terms of the quantity of a particular characteristic. Derives from Stevens' theory of measurement.
Interval variable	Statistical	Variables measured on a numerical scale where the unit of measurement is the same size irrespective of the position on the scale.
Ratio variable	Statistical	Variables measured on an interval numerical scale which has a proper zero point. This allows the researcher to make ratio statements such as person A is twice as tall as person B.
Dummy variable	Statistical	Used to describe the variables created to convert nominal category data to approximate score data.

the important thing about the table is that certain types of variable are primarily of theoretical and conceptual interest whereas others are primarily statistical in nature. Of course, given the very close relationships between psychology and statistics, many variables do not readily fall into just one of these categories. This is sometimes because psychologists have taken statistical terminology and absorbed it into their professional vocabulary to refer to slightly different things. There is an implication of the table which may not appear obvious at first sight. That is, it is very easy to fall into the trap of discussing psychological issues as if they are really statistical issues. This is best exemplified when psychologists seek to identify causal influences of one variable on another. The only way in which it is possible to establish that a relationship between two variables is causal is by employing an appropriate research design to do this. The randomised experiment is the best example of this by far. The statistical analysis employed cannot establish causality.

3.4 Independent and dependent variables

The concepts of independent and dependent variables are common in psychological writings. The distinction between the two is at its clearest when we consider the true experiment and, in an ideal world, would probably best be confined to laboratory and similar true experiments. The variable which is manipulated by the researcher is known as the independent variable. Actually it is totally independent of any other variable in a true experimental design since purely random processes are used to allocate participants to the different experimental treatments. Nothing in the situation, apart from randomness, influences the level of the independent variable. The variable which is measured (rather than manipulated) is the dependent variable since the experimental manipulation is expected to influence how the participants in the experiment behave. In other words, the dependent variable is subject to the influence of the independent variable.

The concepts of independent and dependent variables would appear to be quite simple, that is, the independent variable is the manipulated variable and the dependent variable is the measured variable which is expected to be influenced by the manipulated variable. It becomes rather confusing because the distinction between independent and dependent variables is applied to non-experimental designs. For example, the term independent variable is applied to comparisons between different groups. Thus, if we were comparing men and women in terms of their computer literacy then gender would be the independent variable. Computer literacy would be the dependent variable.

Of course, gender cannot be manipulated by the researcher – it is a fixed characteristic of the participant. Variables which cannot be or were not manipulated and which are characteristic of the participant or subjects are sometimes called *subject variables*. They include such variables as how old the person is, how intelligent they are, how anxious they are and so on. All of these variables may be described as the independent variable by some researchers. However, how can a variable be the independent variable if the causal direction of the relationship between two variables is not known? In non-experiments it may be better to use more neutral terms for these two types of variable such as *predictor variable* for the independent variable and *criterion variable* for the dependent variable. In this case we are trying to predict what the value is of the criterion variable from the values of the predictor variable or variables.

3.5 Measurement characteristics of variables

Measurement is the process of assigning individuals to the categories or values of a variable. Different variables have different measurement characteristics which need to be understood in order to plan and execute research effectively. The most important way in which variables differ is in terms of the nominal versus quantitative measurement.

■ Nominal variables (also known as qualitative, category or categorical variables)

Nominal variables are ones in which measurement consists of categorising cases in terms of two or more named categories. The number of different categories employed is also used to describe these variables:

- *Dichotomous, binomial or binary variables* These are merely variables which are measured using just two different values. (The term dichotomous is derived from the Greek meaning equally divided or cut in two: *dicho-* is Greek for apart, separate or in two parts while '-ous' is Latin for characterised by.) For example, one category could be 'friend' while the other category would be anyone else.

- *Multinomial variables* When a nominal variable has more than two values it is described as a multinomial, polychomous or polytomous variable (*poly* is Greek for many). We could have the four categories of 'friend', 'family member', 'acquaintance' and 'strangers'.

Each value or category of a dichotomous or multinomial variable needs to be identified or labelled. For example, we could refer to the four categories friend, family member, acquaintance and stranger as category A, category B, category C and category D. We could also refer to them as category 1, category 2, category 3 and category 4. The problem with this is that the categories named in this way have been separated from their original labels – friend, family member, acquaintance and stranger. This kind of variable may be known as a nominal, qualitative, category, categorical or frequency variable. Numbers are simply used as names or labels for the different categories. We may have to use numbers for the names of categories when analysing this sort of data on a computer. The only arithmetical operation that can be applied to dichotomous and multinomial variables is to count the frequency of how many cases fall into the different categories.

■ Quantitative variables

When we measure a quantitative variable, the numbers or values we assign to each person or case represent increasing levels of the variable. These numbers are known as scores since they represent amounts of something. A simple example of a quantitative variable might be social class (socio-economic status is a common variable to use in research). Suppose that social class is measured using the three different values of lower, middle and upper class. Lower class may be given the value of 1, middle class the value of 2 and upper class the value of 3. Hence, higher values represent higher social status. The important thing to remember is that the numbers here are being used to indicate different quantities of social class. Many quantitative variables (such as age, income, reaction time, number of errors or the score on a questionnaire scale) are measured using many more than three categories. When a variable is measured quantitatively, then the range of arithmetic operations that can be carried out is extensive – we can, for example, calculate the average value or sum the values.

The term dichotomous can be applied to certain quantitative variables as it was to some nominal variables. For example, we could simply measure a variable such as income using two categories – poor and rich which might be given the values 1 and 2. Quite clearly the rich have greater income than the poor so the values clearly indicate quantities. However, this is true of any dichotomous variable. Take the dichotomous variable sex or gender. For example, females may be given the value of 1 and males the value of 2. These values actually indicate quantity. A person who has the value 2 has more maleness than a person given the value 1. In other words, the distinction between quantitative and qualitative variables is reduced when considering dichotomous variables.

Box 3.1   KEY IDEAS

Mediator versus moderator variables

Conceptually, modern psychologists speak of the distinction between mediator and moderator variables. These present quite different views of the role of third variables in relationships among measures. Mediator and moderator variables are conceptual matters which are important more to research design and methodology than they are to statistical analysis as such. If we consider the relationship between the independent and dependent variable then a *mediator* variable is a variable which is responsible for this relationship. For example, the independent variable might be age and the dependent variable may be scores on a pub quiz or some other measure of general knowledge. Older people do better on the general knowledge quiz.

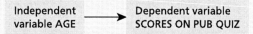

Age, itself, is not responsible for higher scores on the pub quiz. The reason why older people have greater general knowledge might be because they have had more time in their lives to read books and newspapers, watch television, and undertake other educational experiences. It is these learning experiences which are responsible for the relationship between age and general knowledge. In this instance, then, we can refer to these educational experiences as a mediator variable in the relationship between age and general knowledge.

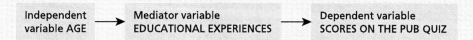

Another way of describing this is that there is an indirect effect of age on the scores on the pub quiz. Of course, there may be more than one mediator variable in the

Box 3.1 continued

relationship between an independent and a dependent variable. There is no substantial difference between a mediator variable and an intervening variable other than that intervening variables are regarded as hypothetical variables whereas mediator variables seem not to be regarded as necessarily hypothetical.

A moderator variable is completely distinct. A moderator variable is one which shows that the relationship between an independent variable and a dependent variable is not consistent throughout the data. For example, imagine that a researcher investigates the relationship between age and scores on a pub quiz but adds a further dimension, that is, they consider the relationship for men and women separately. They may find that the relationship between the two is different for men and women. Perhaps there is a strong correlation of 0.7 between age and scores on the pub quiz for women but a weak one of 0.2 between age and scores on the pub quiz for men. Thus the relationship is not the same throughout the data. This implies quite different conclusions for men and for women. In other words, gender moderates the relationship between age and scores on the pub quiz. Having established that gender is a moderator variable in this case does not explain in itself why the relationship is different for men and women. One possibility is that the pub quiz in question had a gender bias such that most of the questions were about topics which are of interest to women but not to men. Consequently, we might expect that the relationship would be reduced for men.

The interpretation of moderator variables is dependent on whether or not the independent variable in the independent variable–moderator variable–dependent variable chain is a randomised variable or not. Only where it is randomised can the researcher be sure of the causal sequence. Otherwise there is uncertainty about what is causing what.

3.6 Stevens' theory of scales of measurement

The previous section describes the measurement principles underlying variables in the most useful and practical way possible. However, there is another approach which is common in textbooks. Research methods textbooks are full of ideas which appear to be the uncontroversial bedrock of the discipline. A good example of this is the theory of scales of measurement put forward by the psychologist Stanley Stevens in 1946. You may have heard of his ideas: psychologists frequently write about nominal, ordinal, interval and ratio scales of measurement though few could name Stevens as the originator of these ideas. Remarkably, his ideas are surrounded by controversy in specialised statistical publications but one would be forgiven for thinking that they are indisputable 'facts' on the basis of the way they are uncritically presented in research methods and statistics textbooks. So in this section we will look at Stevens' theory in a somewhat critical way unlike other sources that you will find. You might be glad of the enlightenment.

By measurement, Stevens is taken to mean the allocation of a number (or symbol) to things using some consistent rule. So, for example, we could measure sweets in a number of different ways: (a) we could allocate a colour (blue, red, yellow are linguistic symbols, of course) to each sweet; (b) we could measure each sweet's weight as a number of grams;

or (c) we could grade them in terms of how good they taste. Measurement, conceptually, amounts to quite a simple process as these examples illustrate. It is clear that these three ways of measurement are somewhat different in terms of how the measurement was carried out. Stevens argued that there are four different types of measurement which have somewhat different mathematical properties. This means that the mathematical procedures that can be applied to each type of measurement differ. The mathematical operations which are appropriate for one type of measurement may be inappropriate for another. One consequence of this is that the sort of statistical analysis that is appropriate for one sort of variable may be inappropriate for a different type of variable. Choosing a statistical technique appropriate to the sort of data one has is one of the skills that has to be learnt when studying statistics in psychology.

Stevens' four types of measurement are usually put in the order nominal, ordinal, interval and ratio scales of measurement. This is actually a hierarchy from the least powerful data to the most powerful data. The later in the series the scale of measurement is in, the more information is contained within the measurement, thus variables measured so that they constitute a ratio scale are at the highest level of measurement and contain more information all other things being equal. The different measurement scales are often referred to as different levels of measurement which, of course, implies a hierarchy. Let us take each of these in turn starting with the highest level of the hierarchy.

1. *Ratio measurement scales*   The key feature of a ratio measurement scale is that it should be possible to calculate a meaningful ratio between two things which have been measured. This is a simpler idea than it sounds because we are talking ratios when we say things like Grant is twice as tall as Michelle. So if we measure the weights of two chocolates in grams we can say that the coffee cream chocolate was 50 per cent heavier than the strawberry truffle chocolate. In order to have a ratio measurement scale it is necessary for there to be a zero point on the scale which implies zero quantity for the measurement. Weights do have a zero point – zero grams means that there is no weight – weight is a ratio measurement scale. A common measurement which does not have a proper zero (implying zero quantity) is temperature scales such as Celsius or Fahrenheit. To be sure, if you look at a thermometer you will find a zero point on both Celsius and Fahrenheit scales but this is not the lowest temperature possible. Zero on the Celsius scale is the freezing point of water but it can get a lot colder than that. What this means is that for temperature, it is not possible to say that something is twice as hot as something else if we measure on the temperature scales familiar to us all. Thirty degrees Celsius cannot be regarded as twice as hot as 15 degrees Celsius. Any statistical procedure can be applied to ratio data. For example, it is meaningful to calculate the mean of ratio data – as well as ratios. There is another feature of ratio measurement scales, that there should be equal intervals between points on the scale. However, this requirement of equal intervals is also a requirement of the next measurement scale – the interval measurement scale – as we shall see.

2. *(Equal) interval measurement scale*   This involves assigning real numbers (as opposed to ranks or descriptive labels) to whatever is being measured. It is difficult to give common examples of interval measures which are not also ratio measures. But let us look on our bag of sweets: we find a sell-by date. Now sell-by date is part of a measurement scale which measures time. If a bag of sweets has the sell-by date of 22nd February then this is one day less than a sell-by date of 23rd February. Sell-by date is being measured on an equal interval measure on which each unit is a day and that unit is constant throughout the scale of measurement. However, there is not a zero

point on this scale. We all know that the year 0 is not the earliest year that there has ever been since it is the point where BC changes to AD. We could, if we wanted to, work out the average sell-by date on bags of sweets in a shop. The average would be meaningful because it is based on an equal-step scale of measurement. There are many statistical techniques which utilise data which is measured on interval scales of measurement. Indeed, most of the statistical techniques available to researchers can handle interval scale data. Conceptually, there is a clear difference between interval scale measurements and ratio scale measurements though in most instances it makes little difference, say, in terms of statistical analysis – it is only important when one wishes to use ratios which, in truth, is not common in psychology.

3. *Ordinal measurement scales*   This involves giving a value to each of the things being measured which indicates the relative order on some sort of characteristic. For example, you might wish to order the chocolates in a box of chocolates in terms of how much you like each of them. So you could put the ones that you most like on the left-hand side of a table, the ones that you like a bit less to the right of them, and so forth until the ones that you most dislike like are on the far right-hand side of the table. In this way, the chocolates have been placed in order from the most liked to the least liked. This is like ordinal measurement in that your have ordered them from the most to the least. Nothing can really be said about how much more that you like, say, the hazelnut cluster from the cherry delight, only that one is preferred to the other because you put them at different points on the table. It is not possible to say how much more you like one of the chocolates than another. Even if you measured the distance between where you put the hazelnut cluster and where you put the cherry delight, this gives no precise indication of how much more one chocolate is liked than another. Ordinal numbers (first, second, third, fourth . . . last) could be applied to the positions from left to right at which the chocolates were placed. These ordinal numbers correspond to the rank order. The hazelnut cluster might be eighth and the cherry delight might be ninth. However, it still remains the case that although the hazelnut cluster is more liked than the cherry delight, how much more it is liked is not known. Ordinal measurements, it is argued, are not appropriate for calculating statistics such as the mean. This is certainly true for data which has been converted to ranks since the mean rank is totally determined by the number of items ranked. However, psychologists rarely collect data in the form of ranks but in the form of scores. In Stevens' measurement theory any numerical score which is not on a scale where the steps are equal intervals is defined as ordinal. Stevens argued that the mode and the median are more useful statistics for ordinal data and that the mean is inappropriate. Ordinal measurements are frequently analysed using what are known as non-parametric or distribution-free statistics. They vary, but many of these are based on putting the raw data into ranks.

4. *Nominal (or category/categorical) measurement scales*   This measurement scale involves giving labels to the things being measured. It is illustrated by labelling sweets in an assorted bag of sweets in terms of their colour. Colour names are linguistic symbols but one could use letters or numbers as symbols to represent each colour if we so wished. So we could call red Colour A and blue Colour B, for instance. Furthermore, we could use numbers purely as symbols so that we could call red Colour 1 and blue Colour 2. Whether we use words, letters, numbers or some other symbol to represent each colour does not make any practical difference. It has to be recognised that if we use numbers as the code then these numbers do not have

mathematical properties any more than letters would have. So things become a little more complicated when we think about what numerical procedures we can perform on these measurements. We are very restricted. For example, we cannot multiply red by blue – this is meaningless. Actually the only numerical procedure we could perform in these circumstances would be to count the number of red sweets, the number of blue sweets, and the number of yellow sweets, for example. By counting we mean the same thing as calculating the frequency of things so we are actually able to say that red sweets have a frequency of 10, blue sweets have a frequency of 5, and yellow sweets have a frequency of 19 in our particular bag of sweets. We can say which is the most frequent or typical sweet colour (yellow) in our bag of sweets but little else. We cannot meaningfully calculate things like the average red sweet, the average blue sweet, and the average yellow sweet based on giving each sweet a colour label. So in terms of statistical analysis, only statistics which are designed for use with frequencies could be used. Confusions can occur if the symbols used for the nominal scale of measurement are numbers. There is nothing wrong with using numbers as symbols to represent things so long as one remembers that they are merely symbols and that they are no different from words or letters in this context.

It is not too difficult to grasp the differences between these four different scales of measurement. The difficulty arises when one tries to apply what has been learnt to the vast variety of different psychological measures. It will not have escaped your attention how in order to explain interval and ratio data physical measurements such as weight and temperature were employed. This is because these measures clearly meet the requirements of these measurement scales. When it comes to psychological measures, it is much more difficult to find examples of interval and ratio data which everyone would agree about. There are a few examples but they are rare. Reaction time (the amount of time it takes to react to a particular signal) is one obvious exception but largely because it is a physical measure (time) anyway. Examples of more psychological variables which reflect the interval and ratio levels of measurement are difficult to find. Take, for example, IQ (intelligence quotient) scores. It is certainly possible to say that a person with an IQ of 140 is more intelligent than a person with an IQ of 70. Thus we can regard IQ as an ordinal measurement. However, is it possible to say that a person with an IQ of 140 is twice as intelligent as someone with an IQ of 70 which would make it a ratio measurement? Are the units that IQ are measured in equal throughout the scale? Is the difference between an IQ of 70 and an IQ of 71 the same difference as that between an IQ of 140 and an IQ of 141? They need to be the same if IQ is being measured on an equal interval scale of measurement. One thing that should be pointed out is that one unit on our measure of IQ is in terms of the numbers involved the same no matter where it occurs on the scale. The problem is that in terms of what we are really interested in – intelligence – we do not know that each mathematical unit is the same as each psychological unit. If this is not clear, then consider using electric shocks to cause pain. The scale may be from zero volts to 6000 volts. This is clearly an interval and also a ratio scale in terms of the volts, in terms of the resulting pain then this is not the case. We all know that if we touch the terminals of a small battery this has no effect on us which means that at the low voltage levels no pain is caused but this is not true at higher voltage levels. Thus, in terms of pain this scale is not equal interval.

Not surprisingly, Stevens' theory of measurement has caused a majority of students great consternation especially given that it is usually taught in conjunction with statistics which itself is a difficult set of ideas for many students. The situation is that anyone using the theory will generally have great difficulty in arguing that their measures are on either an interval or ratio scale of measurement simply because there is generally no way of specifying that each interval on the scale is in some way equal to all of the others. Furthermore, there are problems with the idea that a measure is ordinal. One reason for this is that psychologists rarely simply gather data in the form of ranks as opposed to some form of score. These scores therefore contain more information than that implied merely by a rank though the precise interpretation of these scores is not known. There is no way of showing that these scores are on an equal interval scale so they should be regarded as ordinal data according to Stevens' theory. Clearly this is entirely unsatisfactory. Non-parametric statistics were frequently advocated in the past for psychological data since these do not assume equality of the measurement intervals. Unfortunately, many powerful statistical techniques are excluded by this strategy.

One argument, which we find convincing, is that it is not the psychological implications of the scores which is important but simply the mathematical properties of the numbers involved. In other words, so long as the scores are on a numerical scale then they can be treated as if they are interval scale data (and, in exceptional circumstances where there is a zero point, as ratio scale data). The truth of the matter, and quite remarkable given the dominance of Stevens' ideas about measurement in psychology, is that researchers usually treat any measure they make involving scores as if it were interval data. This is done without questioning the status of their measures in terms of Stevens' theory. Actually there are statistical studies which partly support this in which ordinal data is subject to statistical analyses which are based on the interval scale of measurement. For many statistics, this makes little or no difference.

Box 3.2 **KEY IDEAS**

Hypothetical constructs

Hypothetical constructs were first defined by Kenneth MacCorquodale and Paul E. Meehl in 1948. They are not variables in the sense we have discussed in this chapter. Essentially a hypothetical construct is a theoretical invention which is introduced to explain more observable facts. It is something which is not directly observable but nevertheless is useful in explaining things such as relationships between variables which can be observed. There is a wide variety of hypothetical constructs in psychology. Self-esteem, intelligence, the ego, the id and the superego are just some examples. None of these things are directly observable yet are discussed as explanations of a number of observable phenomena. Some of them, such as intelligence, might at first sight seem to be observable things but, usually, they are not since they are based on inferences rather than observation. In the case of the hypothetical construct of intelligence, we use observables such as the fact that a child is top of their class, is a chess champion, and has a good vocabulary to infer that they are intelligent. Perhaps more crucially, the Freudian concept of the id is not observable as such but is a way of uniting observable phenomena in a meaningful way which constitutes an explanation of those observables.

3.7 Operationalising concepts and variables

There is a crucial distinction to be made between a variable and the measure of that variable. Variables are concepts or abstractions which are created and refined as part of the advancement of the discipline of psychology. Gender is not a tick on a questionnaire, but we can measure gender by getting participants to tick male or female on a questionnaire. The tick on the questionnaire is an *indicator* of gender, but it is not gender. Operationalisation (Bridgman, 1927) is the steps (or operations) that we take to measure the variable in question. Bridgman was a physical scientist who, at the time that he developed his ideas was concerned that concepts in the physical sciences were extremely poorly defined and lacked clarity. Of course, this is frequently the case in the softer discipline of psychology too. For Bridgman, the solution was to argue that precision is brought to the definition of concepts by specifying precisely the operations by which a concept is measured. So the definition of weight is through describing the measurement process, for example, the steps by which one weighs something using some sort of measurement scale. Of course, operationalising concepts is not guaranteed to provide precision of definition unless the measurement process is close to the concept in question and the measurement process can be precisely defined. So, for example, is it possible to provide a good operational definition of a concept like love? By what operations can love be measured is the question. One possible operational definition might be to measure the amount of time that a couple spends in each other's company in a week. There are obvious problems with this operational definition which suggests that it is not wholly adequate.

Nevertheless, some researchers in psychology argue that the best way of defining the nature of our variables is to describe how they are measured. For example, there are various ways in which we could operationalise the concept or variable of anxiety. We could manipulate it by putting participants in a situation which makes them anxious and compare that situation with one in which they do not feel anxious. We could assess anxiety by asking them how anxious they are, getting other people to rate how anxious they seem to be, or measuring some physiological index of anxiety such as their heart rate. These are different ways of operationalising anxiety. If they all reflect what we consider to be anxiety we should find that these different methods are related to one another. So we would expect participants in a situation which makes them anxious to report being more anxious, be rated as being more anxious and to have a faster heart rate than those in a situation which does not make them anxious. If these methods are not related to one another, then they may not all be measuring anxiety.

Operationalisation has benefits and drawbacks. The benefit is that by defining a concept by the steps involved in measuring it, then the meaning of the concept could not be more explicit. The costs include that operationalisation places less onus on the researcher to explicate the nature of their concepts and encourages the concentration on measurement issues rather than conceptual issues. Of course, ultimately any concept used in research has to be measured using specific and specified operations. However, this should not be at the expense of careful consideration of the nature of the concepts involved. Unfortunately, the tendency is for the idea of operational definition to result in a concentration on measurement in psychology rather than establishing the value of the psychological concepts that the researcher should actually be interested in.

3.8 Conclusion

Perhaps the key thing to have emerged in this chapter is that some of the accepted ideas in psychological research methods were philosophical contributions to the discipline. A concept such as a variable has its own timeline and is not universal in the discipline. Although some of these ideas seem to be consensually accepted that does not alter the fact that they are not the only way of regarding psychological research. While the idea of operational definitions of concepts pervades much of psychology, once again it should be regarded as a notion which may have its advantages but also its disadvantages in that it encourages psychologists to focus on measurement but not in the context of a theoretical examination.

The concept of a variable has many different ramifications in psychology. Many of these are a consequence of the origins of the concept in statistics. Intervening variables, moderator variables, mediating variables, continuous variables, discrete variables, independent variables, dependent variables and so forth are all examples of variables but all are different conceptually. Some have more to do with statistics than others.

Measurement theory introduced the notions of nominal, ordinal, interval and ratio measurement. While these ideas are useful in helping the researcher not to make fundamental mistakes such as suggesting that one person is twice as intelligent as another when such statements require a ratio level of measurement, they are actually out-of-step with psychological practice in terms of the statistical analysis of research data.

Key points

- The concept of variable firmly ties psychology to statistics since it is a statistical concept. There are many different types of variable which relate as much to theoretical issues as empirical issues. For example, the distinction between independent and dependent variables and the distinction between moderator and mediating variables relate to explanations of psychological phenomena and not simply to empirical methods.

- Stevens' measurement theory has an important place in the teaching of statistics but is problematic in relation to the practice of research. Nevertheless, it can help a researcher from making totally erroneous statements based on their data. Most research in psychology ignores measurement theory and simply assumes that data in the form of scores (as opposed to nominal data) can be analysed as if they are based on the interval scale of measurement.

- Psychologists stress operational definitions of concepts in which theoretical concepts are defined in terms of the processes by which they are measured. In the worst cases, this can encourage the concentration of easily measured variables at the expense of trying to understand the fundamental concept better at a conceptual and theoretical level.

1. Try to list the defining characteristics of the concept love. Suggest how love can be defined using operational definitions.

2. Could Stevens' theory of measurement be applied to measures of love? For example, what type of measurement would describe classifying relationships as either platonic or romantic love?

8 Ethics in research

Overview

■ Psychological ethics are the moral principles that govern psychological activity. Research ethics are the result of applying these broader principles to research. Occasions arise when there is a conflict between ethical principles – ethical dilemmas – which are not simply resolved.

■ Psychology's professional bodies (for example, the American Psychological Association and the British Psychological Society) publish detailed ethical guidelines. They overlap significantly. This chapter is based on recent revisions of the ethical principles of these bodies.

■ Deception, potential harm, informed consent and confidentiality are commonly the focus of the debate about ethics. However, ethical issues stretch much more widely. They include responsibilities to other organisations, the law and ethical committees, circumstances in which photos and video recording are appropriate, and the publication of findings, plagiarism and fabricating data.

■ Significantly, ethical considerations are the responsibility of all psychologists including students in training.

8.1 Introduction

Quite simply, ethics are the moral principles by which we conduct ourselves. Psychological ethics, then, are the moral principles by which psychologists conduct themselves. It is wrong to regard ethics as being merely the rules or regulations which govern conduct. The activities of psychologists are far too varied and complex for that. Psychological work inevitably throws up situations which are genuinely dilemmas which no amount of rules or regulations could effectively police. Ethical dilemmas involve conflicts between different principles of moral conduct. Consequently psychologists may differ in terms of their position on a particular matter. Ethical behaviour is not the responsibility of each individual psychologist but a responsibility of the entire psychological community. Monitoring the activities of fellow psychologists, seeking the advice of other psychologists when ethical difficulties come to light and collectively advancing ethical behaviour in their work-place are all instances of the mutual concern that psychologists have about the conduct of the profession. Equally, psychological ethics cannot be entirely separated from personal morality.

The American Psychological Association's most recent ethical code was first published in 2002. It came into effect on 1 June 2003. It amounts to a substantial ethical programme for psychological practitioners, not just researchers. This is important since unethical behaviour reflects on the entire psychological community. The collective strength of psychology lies largely in the profession's ability to control and monitor all aspects of the work of psychologists. The code, nevertheless, only applies to the professional activities of the psychologist – their scientific, professional and educational roles. For example, it requires an ethical stance in psychology teaching – so that there is a requirement of fidelity in the content of psychology courses such that they should accurately reflect the current state of knowledge. These newest ethical standards do not simply apply to members of the American Psychological Association but also to student affiliates/members. Ignorance of the relevant ethical standards is not a defence for unethical conduct and neither is failure to understand the standards properly. Quite simply, this means that all psychology students need a full and mature understanding of the ethical principles which govern the profession. It is not something to be left until the student is professionally qualified. Whenever scientific, professional and educational work in psychology is involved so too are ethics irrespective of the status. We have chosen to focus on the American Psychological Association's ethical guidelines as they are the most recent available but also because they consider more issues than any others. As such, they bring to attention matters which otherwise might be overlooked. We believe that it is no excuse to disregard them simply because they are not mentioned by one's own professional ethics.

What is the purpose of ethics? The answer to this may seem self-evident, that is, psychologists ought to know how to conduct themselves properly. But there is more to it than that. One of the characteristics of the professions (medicine being the prime example) is the desire to retain autonomy. The history of the emergence of professions such as medicine during the nineteenth century illustrates this well (Howitt, 1992*a*). Autonomy implies self-regulation of the affairs of members by the professional body. It is not possible to be autonomous if the activities of members are under the detailed control of legislation. So professions need to stipulate and police standards of conduct. There is another important reason why psychological work should maintain high ethical standards. The good reputation of psychology and psychologists among the general public, for example, is essential for the development of psychology. If psychologists collectively enjoyed a reputation for being dishonest, exploitative, prurient liars then few would employ their services or willingly participate in their research. Trust in the profession is essential.

Failure to adhere to sound ethical principles may result in complaints to professional bodies such as the American Psychological Association, British Psychological Society and so forth. Sanctions may be imposed on those violating ethical principles. Ultimately the final sanction is ending the individual's membership of the professional body, which may result in the individual being unable to practise professionally. Many organisations including universities have ethics committees that both supervise the research carried out by employees but also that of other researchers wishing to do research within the organisation. While this does provide a measure of protection for all parties (including the researcher), it should not be regarded as the final guarantee of good ethical practices in research.

8.2 APA ethics

The APA ethics are based on five general principles. These are:

- *Principle A: Beneficence and nonmaleficence*   Psychologists seek to benefit and avoid harm to those whom they engage with professionally. This includes the animals used in research. Psychologists should both be aware of and guard against those factors which may result in harm to others. The list of factors is long and includes financial, social and institutional considerations.

- *Principle B: Fidelity and responsibility*   Psychologists are in relationships of trust in their professional activities. They are thus required to take responsibility for their actions, adhere to professional standards of conduct, and make clear exactly their role and obligations in all aspects of their professional activities. In relation to research and practice, psychologists are not merely concerned with their own personal activities but with the ethical conduct of their colleagues (widely defined). It is worthwhile quoting word for word one aspect of the professional fidelity ethic: 'Psychologists strive to contribute a portion of their professional time for little or no compensation or personal advantage.'

- *Principle C: Integrity – accuracy, honesty, truthfulness*   Psychologists are expected to manifest integrity in all aspects of their professional work. One possible exception to this is circumstances in which the ratio of benefits to harm of using deception is large. Nevertheless, it remains the duty of psychologists even in these circumstances to seriously assess the possible harmful consequences of the deception including the ensuing distrust. The psychologist has a duty to correct these harmful consequences. The problem of deception is discussed in more detail later.

- *Principle D: Justice – equality of access to the benefits of psychology*   This means that psychologists exercise careful judgement and take care to enable all people to experience just and fair psychological practices. Psychologists should be aware of the nature of their biases (potential and actual). They should not engage in, or condone, unjust practices and need to be aware of the ways in which injustice may manifest itself.

- *Principle E: Respect for people's rights and dignity*   According to the American Psychological Association, individuals have the rights of privacy, confidentiality and self-determination. Consequently, psychologists need to be aware of the vulnerabilities of some individuals that make it difficult for them to make autonomous decisions. Children are an obvious example. The principle also requires psychologists to be aware of and respect differences between cultures, individuals and roles. Age, culture, disability, ethnicity, gender, gender identity, language, national origin, race, religion, sexual orientation and socio-economic status are among these differences. Psychologists should avoid and remove biases related to these differences while being vigilant for, and critical of, those who fail to meet this standard.

Detailed recommendations about ethical conduct are provided on the basis of these principles. In this chapter we will concentrate on those issues which are especially pertinent to research.

8.3 Research ethics

Ethical issues are presented by the American Psychological Association's documentation in the order in which they are likely to be of concern to the researcher. Hence the list starts with the preparatory stages of planning research and culminates with publication.

▪ Institutional approval

Much research takes place in organisations such as the police, prisons, schools and health services. Many, if not all, of these require formal approval before the research may be carried out in that organisation or by members of that organisation. Sometimes this authority to permit research is the responsibility of an individual (for example, a headteacher) but, more likely, it will be the responsibility of a committee which considers ethics. It is incumbent on the researcher to obtain approval for their planned research. Furthermore, the proposal they put forward should be transparent in the sense that the information contained in the documentation and any other communication should accurately reflect the nature of the research. The organisation should be in a position to understand precisely what the researcher intends on the basis of the documentation provided by the researcher and any other communications. So any form of deceit or sharp practice such as lies, lying by omission and partial truths is unacceptable. Finally, the research should be carried out strictly in accordance with the protocol for the research as laid down by the researcher in the documentation. Material changes are not permissible and, if unavoidable, may require additional approval to remain ethical.

The next set of ethical requirements superficially seem rather different from each other. Nevertheless, they all relate to the general principle that participation in research should be a freely made decision of the participant. Undue pressure, fear, coercion and the like should not be present or implied. In addition, participants need to understand just what they are subjecting themselves to by agreeing to be part of the research. Without this, they may inadvertently agree to participate in something which they would otherwise decline to do.

▪ Informed consent to research

The general principle of informed consent applies widely and would include assessment, counselling and therapy as well as research. People have the right to have prior knowledge of just what they are agreeing to before agreeing to it. Only in this way is it possible for them to decide not to participate. Potential participants in research need to have the nature of the research explained to them in terms which they could reasonably be expected to understand. So the explanation given to a child may be different from that given to a university student. According to the ethical principles, sometimes research may be conducted without informed consent if it is allowed by the ethical code or where the law and other regulations specifically permit. (Although one might question whether research is ethical merely because the law permits it.)

The main provisions which need to be in place to justify the claim of informed consent are:

- ▪ The purpose, procedures and approximate duration of the research should be provided to potential participants.

- ▪ Participants should be made aware that they are both free to refuse to take part in the research and also free to withdraw from the research at any stage. Usually researchers accept that this freedom to withdraw involves the freedom to withdraw any data provided up to the point of withdrawal. For example, the shredding of questionnaires and the destruction of recordings are appropriate ways of doing this if the withdrawing participant wishes. Or they may simply be given to the participant to dispose of as they wish.

- The participant should be made aware of the possible outcomes or consequences of refusing to take part in the research or withdrawing. Frequently, there are no consequences but this is not always the case. For example, some organisations require that clients take part in research as part of the 'contract' between the organisation and client. Failure to take part in research might be taken as an indicator of non-cooperation. The sex offender undergoing treatment who declines to take part in the research might be regarded as lacking in contrition. Such judgements may have implications for the future disposal of the client. The researcher cannot be responsible for the original contract but they should be aware of the (subtle) pressure to participate and stress the voluntary nature of participation.

- The participants should be informed of those aspects of the research which might influence their decision to participate. These include discomforts, risks and adverse outcomes. For example, one might include features of the study which might offend the sensibilities of the participant. Research on pornography in which pornographic images will be shown may offend the moral and/or social sensibilities of some participants.

- Similarly, the participant should be informed of the benefits that may emerge from the research. A wide view of this would include benefits for academic research, benefits for the community, and even benefits for the individual participant. In this way, the potential participant is provided with a fuller picture of what the research might achieve which otherwise might not be obvious to them.

- They should be told of any limits to the confidentiality of information provided during the research. Normally, researchers ensure the anonymity of the data that they collect and also the identity of the source of the data. But this is not always possible. For example, if one were researching sex offenders and they disclosed other offences of which authorities were unaware. It may be a requirement placed on the researcher that such undisclosed offences are reported to the authorities. In these circumstances, the appropriate course of action might be to indicate to the participant that the researcher would have to report such previously undisclosed offences to the authorities.

- Participants should be informed of the nature of any incentives being made to participate. Some participants may agree to take part as an act of kindness or because they believe that the research is important. If they are unaware of a cash payment, they may feel that their good intentions for taking part in the research are compromised when the payment is eventually offered.

- Participants should be given contact details of someone whom they may approach for further details about the research and the rights of participants in the research. This information allows potential participants to ask more detailed questions and to obtain clarification. Furthermore, it has the benefit of helping to establish the bona fides of the research. For example, if the contact is a professor at a university, then this would help establish the reputability of the research.

Special provisions apply to experimental research involving potentially beneficial treatments which may not be offered to all participants (see Box 8.1).

Box 8.1   TALKING POINT

Informed consent in intervention experiments

When a psychologist conducts *intervention research* there may be issues of informed consent. This does not refer to every experiment but those in which there may be significant advantages to receiving the treatment and significant disadvantages in *not* receiving the treatment. The treatment, for example, might be a therapeutic drug, counselling or therapy. Clearly, in these circumstances many participants would prefer to receive the treatment rather than not receive the treatment. If this were medical research it would be equivalent to some cancer patients being in the control group and dying because they are not given the newly developed drug that the experimental group benefits from. In psychological research, someone may be left suffering depression simply because they are allocated to the control group not receiving treatment. Due to these possibilities, the researcher in these circumstances should do the following:

- The experimental nature of the treatments should be explained at the outset of the research.

- It should be made clear the services or treatments which will *not* be available should the participant be allocated to the control condition.

- The method of assignment to the experimental or the control conditions should be explained clearly. If the method of selection for the experimental and control conditions is random then this needs to be explained.

- The nature of the services or treatments available to those who choose *not* to take part in the research should be explained.

- Financial aspects of participation should be clarified. For example, the participant may be paid for participation, but it is conceivable that they may be expected to contribute to the cost of their treatment.

The classic study violating the above principles is known as the Tuskegee Experiment (Jones, 1981). Significantly, the study only involved black people as participants. They were suffering from syphilis at a time when this was a killer disease. The researchers, unbeknown to the participants, allocated them to experimental and control conditions. Hence those in the control had effective treatment withheld so were at a serious health risk as a consequence. This may have been bad enough but there was worse. Even when it had become clear that the treatment was effective, the members of the control group were left to suffer from the disease because the researchers also wished to study its natural progression!

Informed consent for recordings and photography

Taking voice recordings, videos or photographs of participants is subject to the usual principle of informed consent. However, exceptions are stipulated in the ethical code:

■ Informed consent is not necessary if the recording or photography takes place in a public place and is naturalistic (that is, there is no experimental intervention). This is ethical only to the extent that there is no risk of the inadvertent participants being identified personally or harmed by the recording or photography.

■ If the research requires deception (and that deception is ethical) then consent for using the recording may be obtained retrospectively during the debriefing session in which the participant is given information about the research and an opportunity to ask questions. Deception is discussed below.

Circumstances in which informed consent may not be necessary

The ethical guidelines do not impose an invariant requirement of informed consent. They suggest circumstances in which it may be permissible to carry out research without prior consent of this sort. The overriding requirement is that the research could not be expected to (i.e. can be regarded as *not* likely to) cause distress or harm to participants. Additionally, at least *one* of the following should apply to the research in question:

■ The study uses anonymous questionnaires or observations in a natural setting or archival materials – even then such participants should not be placed at risk of harm of any sort (even to their reputation) and confidentiality should be maintained.

■ The study concerns jobs or related organisational matters in circumstances where the participant is under no risk concerning employment issues and the requirements of confidentiality are met.

■ The study concerns 'normal educational practices, curricula or classroom management methods' in a context of an educational establishment.

The ethics also permit research not using informed consent *if* the law or institutional regulations permit research without informed consent. This provision of the ethical principles might cause some consternation. Most of us probably have no difficulty with the principle that psychologists should keep to the law in terms of their professional activities. Stealing from clients, for example, is illegal as well as unethical. However, there is a distinction to be made between what is permissible in law and what is ethical. A good example of this is the medical practitioner who has consenting sex with a patient. This may not be illegal and no crime committed in some countries. However, it is unethical for a doctor to do so and the punishment imposed by the medical profession is severe: possibly removal from the register of medical practitioners. There may be a potential conflict between ethics and the law. It seems to be somewhat lame to prefer the permission of the law rather than the constraints of the ethical standards.

■ Research with individuals in a less powerful/subordinate position to the researcher

Psychologists are often in a position of power relative to others. A university professor of psychology has power over his or her students. Clients of psychologists are dependent on the psychologists for help or treatment. Junior members of research staff are dependent on senior research staff and subordinate to them. It follows that some potential research participant may suffer adverse consequences as a result of refusing to take part in research or may be under undue pressure to participate simply because of this power differential.

Any psychologist in such a position of power has an ethical duty to protect these vulnerable individuals from such adverse consequences. Sometimes, participation in research is a requirement of particular university courses or inducements may be given to participate in the form of additional credit. In these circumstances, the ethical recommendation is that fair alternative choices should be made available for individuals who do not wish to participate in research.

Inducements to participate

Financial and other encouragement to participate in research are subject to the following requirements:

- Psychologists should not offer unreasonably large monetary or other inducements (for example, gifts) to potential participants in research. In some circumstances such rewards can become coercive. One simply has to take the medical analogy of offering people large amounts of money to donate organs in order to understand the undesirability of this. While acceptable levels of inducements are not stipulated in the ethics, one reasonable approach might be to limit payments where offered to out-of-pocket expenses (such as travel) and a modest hourly rate for time. Of course, even this provision is probably out of the question for student researchers.

- Sometimes professional services are offered as a way of encouraging participation in research. These might be, for example, counselling or psychological advice of some sort. In these circumstances, it is essential to clarify the precise nature of the services, including possible risks, further obligations and the limitations to the provision of such services. A further requirement, not mentioned in the APA ethics, might be that the researcher should be competent to deliver these services. Once again, it is difficult to imagine the circumstances in which students could be offering such inducements.

The use of deception in research

The fundamental ethical position is that deception should *not* be used in psychological research procedures. There are *no* circumstances in which deception is acceptable if there is a reasonable expectation that physical pain or emotional distress will be caused. However, it is recognised that there are circumstances in which the use of deception may be justified. If the proposed research has 'scientific, educational or applied value' (or the prospect of it) then deception may be considered. The next step is to establish that no effective alternative approach is possible which does not use deception. These are not matters on which individual psychologists should regard themselves as their own personal arbiters. Consultation with disinterested colleagues is an appropriate course of action.

If the use of deception is the only feasible option, it is incumbent on the psychologist to explain the deception as early as possible. This is preferably immediately after the data have been collected from each individual, but it may be delayed until all of the data from all of the participants have been collected. The deceived participant should be given the unfettered opportunity to withdraw their data. Box 8.2 discusses how deception has been a central feature of social psychological research. The ethics of the British Psychological Society indicate that a distinction may be drawn between deliberate lies and omission of particular details about the nature of the research that the individual is participating in. This is essentially the distinction between lying by omission and lying by commission. You might wonder if this distinction is sufficient justification of anything. The British

Psychological Society indicates that a key test of the acceptability is the response of participants at debriefing when the nature of the deception is revealed. If they express anger, discomfort or otherwise object to the deception then the deception was inappropriate and the future of the project should be reviewed. The BPS guidelines do not specify the next step however.

Box 8.2   TALKING POINT

Deception in the history of social psychology

The use of deception has been much more characteristic of the work of social psychologists than any other branch of psychological research. Korn (1997) argues that this was the almost inevitable consequence of using laboratory methods to study social phenomena. Deception first occurred in psychological research in 1897 when Leon Solomons studied how we discriminate between a single point touching our skin and two points touching our skin at the same time. Some participants were led to believe that there were two points and others that there was just one point. Whichever they believed made a difference to what they perceived. Interestingly, Solomons told his participants that they might be being deceived before participation.

In the early history of psychology deception was indeed a rare occurrence, but so was any sort of empirical research. There was a gradual growth in the use of deception between 1921 and 1947. The *Journal of Abnormal and Social Psychology* was surveyed during this period. Fifty-two per cent of articles involved studies using misinformation as part of the procedure while 42 per cent used 'false cover stories' (Korn, 1997). Little fuss was made about deception at this time. According to a variety of surveys of journals, the use of deception increased between 1948 and 1979 despite more and more questions about psychological ethics being asked. Furthermore, there appears to be no moderation in the scale of the sort of deceptions employed during this period. Of course, the purpose of deception in many cases is simply to hide the true purpose of the experiment. Participants threatened with a painful injection might be expected to behave differently if they believe this is necessary for a physiological experiment than if they know that the threat of the injection is simply a way of manipulating their stress levels.

Many of the classic studies in social psychology – ones still discussed in textbooks – used deceit of some sort or another. These did not necessarily involve trivial matters. In Milgram's studies of obedience in which participants were told that they were punishing a third party with electric shock, it appeared at one stage that the victim of the shock had been severely hurt. All of this was a lie and deception (Milgram, 1974). Milgram tended to refer to his deceptions as 'technical illusions' but this would appear to be nothing other than a euphemism. In studies by other researchers, participants believed that they were in an emergency situation when smoke was seeping into a laboratory through a vent – again a deliberate deception (Latane and Darley, 1970).

→

Box 8.2 continued

Deception was endemic and routine in social psychological research. It had to be, given the great stress on laboratory experimentation in the social psychology of the time. Without the staging of such extreme situations by means of deception, experimental social psychological research would be difficult if not impossible.

Sometimes the deceptions seem relatively trivial and innocuous. For example, imagine that one wished to study the effects of the gender of a student on the grades that they get for an essay. Few would have grave concerns about taking an essay and giving it to a sample of lecturers for marking, telling half of them that the essay was by a male and the other half the essay was by a woman. It would seem to be important to know through research whether or not there is a gender bias in marking which favours one gender over the other. Clearly there has been a deception – a lie if one prefers – but it is one which probably does not jeopardise in any way the participants' psychological well-being though there are circumstances in which it could. Believing that you have endangered someone's life by giving them dangerous levels of electric shock is not benign but may fundamentally affect a person's ideas about themselves. In some studies, participants have been deceitfully abused about their abilities or competence in order to make them angry (Berkowitz, 1962).

How would studies like these stand up to ethical scrutiny? Well deception as such is not banned by ethical codes. There are circumstances in which it may be justifiable. Deception may be appropriate when the study has, or potentially has, significant 'scientific, educational or applied value' according to the APA ethical principles. Some might question what this means. For example, if we wanted to study the grieving process, would it be right to tell someone that the university had just been informed that their mother had just died? Grief is an important experience and clearly it is of great importance to study the phenomenon. Does that give the researcher carte blanche to do anything?

Deception is common in our society. The white lie is a deception, for example. Does the fact that deception is endemic in society justify its use in research? Psychologists are professionals who as a group do not benefit from developing a reputation as tricksters. The culture of deception in research may lead to suspicion and hostility towards participation in the research.

■ Debriefing

As soon as the research is over (or essential stages are complete), debriefing should be carried out. There is a mutual discussion between researcher and participant to fully inform the participant about matters such as the nature of the result, the results of the research and the conclusions of the research. The researcher should try to correct the misconceptions of the participant that may have developed about any aspect of research. Of course, there may be good scientific or humane reasons for withholding some information – or delaying the main debriefing until a suitable time. For example, it may be that the research involves two or more stages separated by a considerable interval of time. Debriefing participants after the first stage may considerably contaminate the results at the second stage.

Box 8.3 TALKING POINT

Ethics and research with animals

Nowadays, few students have contact with laboratory animals during their education and training. Many universities simply do not have any facilities at all for animal research. However, many students have active concerns about the welfare of animals and so may be particularly interested in the ethical provision for such research in psychology. It needs to be stressed that this is an area where the law in many countries has exacting requirements that may be even more stringent than those required ethically. The first principle is that psychologists involved in research with animals must adhere to the pertinent laws and regulations. This includes the means by which laboratory animals are acquired, the ways in which the animals are cared for, the ways in which the animals are used, and the way in which laboratory animals are disposed of or retired from research.

Some further ethical requirements are:

- Psychologists both experienced and trained in research methods with laboratory animals should adopt a supervisory role for all work involving animals. Their responsibilities include consideration of the 'comfort, health and humane treatment' of animals under their supervision.

- It should be ensured that all individuals using animals have training in animal research methods and the care of animals. This should include appropriate ways of looking after the particular species of animal in question and the ways in which they should be handled. The supervising psychologist is responsible for this.

- Psychologists should take appropriate action in order that the adverse aspects of animal research should be minimised. This includes matters such as the animals' pain, comfort, freedom from infection and illnesses.

- While in some circumstances it may be ethically acceptable to expose animals to stress, pain or some form of privation of its bodily needs, this is subject to requirements. There must be no alternative way of doing the research. Furthermore, it should only be done when it is possible to justify the procedures on the basis of its 'scientific, educational or applied value'.

- Anaesthesia before and after surgery is required to minimise pain. Techniques which minimise the risk of infection are also required.

- Should it be necessary and appropriate to terminate the animal's life, this should be done painlessly and as quickly as possible. The accepted procedures for doing so should be employed.

One suspects that many will regard this list as inadequate. The list makes a number of assumptions – not the least being that it is ethically justifiable to carry out research on animals in certain conditions. But is this morally acceptable? Some might question whether cruelty to animals (and the unnecessary infliction of pain is cruel) is defensible in any circumstances. Others may be concerned about the lack of clarity in terms of when animal research is appropriate. Isn't any research defensible on the grounds of scientific progress? What does scientific progress mean? Is it achieved by publication in an academic psychology journal?

Debriefing cannot be guaranteed to deal effectively with the harm done to participants by deception. Whenever a researcher recognises that a particular participant appears to have been (inadvertently) harmed in some way by the procedures then reasonable efforts should be made to deal with this harm. It should be remembered that researchers are not normally qualified to offer counselling, and other forms of help and referral to relevant professionals may be the only appropriate course of action. There is a body of research on the effects of debriefing (for example, Epley and Huff, 1998; Smith and Richardson, 1983).

8.4 Ethics and publication

The following few ethical standards for research might have particular significance for student researchers.

Ethical standards in reporting research

It is ethically wrong to fabricate data. Remember that this applies to students. Of course, errors may inadvertently be made in published data. This is most likely to be a computational or statistical error. The researcher, on spotting the error, should take reasonable efforts to correct this. Among the possibilities are corrections or retractions in the journal in question.

Plagiarism

Plagiarism is when the work of another person is used without acknowledgement and as if it was one's own work. Psychologists do *not* plagiarise. Ethical principles hold that merely occasionally citing the original source is insufficient to militate against the charge of plagiarism. So, copying chunks of other people's work directly is inappropriate even if they are occasionally cited during this procedure. Of course, quotations clearly identified as such by the use of quotation marks, attribution of authorship, and citation of the source are normally acceptable. Even then, quotations should be kept short and within the limits set by publishers, for example.

Proper credit for publications

It is ethically inappropriate to stake a claim on work which one has not actually done or in some way contributed to substantially. This includes claiming authorship on publications. The principal author of a publication (the first-named) should be the individual who has contributed the most to the research. Of course, sometimes such a decision will be arbitrary where contributions cannot be ranked. Being senior in terms of formal employment role should not be a reason for principal authorship. Being in charge of a research unit is no reason for being included in the list of publications. There are often circumstances in which an individual makes a contribution but less than a significant one. This should be dealt with by a footnote acknowledging their contribution or some similar means. Authorship is not the reward for a minor contribution of this sort.

It is of particular importance to note that publications based on the dissertations of students should credit the student as principal (first) author. The issue of publication credit should be raised with students as soon as practicable by responsible academics.

■ Publishing the same data repeatedly

When data are published for the second or more time then the publication should clearly indicate the fact of republication. This is acceptable. It is not acceptable to repeatedly publish the same data as if for the first time.

■ The availability of data for verification

Following the publication of the results of research, they should be available for checking or verification by others competent to do so. This is not carte blanche for anyone to take another person's data for publication in some other form – that would require agreement. It merely is a safeguard for the verification of substantive claims made by the original researcher. The verifying psychologist may have to meet the costs of supplying the data for verification. Exceptions to this principle of verification are:

■ Circumstances in which the participants' confidentiality (e.g. anonymity) cannot be ensured.
■ If the data may not be released because another party has proprietary rights over the data which prevent their release.

8.5 Conclusion

Research ethics cover virtually every stage of the research process. The literature review, for example, is covered by the requirements of fidelity and other stages of the process have specific recommendations attached to them. It is in the nature of ethics that they do not simply list proscribed behaviours. Frequently they offer advice on what aspects of research require ethical attention and the circumstances in which exceptions to the generally accepted standards may be considered. They impose a duty on all psychologists to engage in consideration and consultation about the ethical standing of their research as well as that of other members of the psychological community. Furthermore, the process does not end prior to the commencement of data collection but requires attention and vigilance throughout the research process since new information may indicate ethical problems where they had not been anticipated.

One important thing about ethics is that they require a degree of judgement in their application. It is easy for students to seek rules for their research. For example, is it unethical to cause a degree of upset in the participants in your research? What if your research was into experiences of bereavement? Is it wrong to interview people about bereavement knowing that it will distress some of them? Assume that you have carefully explained to participants that the interviews are about bereavement. Is it wrong then to cause them any distress in this way? What if the research was just a Friday afternoon practical class on interviewing? Is it right to cause distress in these circumstances? What if it were a Friday workshop for trainee clinical psychologists on bereavement counselling? Is it any more acceptable? All of this reinforces the idea that ethics are fine judgements not blanket prohibitions for the most part.

The consideration of ethics is a fundamental requirement of the research process that cannot be avoided by any psychologist – including students at any level. It starts with not fiddling the data and not plagiarising. And what if your best friend fiddles the data and plagiarises?

■ Psychological associations such as the American Psychological Association and the British Psychological Society publish ethical guidelines to help their members behave morally in relation to their professional work. Self-regulation of ethics is a characteristic of professions.

■ Ethics may be based on broad principles, but frequently advice is provided in guidelines about their specific application, for example, in the context of research. So one general ethical principle is that of integrity meaning accuracy, honesty and truthfulness. This principle clearly has different implications to the use of deception in research from those when reporting data.

■ Informed consent is the principle that participants in research should willingly consent to taking part in research in the light of a clear explanation by the researcher about what the research entails. At the same time, participants in research should feel in a position to withdraw from the research at any stage with the option of withdrawing any data that has already been provided. There are exceptions where informed consent is not deemed necessary – especially naturalistic observations of people who might expect to be observed by someone since they are in a public place.

■ Deception of participants in research is regarded as problematic in modern psychology despite being endemic in some fields, particularly social psychology. Nevertheless, there is no complete ban on deception only the requirements that the deception is absolutely necessary since the research is important and there is no effective alternative deception-free way of conducting it. The response of participants during debriefing to the deception may be taken as an indicator of the risks inherent in that deception.

■ The publication of research is subject to ethical constraints. The fabrication of data, plagiarism of the work of others, claiming the role of author on a publication to which one has only minimally contributed, and the full acknowledgement by first authorship of students' research work are all covered in recent ethical guidelines.

Activities

1. Are any principles of ethical conduct violated in the following examples? What valid arguments could be made to justify what occurs? These are matters that could be debated. Alternatively, you could list the ethical pros and cons of each before reaching a conclusion.

    (a) Ken is researching memory and Dawn volunteers to be a participant in the research. Ken is very attracted to Dawn and asks for her address and mobile phone number, explaining that she may need to be contacted for a follow-up interview. This is a lie as no such interviews are planned. He later phones her up for a date.

    (b) A research team is planning to study Internet sex offenders. They set up a bogus Internet pornography site – 'All tastes sex'. The site contains a range of links to specialised pages devoted to a specific sexual interest – bondage, mature sex,

Asian women and the like. Visitors to the site who press these links see mild pornographic pictures in line with the theme of the link. The main focus of the researchers is on child pornography users on the Internet. To this end they have a series of links labelled '12 year olds and under', 'young boys need men friends', 'schoolgirls for real', 'sexy toddlers' and so forth. These links lead nowhere but the researchers have the site programmed such that visitors to the different pages can be counted. Furthermore, they have a 'data miner' which implants itself onto the visitor's computer and can extract information from that computer and report back to the researchers. They use this information in order to send out an e-mail questionnaire concerning the lifestyle of the visitor to the porn site – details such as their age, interests, address and so forth as well as psychological tests. To encourage completion, the researchers claim that in return for completing the questionnaire, they have a chance of being selected for a prize of a Caribbean holiday. The research team is approached by the police who believe that the data being gathered may be useful in tracking down paedophiles.

(c)   A student researcher is studying illicit drug use on a university campus. She is given permission to distribute questionnaires during an introductory psychology lecture. Participants are assured anonymity and confidentiality, although the researcher has deliberately included questions about demographic information such as the participants' exact date of birth, their home town, the modules they are taking and so forth. However, the student researcher is really interested in personality factors and drug taking. She gets another student to distribute personality questionnaires to the same class a few weeks later. The same information about exact date of birth, home town, place of birth and so forth is collected. This is used to match each drugs questionnaire with that same person's personality questionnaire. However, the questionnaires are anonymous since no name is requested.

(d)   Professor Green is interested in fascist and other far-right political organisations. Since he believes that these organisations would not permit a researcher to observe them, he poses as a market trader and applies for and is given membership of several of these organisations. He attends the meetings and other events with other members. He is carrying out participant observation and is compiling extensive notes of what he witnesses for eventual publication.

(e)   A researcher studying sleep feels that a young woman taking part in the research is physically attracted to him. He tries to kiss her.

(f)   Some researchers believe that watching filmed violence leads to violence in real life. Professor Jenkins carries out a study in which scenes of extreme violence taken from the film *Reservoir Dogs* are shown to a focus group. A week later, one of the participants in the focus group is arrested for the murder of his partner on the day after seeing the film.

(g)   A discourse analyst examines President Bill Clinton's television claim that he did not have sexual intercourse with Monica Lewinsky in order to assess discursive strategies that he employed and to seek any evidence of lying. The results of this analysis are published in a psychology journal.

(h)   'Kitty Friend complained to an ethics committee about a psychologist she read about in the newspaper who was doing research on evoked potentials in cat brains. She asserted that the use of domesticated cats in research was unethical, inhumane, and immoral' (Keith-Spiegel and Koocher, 1985, p. 35). The ethics committee chooses not to consider the complaint.

(i)   A psychology student chooses to investigate suicidal thoughts in a student population. She distributes a range of personality questionnaires among her friends. Scoring the test she notices that one of her friends, Tom, has scored heavily on a measure of suicide ideation and has written at the end of the questionnaire that he feels desperately depressed. She knows that it is Tom from the handwriting which is very distinctive.

(j)   Steffens (1931) describes how along with others he studied the laboratory records of a student of Wilhelm Wundt, generally regarded as the founder of the first psychological laboratory. This student went on to be a distinguished professor in America. Basically the student's data failed to support aspects of Wundt's psychological writings. Steffens writes that the student

> . . . must have thought . . . that Wundt might have been reluctant to crown a discovery which would require the old philosopher [Wundt] to rewrite volumes of his lifework. The budding psychologist solved the ethical problem before him by deciding to alter his results, and his papers showed how he did this, by changing the figures item by item, experiment by experiment, so as to make the curve of his averages come out for instead of against our school. After a few minutes of silent admiration of the mathematical feat performed on the papers before us, we buried sadly these remains of a great sacrifice to loyalty, to the school spirit, and to practical ethics.

[p. 151]

1 Why you need statistics
Types of data

Overview

- Statistics are used to describe our data but also assess what reliance we can place on information based on samples.

- A variable is any concept that we can measure and that varies between individuals or cases.

- Variables should be identified as nominal (also known as category, categorical and qualitative) variables or score (also known as numerical) variables.

- Formal measurement theory holds that there are more types of variable – nominal, ordinal, interval and ratio. These are generally unimportant in the actual practice of doing statistical analyses.

- Nominal variables consist of just named categories whereas score variables are measured in the form of a numerical scale which indicates the quantity of the variable.

1.1 Introduction

Imagine a world in which everything is the same; people are identical in all respects. They wear identical clothes; they eat the same meals; they are all the same height from birth; they all go to the same school with identical teachers, identical lessons and identical facilities; they all go on holiday in the same month; they all do the same job; they all live in identical houses; and the sun shines every day. They do not have sex as we know it since there are no sexes so everyone self-reproduces at the age of 30; their gardens have the same plants and the soil is exactly the same no matter whose garden; they all die on their 75th birthdays and are all buried in the same wooden boxes in identical plots of land. They are all equally clever and they all have identical personalities. Their genetic make-up never varies. Mathematically speaking all of these characteristics are constants. If this world seems less than realistic then have we got news for you – you need statistics! Only in a world of standardisation would you not need statistics – in a richly varying world statistics is essential.

If nothing varies, then everything that is to be known about people could be guessed from information obtained from a single person. No problems would arise in generalising since what is true of Sandra Green is true of everyone else – they're all called Sandra Green after all. Fortunately, the world is not like that. Variability is an essential characteristic of life and the social world in which we exist. The sheer quantity of variability has to be tamed when trying to make statements about the real world. Statistics is largely about making sense of variability.

Statistical techniques perform three main functions:

1. They provide ways of summarising the information that we collect from a multitude of sources. Statistics is partly about tabulating your research information or data as clearly and effectively as possible. As such it merely describes the information collected. This is achieved using tables and diagrams to summarise data, and simple formulae which turn fairly complex data into simple indexes that describe numerically the main features of the data. This branch of statistics is called *descriptive statistics* for very obvious reasons – it describes the information you collect as accurately and succinctly as possible. The first few chapters of this book are largely devoted to descriptive statistics.

2. Another branch of statistics is far less familiar to most of us: *inferential statistics*. This branch of statistics is really about economy of effort in research. There was a time when in order to find out about people, for example, everyone in the country would be contacted in order to collect information. This is done today when the government conducts a *census* of everyone in order to find out about the population of the country at a particular time. This is an enormous and time-consuming operation that cannot be conducted with any great frequency. But most of us are familiar with using relatively small *samples* in order to approximate the information that one would get by studying everybody. This is common in public-opinion surveying where the answers of a sample of 1000 or so people may be used, say, to predict the outcome of a national election. Granted that sometimes samples can be misleading, nevertheless it is the principle of sampling that is important. *Inferential statistics* is about the confidence with which we can generalise from a sample to the entire population.

3. The amount of data that a researcher can collect is potentially massive. Some statistical techniques enable the researcher to clarify trends in vast quantities of data using a number of powerful methods. Data simplification, data exploration and data reduction are among the names given to the process. Whatever the name, the objective is the same – to make sense of large amounts of data that otherwise would be much too confusing. These *data exploration techniques* are mainly dealt with in later chapters.

1.2   Variables and measurement

The concept of a *variable* is basic but vitally important in statistics. It is also as easy as pie. *A variable is anything that varies and can be measured.* These measurements need *not* correspond very well with everyday notions of measurement such as weight, distance and temperature. So the sex of people is a variable since it can be measured as either male or female – and sex varies between people. Similarly, eye colour is a variable because a set of people will include some with brown eyes, some with blue eyes and some with green eyes. Thus measurement can involve merely categorisation. Clinical psychologists might use different diagnostic categories such as schizophrenia, manic depression and anxiety in research. These diagnostic categories constitute a variable since they are different mental and emotional problems to which people can be allocated. Such categorisation techniques are an important type of measurement in statistics.

Another type of measurement in statistics is more directly akin to everyday concepts of measurement in which numerical values are provided. These *numerical* values are assigned to variables such as weight, length, distance, temperature and the like – for example, 10 kilometres or 30 degrees. These numerical values are called *scores*. In psychological research many variables are measured and *quantified* in much the same way. Good examples are the many tests and scales used to assess intelligence, personality, attitudes and mental abilities. In most of these, people are assigned a number (or score) in order to describe, for example, how neurotic or how extraverted an individual is. Psychologists will speak of a person having an IQ of 112 or 93, for example, or they will say an individual has a low score of 6 on a measure of psychoticism. Usually these numbers are used as if they corresponded exactly to other forms of measurement such as weight or length. For these, we can make statements such as that a person has a weight of 60 kilograms or is 1.3 metres tall.

1.3 Major types of measurement

Traditionally, statistics textbooks for psychologists emphasise different types of measurement – usually using the phrase *scales of measurement*. However, *for virtually all practical purposes there are only two different types of measurement in statistics*. These have already been discussed, but to stress the point:

1. **Score/numerical measurement** This is the assignment of a *numerical* value to a measurement. This includes most physical and psychological measures. In psychological jargon these numerical measurements are called *scores*. We could record the IQ scores of five people as in Table 1.1. Each of the numerical values in the table indicates the named individual's *score* on the variable IQ. It is a simple point, but note that the numbers contain information that someone with an IQ of 150 has a higher intelligence than someone with an IQ of 80. In other words, the numbers *quantify* the variable.

Table 1.1 IQ scores of five named individuals

Individual	IQ score
Stan	80
Mavis	130
Sanjit	150
Sharon	145
Peter	105

2. ***Nominal/category measurement*** This is deciding to which category of a variable a particular case belongs. It is also appropriate to refer to it as a *qualitative measure*. So, if we were measuring a person's job or occupation, we would have to decide whether or not he or she was a lorry driver, a professor of sociology, a debt collector, and so forth. This is called *nominal* measurement since usually the categories are described in words and, especially, given names. Thus the category 'lorry driver' is a name or verbal description of what sort of case should be placed in that category.

Notice that there are no numbers involved in the process of categorisation as such. A person is either a lorry driver or not. *However, you need to be warned of a possible confusion that can occur*. If you have 100 people whose occupations are known you might wish to count how many are lorry drivers, how many are professors of sociology, and so forth. These counts could be entered into a data table like Table 1.2. Notice that the numbers this time correspond to a count of the *frequency* or number of cases falling into each of the four occupational categories. *They are not scores*, but frequencies. The numbers do not correspond to a single measurement but are the aggregate of many separate (nominal) measurements.

The distinction between numerical scores and frequencies is important so always take care to check whether what appear to be numerical scores in a table are actually frequencies.

Make a habit of mentally labelling variables as numerical scores or nominal categories. Doing so is a big step forward in thinking statistically. This is all you really need to know about types of measurement. However, you should be aware that others use more complex systems. Read the following section to learn more about scales of measurement.

Formal measurement theory

You may find it unnecessary to learn the contents of this section in detail. However, it does contain terms with which you ought to be familiar since other people might make reference to them.

Many psychologists speak of four different scales of measurement. Conceptually they are distinct. Nevertheless, for most practical situations in psychologists' use of statistics the nominal category versus numerical scores distinction discussed above is sufficient.

The four 'theoretical' scales of measurement are as follows. The scales numbered 2, 3 and 4 are different types of *numerical* scores.

1. ***Nominal categorisation*** This is the placing of cases into *named* categories – nominal clearly refers to names. It is exactly the same as our nominal measurement or categorisation process.

Table 1.2 Frequencies of different occupations

Occupational category	Number of frequency in set
Lorry drivers	27
Sociology professors	10
Debt collectors	15
Others occupations	48

2. ***Ordinal (or rank) measurement***   The assumption here is that the values of the numerical scores tell us little else other than which is the smallest, the next smallest and so forth up to the largest. In other words, we can place the scores in *order* (hence ordinal) from the smallest to the largest. It is sometimes called rank measurement since we can assign ranks to the first, second, third, fourth, fifth, etc. in order from the smallest to the largest numerical value. These ranks have the numerical value 1, 2, 3, 4, 5, etc. You will see examples of this later in the book, especially in Chapters 7 and 18. However, few psychologists collect data directly as ranks.

3. ***Interval or equal-interval measurement***   The basic idea here is that in some cases the intervals between numbers on a numerical scale are equal in size. Thus, if we measure distance on a scale of centimetres then the distance between 0 and 1 centimetre on our scale is exactly the same as the difference between 4 and 5 centimetres or between 11 and 12 centimetres on that scale. This is obvious for some standard physical measurements such as temperature.

4. ***Ratio measurement***   This is exactly the same as interval scale measurement with one important proviso. A ratio scale of measurement has an absolute zero point that is measured as 0. Most physical measurements such as distance and weight have zero points that are absolute. Thus zero on a tape measure is the smallest distance one can have – there is no distance between two coincident points. With this sort of scale of measurement it is possible to work out ratios between measures. So, for example, a town that is 20 kilometres away is twice as far away as a town that is only 10 kilometres away. A building that is 15 metres high is half the height of a building that is 30 metres high. (Not all physical measures have a zero that is absolute zero – this applies particularly to several measures of temperature. Temperatures measured in degrees Celsius or Fahrenheit have points that are labelled as zero. However, these zero points do not correspond to the lowest possible temperature you can have. It is then meaningless to say, for example, that it is twice as hot if the temperature is 20 degrees Celsius than if it were 10 degrees Celsius.)

It is very difficult to apply the last three types of measure to psychological measurements with certainty. Since most psychological scores do not have any directly observable physical basis, it is impossible to decide whether they consist of equal intervals or have an absolute zero. For many years this problem caused great controversy and confusion among psychologists. For the most part, much current usage of statistics in psychology ignores the distinctions between the three different types of numerical scores. This has the support of many statisticians. On the other hand, some psychologists prefer to emphasise that some data are best regarded as rankable and lack the qualities which are characteristic of interval/ratio data. They are more likely to use the statistical techniques to be found in Chapter 18 and the ranking correlation coefficient (Chapter 7) than others. In other words, for precisely the same data, different psychologists will adopt different statistical techniques. Usually this will make little difference to the outcomes of their statistical analyses – the results. In general, it will cause you few, if any, problems if you ignore the three subdivisions of numerical score measurement in your practical use of statistics. The exceptions to this are discussed in Chapters 7 and 18. Since psychologists rarely if ever collect data in the form of ranks, Chapters 2 to 6 are unaffected by such considerations.

Key points

■ Always ask yourself what sort of measurement it is you are considering – is it a numerical score on a variable or is it putting individuals into categories?

■ Never assume that a number is necessarily a numerical score. Without checking, it could be a *frequency* of observations in a named category.

■ Clarity of thinking is a virtue in statistics – you will rarely be expected to demonstrate great creativity in your statistical work. Understanding precisely the meaning of terms is an advantage in statistics.

For further resources including data sets and questions, please refer to the CD accompanying this book.

2 Describing variables
Tables and diagrams

Overview

■ Tables and diagrams are important aspects of descriptive statistics (the description of the major features of the data). Examining data in this sort of detail is a vital stage of any statistical analysis and should never be omitted.

■ This chapter describes how to create and present tables and diagrams for individual variables.

■ Statistical tables and diagrams should effectively communicate information about your data. Beware of complexity.

■ The type of data (nominal versus score) largely determines what an appropriate table and diagram will be.

■ If the data are nominal, then simple frequency tables, bar charts or pie charts are most appropriate. The frequencies are simply the numbers of cases in each of the separate categories.

■ If the data are scores, then frequency tables or histograms are appropriate. However, to keep the presentation uncluttered and to help clarify trends, it is often best to put the data into bands (or ranges) of adjacent scores.

Preparation Remind yourself what a variable is from Chapter 1. Similarly, if you are still not sure of the nominal (categorisation) form of measurement and the use of numerical scores in measurement then revise these too.

2.1 Introduction

You probably know a lot more about statistics than you think. The mass media regularly feature statistical tables and diagrams; children become familiar with statistical tables and diagrams at school. Skill with these methods is essential because researchers collect large amounts of data from numerous people. If we asked 100 people their age, sex, marital status (divorced, married, single, etc.), their number of children and their occupation this would yield 500 separate pieces of information. Although this is small fry compared with much research, it is not very helpful to present these 500 measurements in your research report. Such unprocessed information is called *raw data*. Statistical analysis has to be more than describing the raw ingredients. It requires the data to be structured in ways that *effectively communicate* the major trends. If you fail to structure your data, you may as well just give the reader copies of your questionnaires or observation schedules to interpret themselves.

There are very few rules regulating the production of tables and diagrams in statistics so long as they are clear and concise; they need to communicate quickly the important trends in the data. There is absolutely no point in using tables and diagrams that do not ease the task of communication. Probably the best way of deciding whether your tables and diagrams do their job well is to ask other people to decipher what they mean. Tables which are unclear to other people are generally useless.

Descriptive statistics are, by and large, relatively simple visual and numerical techniques for describing the major features of one's data. Researchers may produce descriptive statistics in order to communicate the major characteristics of the data to others, but in the first instance they are used by researchers themselves in order to understand the distribution of participants' responses in the research. Never regard descriptive statistical analysis as an unnecessary or trivial stage in research. It is probably more informative than any other aspect of data analysis.

The distinction between nominal (category) data and numerical scores discussed in the previous chapter is important in terms of the appropriate tables and diagrams to use.

Research design issue

One of the easiest mistakes to make in research is to allow participants in your research to give more than one answer to a question. So, for example, if you ask people to name their favourite television programme and allow each person more than one answer you will find that the data can be very tricky to analyse thoroughly. Take our word for it for now: statistics in general does not handle multiple responses very well. Certainly it is possible to draw up tables and diagrams but some of the more advanced statistical procedures become difficult to apply. You will sometimes read comments to the effect that the totals in a table exceed the number of participants in the research. This is because the researcher has allowed multiple responses to a single variable. So only allow the participants in your research to give one piece of data for each variable you are measuring to avoid digging a pit for yourself. If you plan your data analysis in detail before you collect your data you should be able to anticipate any difficulties.

2.2 Choosing tables and diagrams

So long as you are able to decide whether your data are either numerical scores or nominal (category) data, there are few other choices to be made since the available tables and diagrams are essentially dependent upon this distinction.

Tables and diagrams for nominal (category) data

One of the main characteristics of tables and diagrams for nominal (category) data is that they have to show the *frequencies* of cases in each category used. While there may be as many categories as you wish, it is *not* the function of statistical analysis to communicate all of the data's detail; the task is to identify the major trends. For example, imagine you are researching the public's attitudes towards private health care. If you ask participants in your research their occupations then you might find that they mention tens if not hundreds of different job titles – newsagents, homemakers, company executives and so forth. Simply counting the frequencies with which different job titles are mentioned results in a vast number of categories. You need to think of relevant and meaningful ways of reducing this vast number into a smaller number of much broader categories that might reveal important trends. For example, since the research is about a health issue you might wish to form a category made up of those involved in health work – some might be dentists, some nurses, some doctors, some paramedics and so forth. Instead of keeping these as different categories, they might be combined into a category 'health worker'. There are no hard-and-fast rules about combining to form broader categories. The following might be useful rules of thumb:

1. Keep your number of categories low, especially when you have only small numbers of participants in your research.
2. Try to make your 'combined' categories meaningful and sensible in the light of the purposes of your research. It would be nonsense, for example, to categorise jobs by the letter of the alphabet with which they start – nurses, nuns, nursery teachers and national footballers. All of these have jobs beginning with the same letter but it is very difficult to see any other common thread which allows them to be combined meaningfully.

In terms of drawing tables, all we do is to list the categories we have chosen and give the frequency of cases that fall into each of the categories (Table 2.1). The frequencies are presented in two ways in this table – *simple* frequencies and *percentage* frequencies.

Table 2.1   Occupational status of participants in the research expressed as frequencies and percentage frequencies

Occupation	Frequency	Percentage frequency
Nuns	17	21.25
Nursery teachers	3	3.75
Television presenters	23	28.75
Students	20	25.00
Other	17	21.25

A percentage frequency is the frequency expressed as a percentage of the total of the frequencies (or total number of cases, usually).

Notice also that one of the categories is called 'other'. This consists of those cases which do not fit into any of the main categories. It is, in other words, a 'rag bag' category or miscellany. Generally, all other things being equal, it is best to have a small number of cases in the 'other' category.

CALCULATION 2.1

Percentage frequencies

Many readers will not need this, but if you are a little rusty with simple maths, it might be helpful.

The percentage frequency for a particular category, say for students, is the frequency in that category expressed as a percentage of the total frequencies in the data table.

Step 1   What is the category frequency? For students in Table 2.1:

category frequency$_{[students]}$ = 20

Step 2   Add up all of the frequencies in Table 2.1:

total frequencies = nuns + nursery teachers + TV presenters + students + other
$$= 17 + 3 + 23 + 20 + 17$$
$$= 80$$

Step 3

$$\text{percentage frequency[students]} = \frac{\text{category frequency}_{[students]} \times 100}{\text{total frequencies}}$$

$$= \frac{20 \times 100}{80} = \frac{2000}{80}$$

$$= 25\%$$

One advantage of using computers is that they enable experimentation with different schemes of categorising data in order to decide which is best for your purposes. In this you would use initially narrow categories for coding your data. Then you can tell the computer which of these to combine into broader categories.

Sometimes it is preferable to turn frequency tables into diagrams. Good diagrams are quickly understood and add variety to the presentation. The main types of diagram for nominal (category) data are *pie diagrams* and *bar charts*. A pie diagram is a very familiar form of presentation – it simply expresses each category as a slice of a pie which represents all cases (see Figure 2.1).

Notice that the *number* of slices is small – a multitude of slices can be confusing. Each slice is clearly marked with its category name, and the percentage frequency in each category also appears.

Figure 2.1   A simple pie diagram

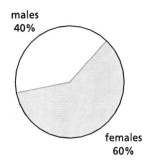

CALCULATION 2.2

Slices for a pie diagram

There is nothing difficult in constructing a pie diagram. Our recommendation is that you turn each of your frequencies into a percentage frequency. Since there are 360 degrees in a circle, if you multiply each percentage frequency by 3.6 you will obtain the angle (in degrees) of the slice of the pie which you need to mark out. In order to create the diagram you will require a protractor to measure the angles. However, computer graph packages are standard at any university or college and do an impressive job.

In Table 2.1, 25.00% of cases were students. In order to turn this into the correct angle for the slice of the pie you simply need to multiply 25.00 by 3.6 to give an angle of 90 degrees.

Figure 2.2   A poor pie diagram

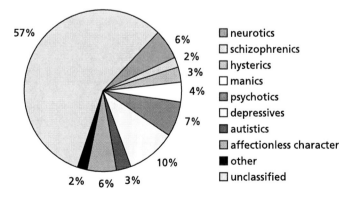

Figure 2.2 shows a *bad* example of a pie diagram for purposes of comparison. There are several problems with this pie diagram:

1. There are too many small slices identified by different shading patterns and the legend takes time to decode.

Figure 2.3 Bar chart showing occupational categories in Table 2.1

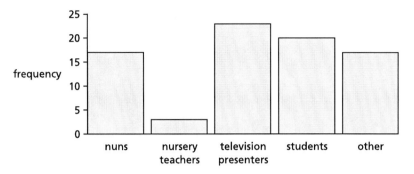

2. It is not too easily seen what each slice concerns and the relative sizes of the slices are difficult to judge. We have the size of the slices around the figure and a separate legend or key to identify the components to help cope with the overcrowding problem. In other words, too many categories have resulted in a diagram which is far from easy to read – a cardinal sin in any statistical diagram.

A simple frequency table might be more effective in this case.

Another very familiar form of statistical diagram for nominal (category) data is the *bar chart*. Again these charts are very common in the media. Basically they are diagrams in which bars represent the size of each category. An example is shown in Figure 2.3.

The relative lengths (or heights) of the bars quickly reveal the main trends in the data. With a bar chart there is very little to remember other than that the bars have a standard space separating them. The spaces indicate that the categories are not in a numerical order; they are frequencies of categories, *not* scores.

It is hard to go wrong with a bar chart (that is not a challenge!) so long as you remember the following:

1. The heights of the bars represent frequencies (number of cases) in a category.
2. Each bar should be clearly labelled as to the category it represents.
3. Too many bars make bar charts hard to follow.
4. Avoid having *many* empty or near-empty categories which represent very few cases. Generally, the information about substantial categories is the most important. (Small categories can be combined together as an 'other' category.)
5. Nevertheless, if *important* categories have very few entries then this needs recording. So, for example, a researcher who is particularly interested in opportunities for women surveys people in top management and finds very few women employed in such jobs. It is important to draw attention to this in the bar chart of males and females in top management. Once again, there are no hard-and-fast rules to guide you – common sense will take you a long way.
6. Make sure that the vertical axis (the heights of the bars) is clearly marked as being frequencies or percentage frequencies.
7. The bars should be of equal width.

In newspapers and on television you are likely to come across a variant of the bar chart called the *pictogram*. In this, the bars of the bar chart are replaced by varying sized drawings of something eye-catching to do with your categories. Thus, pictures of men or women of varying heights, for example, replace the bars. Pictograms are rarely used in professional presentations. The main reason is that pictures of things get wider as well as taller as they increase in size. This can misrepresent the relative sizes of the categories, given that readers forget that it is only the height of the picture that counts.

Tables and diagrams for numerical score data

One crucial consideration when deciding what tables and diagrams to use for score data is the number of separate scores recorded for the variable in question. This can vary markedly. So, for example, age in the general population can range from newly born to over 100 years of age. If we merely recorded ages to the nearest whole year then a table or diagram may have entries for 100 different ages. Such a table or diagram would look horrendous. If we recorded age to the nearest month, then we could multiply this number of ages by 12! Such scores can be grouped into bands or ranges of scores to allow effective tabulation (Table 2.2).

Table 2.2   Ages expressed as age bands

Age range	Frequency
0–9 years	19
10–19 years	33
20–29 years	17
30–39 years	22
40–49 years	17
50 years and over	3

Many psychological variables have a much smaller range of numerical values. So, for example, it is fairly common to use questions which pre-specify just a few response alternatives. The so-called Likert-type questionnaire item is a good case in point. Typically this looks something like this:

Statistics is my favourite university subject:
Strongly agree   Agree   Neither agree nor disagree   Disagree   Strongly disagree

Participants completing this questionnaire circle the response alternative which best fits their personal opinion. It is conventional in this type of research to code these different response alternatives on a five-point scale from one to five. Thus strongly agree might be coded 1, neither agree nor disagree 3, and strongly disagree 5. This scale therefore has only five possible values. Because of this small number of possible answers, a table based on this question will be relatively simple. Indeed, if students are not too keen on statistics, you may well find that they select only the disagree and strongly disagree categories.

Tabulating such data is quite straightforward. Indeed you can simply report the numbers or frequencies of replies for each of the different categories or scores as in Table 2.3.

A *histogram* might be the best form of statistical diagram to represent these data. At first sight histograms look very much like bar charts but without gaps between the bars. This is because the histogram does not represent distinct unrelated categories but different points on a *numerical* measurement scale. So a histogram of the above data might look like Figure 2.4.

Table 2.3   Distribution of students' attitudes towards statistics

Response category	Value	Frequency
Strongly agree	1	17
Agree	2	14
Neither agree nor disagree	3	6
Disagree	4	2
Strongly disagree	5	1

Figure 2.4   Histogram of students' attitudes towards statistics

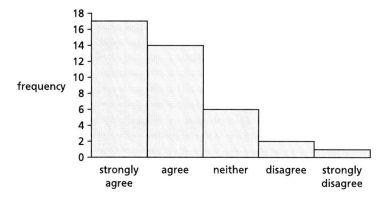

But what if your data have numerous different possible values of the variable in question? One common difficulty for most psychological research is that the number of respondents tends to be small. The large number of possible different scores on the variable is therefore shared between very few respondents. Tables and diagrams should present major features of your data in a simple and easily assimilated form. So sometimes you will have to use *bands of scores* rather than individual score values just as you did for Table 2.2. So if we asked 100 people their ages we could categorise their replies into bands such as 0–9 years, 10–19 years, 30–39 years, 40–49 years and a final category of those 50 years and over. By using bands we reduce the risk of empty parts of the table and allow any trends to become clear (Figure 2.5).

How one chooses the bands to use is an important question. The answer is a bit of luck and judgement, and a lot of trial and error. It is very time consuming to rejig the ranges of the bands when one is analysing the data by hand. One big advantage of computers is that they will recode your scores into bands repeatedly until you have tables which seem to do the job as well as possible. The criterion is still whether the table communicates information effectively.

The one rule is that the bands ought to be of the same size – that is cover, for example, equal ranges of scores. Generally this is easy except at the upper and lower ends of the distribution. Perhaps you wish to use 'over 70' as your upper range. This, in modern practice, can be done as a bar of the same width as the others, but must be very carefully marked. (Strictly speaking, the width of the band should represent the range of scores involved and the height reduced in the light of this. However, this is rarely done in modern psychological statistics.)

Figure 2.5   Use of bands of scores to enable simple presentation

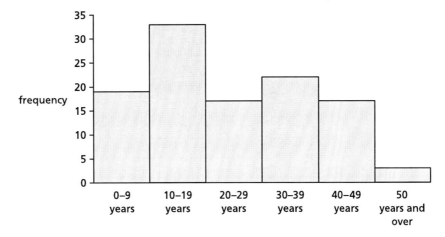

Figure 2.6   Histogram showing 'collapsed' categories

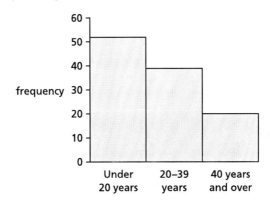

One might redefine the bands of scores and generate another histogram based on identical data but a different set of bands (Figure 2.6).

It requires some thought to decide which of the diagrams is best for a particular purpose. There are no hard-and-fast rules.

2.3   Errors to avoid

There are a few mistakes that you can make in drawing up tables and diagrams:

1. *Do not* forget to head the table or diagram with a succinct description of what it concerns. You will notice that we have done our best throughout this chapter to supply each table and diagram with a clear title.
2. Label everything on the table or diagram as clearly as possible. What this means is that you have to mark your bar charts and histograms in a way that tells the reader what each bar means. Then you must indicate what the height of the bar refers to – probably either frequency or percentage frequency.

Note that this chapter has concentrated on describing a *single* variable as clearly as possible. In Chapter 6, methods of making tables and diagrams showing the relationships between two or more variables are described.

Key points

- Try to make your tables and diagrams useful. It is not usually their purpose to record the data as you collected it in your research. Of course you can list your data in the appendix of projects that you carry out, but this is not useful as a way of illustrating trends. It is part of a researcher's job to make the data accessible to the reader in a structured form that is easily understood by the reader.

- Especially when using computers, it is very easy to generate *useless* tables and diagrams. This is usually because computer analysis encourages you not to examine your raw data in any detail. This implies that you should always regard your first analyses as tentative and merely a step towards something better.

- If a table is not clear to you, it is unlikely to be any clearer to anyone else.

- Check each table and diagram for clear and full labelling of each part. Especially, check that frequencies are clearly marked as such.

- Check that there is a clear, helpful title to each table and diagram.

Computer analysis

The SPSS instruction book to this text is Dennis Howitt and Duncan Cramer (2008), *Introduction to SPSS in Psychology*, Harlow: Pearson. Chapter 2 in that book gives detailed step-by-step procedures for the statistics described in this chapter together with advice on how to report the results.

For further resources including data sets and questions, please refer to the CD accompanying this book.

3 Describing variables numerically
Averages, variation and spread

Overview

- Scores can be described numerically – for example the average of a sample of scores can be given.

- There are several measures of central tendency – the most typical or most likely score.

- The mean score is simply the average score assessed by the total of the scores divided by the number of scores.

- The mode is the numerical value of the most frequently occurring score.

- The median is the score in the middle if the scores are ordered from smallest to largest.

- The spread of scores can be expressed as the range (which is the difference between the largest and the smallest score).

- Variance (an indicator of variability around the average) indicates the spread of scores in the data. Unlike the range, variance takes into account all of the scores. It is a ubiquitous statistical concept.

- Nominal data can only be described in terms of the numbers of cases falling in each category. The mode is the only measure of central tendency that can be applied to nominal (category) data.

Preparation Revise the meaning of nominal (category) data and numerical score data.

3.1 Introduction

Tables and diagrams take up a lot of space. It can be more efficient to use numerical indexes to describe the distributions of variables. For this reason, you will find relatively few pie charts and the like in published research. One numerical index is familiar to everyone – the numerical average (or arithmetic mean). Large amounts of data can be described adequately using just a few numerical indexes.

Table 3.1 Two different sets of scores

Variable A scores	Variable B scores
2	27
2	29
3	35
3	40
3	41
4	42
4	45
4	45
4	49
4	49
5	49
5	
5	

What are the major features of data that we might attempt to summarise in this way? Look at the two different sets of scores in Table 3.1. The major differences between these two sets of data are:

1. The sets of scores differ substantially in terms of their typical value – in one case the scores are relatively large (variable B); in the other case the scores are much smaller (variable A).
2. The sets of scores differ in their spread or variability – one set (variable B) seems to have more spread or a greater variability than the other.
3. If we plot these two sets of scores as histograms then we also find that the shapes of the distributions differ markedly. Variable A is much steeper and less spread out than variable B.

Each of these different features of a set of scores can be described using various indexes. They do not generally apply to nominal (category) variables.

3.2 Typical scores: mean, median and mode

Researchers sometimes speak about the central tendency of a set of scores. By this they are raising the issue of what are the most typical and likely scores in the distribution of measurements. We could speak of the average score but that can mislead us into thinking that the arithmetic mean is the average score when it is just one of several possibilities.

There are three main measures of the typical scores: the arithmetic mean, the mode and the median. These are quite distinct concepts but generally simple enough in themselves.

■ The arithmetic mean

The arithmetic mean is calculated by summing all of the scores in a distribution and dividing by the number of scores. This is the everyday concept of average. In statistical notation we can express this mean as follows:

$$\bar{X}_{[mean]} = \frac{\Sigma X_{[scores]}}{N_{[number\ of\ scores]}}$$

As this is the first statistical formula we have presented, you should take very careful note of what each symbol means:

X is the statistical symbol for a score
Σ is the summation or sigma sign
ΣX means add up all of the scores X
N is the number of scores
$\bar{X}$ is the statistical symbol for the arithmetic mean of a set of scores

We have added a few comments in small square brackets [just like this]. Although mathematicians may not like them very much, you might find they help you to interpret a formula a little more quickly.

CALCULATION 3.1

The numerical or arithmetic mean

Although you probably do not need the formula to work out the arithmetic mean, it is useful at this stage to make sure that you understand how to decode the symbols. It is a simple example but contains several of the important elements of statistical formulae. It is good preparation to go through the calculation using the formula.

To illustrate the calculation of the arithmetic mean we can use the following six scores:

$X_1 = 7$ $X_4 = 7$
$X_2 = 5$ $X_5 = 7$
$X_3 = 4$ $X_6 = 5$

The subscripts following the Xs above define a particular score.

$$\bar{X}_{[mean]} = \frac{\Sigma X_{[scores]}}{N_{[number\ of\ scores]}}$$

$$= \frac{X_1 + X_2 + X_3 + X_4 + X_5 + X_6}{N}$$

$$= \frac{7 + 5 + 4 + 7 + 7 + 5}{6} = \frac{35}{6} = 5.83$$

Table 3.2   Frequency distribution of 40 scores

Score	Frequency (f)
1	1
2	2
3	4
4	6
5	7
6	8
7	5
8	3
9	2
10	1
11	0
12	1

The median

The median is the middle score of a set if the scores are organised from the smallest to the largest. Thus the scores 7, 5, 4, 7, 7, 5, 3, 4, 6, 8, 5 become 3, 4, 4, 5, 5, 5, 6, 7, 7, 7, 8 when put in order from the smallest to the largest. Since there are 11 scores and the median is the middle score from the smallest to the largest, the median has to be the sixth score, i.e. 5.

With odd numbers of scores all of which are different, the median is easily calculated since there is a single score that corresponds to the middle score in the set of scores. However, if there is an even number of all different scores in the set then the mid-point will not be a single score but two scores. So if you have 12 different scores placed in order from smallest to largest, the median will be somewhere between the sixth and seventh score from smallest. There is no such score, of course, by definition – the 6.5th score just does not exist. What we could do in these circumstances is to take the average of the sixth and seventh scores to give us an estimate of the median.

For the distribution of 40 scores shown in Table 3.2, the middle score from the smallest is somewhere between the 20th and 21st scores. Thus the median is somewhere between score 5 (the 20th score) and score 6 (the 21st score). One could give the average of these two as the median score – that is, the median is 5.5. For most purposes this is good enough.

You may find that computer programs give different values from this. The computer program is making adjustments since there may be several identical scores near the median but you need only a fraction of them to reach your mid-point score. So in the above example the 21st score comes in score category 6 although there are actually eight scores in that category. So in order to get that extra score we need take only one-eighth of score category 6. One-eighth equals 0.125 so the estimated median equals 5.125. To be frank, it is difficult to think of many circumstances in which this level of precision about the value of the median is required in psychological statistics. You ought to regard this feature of computer output as a bonus and adopt the simpler method for your hand calculations.

The mode

The mode is the most frequently occurring category of score. It is merely the most common score or most frequent category of scores. In other words, you can apply the mode to any

Table 3.3   Frequencies of scores

Score	Frequency (f)
4	1
5	2
6	0
7	3

Table 3.4   A bimodel frequency distribution

Score	Frequency (f)
3	1
4	2
5	3
6	1
7	3
8	1

category of data and not just scores. In the above example where the scores were 7, 5, 4, 7, 7, 5 we could represent the scores in terms of their frequencies of occurrence (Table 3.3).

Frequencies are often represented as f in statistics. It is very easy to see in this example that the most frequently occurring score is 7 with a frequency of 3. So the mode of this distribution is 7.

If we take the slightly different set of scores 7, 5, 4, 7, 7, 5, 3, 4, 6, 8, 5, the frequency distribution of these scores is shown in Table 3.4. Here there is no single mode since scores 5 and 7 jointly have the highest frequency of 3. This sort of distribution is called bimodal and the two modes are 5 and 7. The general term multimodal implies that a frequency distribution has several modes.

The mode is the only measure in this chapter that applies to nominal (category) data as well as numerical score data.

Identifying outliers statistically

Outliers, potentially, put your analysis at risk of erroneous conclusions. This is because they are scores which are so atypical of your data in general that they distort any trend in the data because they are unusually large or small. In other words, outliers are a few cases which are out of step with the rest of the data and can mislead the researcher. Routinely, good researchers examine their data for possible outliers simply by inspecting tables of frequencies or scatterplots, for example. This is normally sufficient but does involve an element of judgement which you may not be comfortable with. There are more objective ways of identifying outliers which reduce this subjective element. Essentially what is done is to define precise limits beyond which a score is suspected

$\rightarrow$

of being an outlier. One simple way of doing this is based on the interquartile range which is not affected by outliers since it is based on the middle 50% of scores put in order of their size (p.22).

To calculate the interquartile range, essentially the scores on a variable are arranged from smallest to largest and the 25% of smallest scores and the 25% of largest scores ignored. This leaves the 50% of scores in the middle of the original distribution. The difference between the largest and the smallest score in this middle 50% is the interquartile range. Outliers, which by definition are unusually large or small scores, cannot affect the interquartile range since they will be in the top or bottom 25% of scores and thus eliminated in calculating the interquartile range.

Imagine that we had the following scores for the IQs (Intelligence Quotients) from a sample of 12 individuals:

120, 115, 65, 140, 122, 142, 125, 135, 122, 138, 144, 118

Common sense would suggest that the score of 65 is uncharacteristic of the sample's IQs in general so we would probably identify it as a potential outlier anyway.

To calculate the interquartile range we would first rearrange the scores from smallest to largest (or get a computer to do all of the work for us). This gives us:

65, 115, 118, 120, 122, 122, 125, 135, 138, 140, 142, 144

Since there are 12 scores, to calculate the interquartile range we delete the three (i.e. 25%) lowest scores and also delete the three (i.e. 25%) highest scores. The three lowest scores are 65, 115 and 118 and the three highest scores are 140, 142 and 144. With the extreme quarters deleted, we have the following six scores which are the middle 50% of scores:

120, 122, 122, 125, 135, 138

The interquartile range is the largest of these scores minus the smallest. Thus the interquartile range is $138 - 120 = 16$ in this case.

This interquartile range is multiplied by 1.5 which gives us $1.5 \times 16 = 24$. Outliers among the low scores are defined as any score which is smaller than the smallest score in the interquartile range $- 24 = 120 - 24 = 96$. Outliers among the high scores are defined as any score which is bigger than the largest score in the interquartile range $+ 24 = 138 + 24 = 162$. In other words, scores which are not between 96 and 162 are outliers in this example. The IQ of 65 is thus regarded as an outlier. On the assumption that the scores are normally distributed, then less than 1% of scores would be defined as outliers. This method identifies the moderate outliers.

Extreme outliers are identified in much the same way but the interquartile range is multiplied by 3 (rather than 1.5). This gives us $3 \times 16 = 48$. Extreme outliers among the low scores are scores which are smaller than $120 - 48 = 72$. Extreme outliers among the high scores are scores larger than $138 + 48 = 186$. Thus the participant who has an IQ of 65 would be identified as an extreme outlier. In normally distributed scores, extreme outliers will occur only about once in half a million scores.

It would be usual practice to delete outliers from your data. You might also wish to compare the outcome of the analysis with the complete data and with outliers excluded.

3.3 Comparison of mean, median and mode

Usually the mean, median and mode will give different values of the central tendency when applied to the same set of scores. It is only when a distribution is perfectly symmetrical and the distribution peaks in the middle that they coincide completely. Regard big differences between the mean, median and mode as a sign that your distribution of scores is rather asymmetrical or lopsided.

Distributions of scores do not have to be perfectly symmetrical for statistical analysis but symmetry tends to make some calculations a little more accurate. It is difficult to say how much lack of symmetry there can be without it becoming a serious problem. There is more about this later, especially in Chapter 18 and Appendix A which makes some suggestions about how to test for asymmetry. This is done relatively rarely in our experience.

3.4 The spread of scores: variability

The concept of variability is essential in statistics. Variability is a non-technical term and is related to (but is not identical with) the statistical term variance. Variance is nothing more or less than a mathematical formula that serves as a useful indicator of variability. But it is not the only way of assessing variability.

The following set of ages of 12 university students can be used to illustrate some different ways of measuring variability in our data:

18 years	21 years	23 years	18 years	19 years	19 years
19 years	33 years	18 years	19 years	19 years	20 years

These 12 students vary in age from 18 to 33 years. In other words, the range covers a 15-year period. The interval from youngest to oldest (or tallest to shortest, or fattest to thinnest) is called the range – a useful statistical concept. As a statistical concept, range is always expressed as a single number such as 20 centimetres and seldom as an interval, say, from 15 to 25 centimetres.

One trouble with range is that it can be heavily influenced by extreme cases. Thus the 33-year-old student in the above set of ages is having a big influence on the range of ages of the students. This is because he or she is much older than most of the students. For this reason, the interquartile range has advantages. To calculate the interquartile range we split the age distribution into quarters and take the range of the middle two quarters (or middle 50%), ignoring the extreme quarters. Since we have 12 students, we delete the three youngest (the three 18-year-olds) and the three oldest (aged 33, 23 and 21). This leaves us with the middle two quarters (the middle 50%) which includes five 19-year-olds and one 20-year-old. The range of this middle two quarters, or the interquartile range, is one year (from 19 years to 20 years). The interquartile range is sometimes a better indicator of the variability of, say, age than the full range because extreme ages are excluded.

Useful as the range is, a lot of information is ignored. It does not take into account all of the scores in the set, merely the extreme ones. For this reason, measures of spread or variability have been developed which include the extent to which each of the scores in the set differs from the mean score of the set.

One such measure is the mean deviation. To calculate this we have to work out the mean of the set of scores and then how much each score in the set differs from that mean.

Table 3.5   Deviations from the mean

Score – mean	Deviation from mean
18 – 20.5	–2.5
21 – 20.5	0.5
23 – 20.5	2.5
18 – 20.5	–2.5
19 – 20.5	–1.5
19 – 20.5	–1.5
19 – 20.5	–1.5
33 – 20.5	12.5
18 – 20.5	–2.5
19 – 20.5	–1.5
19 – 20.5	–1.5
20 – 20.5	–0.5

These deviations are then added up, ignoring the negative signs, to give the total of deviations from the mean. Finally we can divide by the number of scores to give the average or mean deviation from the mean of the set of scores. If we take the ages of the students listed above, we find that the total of the ages is 18 + 21 + 23 + 18 + 19 + 19 + 19 + 33 + 18 + 19 + 19 + 20 = 246. Divide this total by 12 and we get the average age in the set to be 20.5 years. Now if we subtract 20.5 years from each of the student's ages we get the figures in Table 3.5.

The average amount of deviation from the mean (ignoring the sign) is known as the mean deviation (for the above deviations this would give a value of 2.6 years). Although frequently mentioned in statistical textbooks it has no practical applications in psychological statistics and is best forgotten. However, there is a very closely related concept, variance, that is much more useful and has widespread and extensive applications. Variance is calculated in an almost identical way to mean deviation but for one thing. When we draw up a table to calculate the variance, we square each deviation from the mean before summing the total of these squared deviations as shown in Table 3.6.

Table 3.6   Squared deviations from the mean

Score – mean	Deviation from mean	Square of deviation from mean
18 – 20.5	–2.5	6.25
21 – 20.5	0.5	0.25
23 – 20.5	2.5	6.25
18 – 20.5	–2.5	6.25
19 – 20.5	–1.5	2.25
19 – 20.5	–1.5	2.25
19 – 20.5	–1.5	2.25
33 – 20.5	12.5	156.25
18 – 20.5	–2.5	6.25
19 – 20.5	–1.5	2.25
19 – 20.5	–1.5	2.25
20 – 20.5	–0.5	0.25
	Total = 0	**Total = 193**

The total of the squared deviations from the mean is 193. If we divide this by the number of scores (12), it gives us the value of the variance, which equals 16.08 in this case.

Expressing the concept as a formula:

$$\text{Variance} = \frac{\Sigma(X - \bar{X})^2}{N}$$

This formula defines what variance is – it is the defining formula. The calculation of variance above corresponds to this formula. However, in statistics there are often quicker ways of doing calculations. These quicker methods involve computational formulae. The computational formula for variance is important and worth memorising as it occurs in many contexts.

Using negative (−) values

Although psychologists rarely collect data that involve negative signs, some statistical techniques can generate them. Negative values occur in statistical analyses because working out differences between scores is common. The mean is often taken away from scores, for example, or one score is subtracted from another. Generally speaking, negative values are not a problem since either the computer or the calculator will do them for you. A positive value is one which is bigger than zero. Often the + sign is omitted as it is taken for granted.

A negative value (or minus value or − value) is a number which is smaller than (less than) zero. The negative sign is never omitted. A value of −20 is a smaller number than −3 (whereas a value of +20 is a bigger number than +3).

Negative values should cause few problems in terms of calculations – the calculator or computer has no difficulties with them. With a calculator you will need to enter that a number is a negative. A key labelled +/− is often used to do this. On a computer, the number must be entered with a − sign.

Probably, the following are the only things you need to know to be able to understand negative numbers in statistics:

- If a negative number is multiplied by another negative number the outcome is a positive number. So −2 × −3 = +6. This is also the case when a number is squared. Thus −3² = +9. You need this information to understand how the standard deviation and variance formulae work, for example.
- Psychologists often speak of negative correlations and negative regression weights. This needs care because the negative in this case indicates that there is a *reverse* relationship between two sets of scores. That is, for example, the more intelligent a person is, the less time will they take to complete a crossword puzzle.
- If you have got negative values for your scores, it is usually advantageous to add a number of sufficient size to make all of the scores positive. This normally makes absolutely no difference to the outcome of your statistical analysis. For example, the variance and standard deviation of −2, −5 and −6 are exactly the same if we add 6 to each of them. That is, calculate the variance and standard deviation of +4, +1 and 0 and you will find them to be identical to those for −2, −5 and −6. It is important that the same number is added to all of your scores. Doing this is helpful since many of us experience anxiety about negative values and prefer it if they are not there.

Standard deviation (see Chapter 5) is a concept which computationally is very closely related to variance. Indeed, many textbooks deal with them at the same time. Unfortunately, this tends in our view to confuse two very distinct concepts and adds nothing to clarity.

CALCULATION 3.2

Variance using the computational formula

The computational formula for variance speeds the calculation since it saves having to calculate the mean of the set of scores and subtract this mean from each of the scores. The formula is:

$$\text{variance}_{\text{[computational formula]}} = \frac{\Sigma X^2 - \dfrac{(\Sigma X)^2}{N}}{N}$$

Take care with elements of this formula:

X	= the general symbol for each member of a set of scores
Σ	= sigma or the summation sign, i.e. add up all the things which follow
ΣX^2	= the sum of the square of each of the scores
$(\Sigma X)^2$	= sum all the scores and square that total
N	= the number of scores

Step 1 Applying this formula to our set of scores, it is useful to draw up a table (Table 3.7) consisting of our scores and some of the steps in the computation. N (number of scores) equals 12.

Table 3.7   A set of scores and their squares for use in the computing formula for variance

Score X	Squared score X^2
18	324
21	441
23	529
18	324
19	361
19	361
19	361
33	1089
18	324
19	361
19	361
20	400
$\Sigma X = 246$	$\Sigma X^2 = 5236$
$(\Sigma X)^2 = 246^2 = 60\ 516$	

Step 2   Substituting these values in the computational formula:

$$\text{Variance}_{\text{[computational formula]}} = \frac{\Sigma X^2 - \dfrac{(\Sigma X)^2}{N}}{N} = \frac{5236 - \dfrac{60\ 516}{12}}{12} = \frac{5236 - 5043}{12} = \frac{193}{12} = 16.08$$

Calculation 3.2 continued

Interpreting the results   Variance is difficult to interpret in isolation from other information about the data since it is dependent on the measurement in question. Measures which are based on a wide numerical scale for the scores will tend to have higher variance than measures based on a narrow scale. Thus if the range of scores is only 10 then the variance is likely to be less than if the range of scores is 100. Frequently variance is treated comparatively – that is, variances of different groups of people are compared (see Chapter 19).

Reporting the results   Usually variance is routinely reported in tables which summarise a variable or a number of variables along with other statistics such as the mean and range. This is shown in Table 3.8.

Table 3.8   Illustrating the table for descriptive statistics

Variable	*N*	Mean	Variance	Range
Age	12	20.50 years	16.08	15 years

Variance estimate

There is a concept called the *variance estimate* (or estimated variance) which is closely related to variance. The difference is that the variance estimate is your best guess as to the variance of a population of scores *if* you only have the data from a small set of scores from that population on which to base your estimate. The variance estimate is described in Chapter 11. It involves a slight amendment to the variance formula in that instead of dividing by N one divides by $N - 1$.

The formula for the estimated variance is:

$$\text{estimated variance} = \frac{\sum X^2 - \dfrac{(\sum X)^2}{N}}{N - 1}$$

Some psychologists prefer to use this formula in all practical circumstances. Similarly, some textbooks and some computer programs give you calculations based on this formula rather than the one we used in Calculation 3.2. Since virtually all statistical analyses in psychology are based on samples and we normally wish to generalise from these samples to all cases, then the estimated variance is likely to be used in practice. Hence it is reasonable to use the estimated variance as the general formula for variance. The drawback to this is that if we are merely describing the data, this practice is theoretically imprecise.

Key points

- Because they are routine ways of summarising the typical score and the spread of a set of scores, it is important always to report the following information for each of your variables:

  - mean, median and mode
  - range and variance
  - number of scores in the set of scores.

- *The above does not apply to nominal categories.* For these, the frequency of cases in each category exhausts the main possibilities.

- It is worth trying to memorise the definitional and computational formulae for variance. You will be surprised how often these formulae appear in statistics.

- When using a computer, look carefully for variables that have zero variance. They can cause problems and generally ought to be omitted from your analyses (see Chapter 7). Normally the computer will not compute the calculations you ask for in these circumstances. The difficulty is that if all the scores of a variable are the same, it is impossible to calculate many statistical formulae. If you are calculating by hand, variables with all the scores the same are easier to spot.

Computer analysis

The SPSS instruction book to this text is Dennis Howitt and Duncan Cramer (2008), *Introduction to SPSS in Psychology*, Harlow: Pearson. Chapter 3 in that book gives detailed step-by-step procedures for the statistics described in this chapter together with advice on how to report the results.

For further resources including data sets and questions, please refer to the CD accompanying this book.

4 Shapes of distributions of scores

Overview

- The shape of the distribution of scores is a major consideration in statistical analysis. It simply refers to the characteristics of the frequency distribution (i.e. histogram) of the scores.

- The normal distribution is an ideal because it is the theoretical basis of many statistical techniques. It is best remembered as a bell-shaped frequency diagram.

- The normal distribution is a symmetrical distribution. That is, it can be folded perfectly on itself at the mean. Symmetry is another ideal in many statistical analyses. Distributions which are not symmetrical are known as skewed distributions.

- Kurtosis indicates how steep or flat a curve is compared with the normal (bell-shaped) curve.

- Cumulative frequencies are ones which include all of the lower values on an accumulating basis. So the highest score will always have a cumulative frequency of 100% since it includes all of the smaller scores.

- Percentiles are the numerical values of the score that cut off the lowest 10%, 30%, 95%, or what have you, of the distribution of scores.

Preparation   Be clear about numerical scores and how they can be classified into ranges of scores (Chapter 2).

4.1   Introduction

The final important characteristic of sets of scores is the particular shape of their distribution. It is useful for a researcher to be able to describe this shape succinctly. Obviously it is possible to find virtually any shape of distribution amongst the multitude of variables that could be measured. So, intuitively, it seems unrealistic to seek to describe just a few different shapes. But there are some advantages in doing so, as we shall see.

4.2   Histograms and frequency curves

Most of us have very little difficulty in understanding histograms; we know that they are plots of the frequency of scores (the vertical dimension) against a numerical scale (the horizontal dimension). Figure 4.1 is an example of a histogram based on a relatively small set of scores. This histogram has quite severe steps from bar to bar. In other words, it is quite angular and not a smooth shape at all. Part of the reason for this is that the horizontal numerical scale moves along in discrete steps, so resulting in this pattern. Things would be different if we measured on a *continuous scale* on which every possible score could be represented to the smallest fraction. For example, we might decide to measure people's heights in centimetres to the nearest whole centimetre. But we know that heights do not really conform to this set of discrete steps or points; people who measure 120 centimetres actually differ in height by up to a centimetre from each other. Height can be measured in fractions of centimetres, not just whole centimetres. In other words height is a continuous measurement with infinitesimally small steps between measures so long as we have sufficiently precise measuring instruments.

So a histogram of heights measured in centimetre units is at best an approximation to reality. Within each of the blocks of the histogram is a possible multitude of smaller steps. For this reason, it is conventional when drawing frequency curves for theoretical purposes to smooth out the blocks to a continuous curve. In essence this is like taking much finer and more precise measurements and redrawing the histogram. Instead of doing this literally we approximate it by drawing a smooth curve through imaginary sets of extremely small steps. When this is done our histogram is 'miraculously' turned into a continuous unstepped curve (Figure 4.2).

A frequency curve can, of course, be of virtually any shape but one shape in particular is of concern in psychological statistics – the normal curve.

Figure 4.1   Histogram showing steep steps

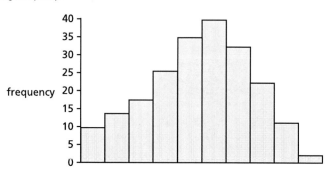

Figure 4.2 A smooth curve based on small blocks

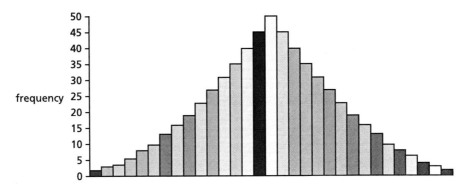

4.3 The normal curve

The normal curve describes a particular shape of the frequency curve. Although this shape is defined by a formula and can be described mathematically, for most purposes it is sufficient to regard it as a symmetrical bell shape (Figure 4.3).

It is called the 'normal' curve because it was once believed that distributions in the natural world corresponded to this shape. Even though it turns out that the normal curve is not universal, it is important because many distributions are more or less this shape – at least sufficiently so for most practical purposes. The crucial reason for its use in statistics is that theoreticians developed many statistical techniques on the assumption that the distributions of scores were bell shaped, or normal. It so happens that these assumptions which are useful in the development of statistical techniques have little bearing on their day-to-day application. The techniques may generally be applied to data which are only very roughly bell shaped without too much inaccuracy. In run-of-the-mill psychological statistics, the question of whether a distribution is normal or bell shaped is relatively unimportant. Exceptions to this will be mentioned as appropriate in later chapters.

Don't forget that for the perfectly symmetrical, bell-shaped (normal) curve the values of the mean, median and mode are identical. Disparities between the three are indications that you have an asymmetrical curve.

Figure 4.3 A normal (bell-shaped) frequency curve

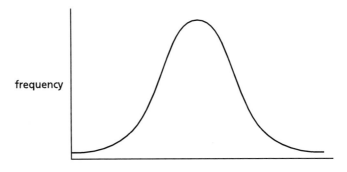

Research design issue

One thing which may trouble you is the question of how precisely your data need fit this normal or bell-shaped ideal. Is it possible to depart much from the ideal without causing problems? The short answer is that usually a lot of deviation is possible without its affecting things too much. So, in the present context, you should not worry too much if the mean, median and mode do differ somewhat; for practical purposes you can disregard deviations from the ideal distribution, especially when dealing with about 30 or more scores. Unfortunately, all of this involves a degree of subjective judgement since there are no useful ways of assessing what is an acceptable amount of deviation from the ideal when faced with the small amounts of data that student projects often involve.

4.4   Distorted curves

The main concepts which deal with distortions in the normal curve are *skewness* and *kurtosis*.

Skewness

It is always worth examining the shape of your frequency distributions. Gross skewness is the exception to our rule of thumb that non-normality of data has little influence on statistical analyses. By skewness we mean the extent to which your frequency curve is lopsided rather than symmetrical. A mid-point of a frequency curve may be skewed either to the left or to the right of the range of scores (Figures 4.4 and 4.5).

There are special terms for left-handed and right-handed skew:

- *Negative skew:*
  - more scores are to the left of the mode than to the right
  - the mean and median are smaller than the mode.
- *Positive skew:*
  - more scores are to the right of the mode than to the left
  - the mean and median are bigger than the mode.

Figure 4.4   Negative skew

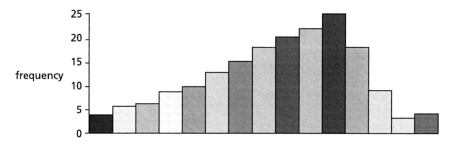

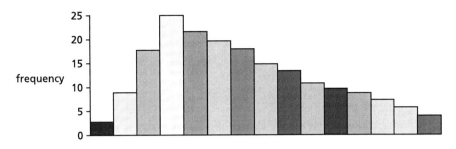

Figure 4.5   Positive skew

There is also an index of the amount of skew shown in your set of scores. With hand-calculated data analyses the best approach is usually to look at your frequency curve. With computer analyses the ease of obtaining the index of skewness makes using complex formulae methods unnecessary. The index of skewness is positive for a positive skew and negative for a negative skew. Appendix A explains how to test for skewness in your data.

■ Kurtosis (or steepness/shallowness)

Some symmetrical curves may look rather like the normal bell-shaped curve except that they are excessively steep or excessively flat compared to the mathematically defined normal bell-shaped curve (Figures 4.6 and 4.7).

Kurtosis is the term used to identify the degree of steepness or shallowness of a distribution. There are technical words for different types of curve:

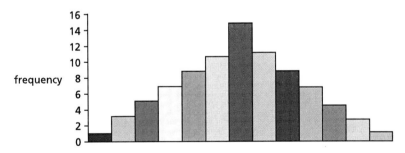

Figure 4.6   A shallow curve

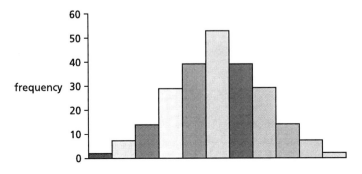

Figure 4.7   A steep curve

- a steep curve is called *leptokurtic*
- a normal curve is called *mesokurtic*
- a flat curve is called *platykurtic*.

Although they are terms beloved of statistics book writers, since the terms mean nothing more than steep, middling and flat there seems to be good reason to drop the Greek words in favour of everyday English.

It is possible to obtain indexes of the amount of shallowness or steepness of your distribution compared with the mathematically defined normal distribution. These are probably most useful as part of a computer analysis. For most purposes an inspection of the frequency curve of your data is sufficient in hand analyses. Knowing what the index means should help you cope with computer output; quite simply:

- a positive value of kurtosis means that the curve is steep
- a zero value of kurtosis means that the curve is middling
- a negative value of kurtosis means that the curve is flat.

Steepness and shallowness have little or no bearing on the statistical techniques you use to analyse your data, quite unlike skewness.

4.5 Other frequency curves

Bimodal and multimodal frequency distributions

Of course, there is no rule that says that frequency curves have to peak in the middle and tail off to the left and right. As we have already explained, it is perfectly possible to have a frequency distribution with twin peaks (or even multiple peaks). Such twin-peaked distributions are called *bimodal* since they have two modes – most frequently occurring scores. Such a frequency curve might look like Figure 4.8.

Figure 4.8   A bimodal frequency histogram

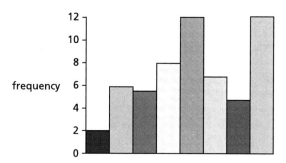

Cumulative frequency curves

There are any number of different ways of presenting a single set of data. Take, for example, the 50 scores in Table 4.1 for a measure of extraversion obtained from airline pilots.

One way of tabulating these extraversion scores is simply to count the number of pilots scoring at each value of extraversion from 1 to 5. This could be presented in several forms, for example Tables 4.2 and 4.3, and Figure 4.9.

Table 4.1   Extraversion scores of 50 airline pilots

3	5	5	4	4	5	5	3	5	2
1	2	5	3	2	1	2	3	3	3
4	2	5	5	4	2	4	5	1	5
5	3	3	4	1	4	2	5	1	2
3	2	5	4	2	1	2	3	4	1

Table 4.2   Frequency table based on data in Table 4.1

Number scoring 1	7
Number scoring 2	11
Number scoring 3	10
Number scoring 4	9
Number scoring 5	13

Table 4.3   Alternative layout for data in Table 4.1

Number of pilots scoring				
1	2	3	4	5
7	11	10	9	13

Figure 4.9   Histogram of Table 4.1

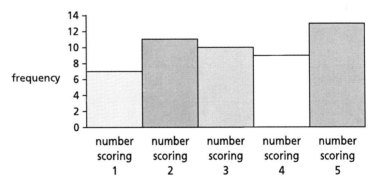

Exactly the same distribution of scores could be represented using a *cumulative* frequency distribution. A simple frequency distribution merely indicates the number of people who achieved any particular score. A cumulative frequency distribution gives the number scoring, say, one, two or less, three or less, four or less, and five or less. In other words, the frequencies accumulate. Examples of cumulative frequency distributions are given in Tables 4.4 and 4.5, and Figure 4.10. Cumulative frequencies can be given also as cumulative percentage frequencies in which the frequencies are expressed as percentages and these percentages accumulated. This is shown in Table 4.4.

There is nothing difficult about cumulative frequencies – but you must label such tables and diagrams clearly or they can be very misleading.

Table 4.4   Cumulative frequency distribution of pilots' extraversion scores from Table 4.1

Score range	Cumulative frequency	Cumulative percentage frequency
1	7	14%
2 or less	18	36%
3 or less	28	56%
4 or less	37	74%
5 or less	50	100%

Table 4.5   Alternative style of cumulative frequency distribution of pilots' extraversion scores from Table 4.1

Number of pilots scoring				
1	2 or less	3 or less	4 or less	5 or less
7	18	28	37	50

Figure 4.10   Cumulative histogram of the frequencies of pilots' extraversion scores from Table 4.1

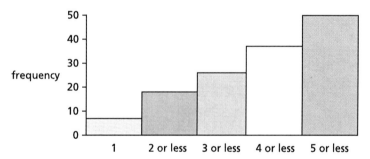

Percentiles

Percentiles are merely a form of cumulative frequency distribution, but instead of being expressed in terms of accumulating scores from lowest to highest, the categorisation is in terms of whole numbers of percentages of people. In other words, the percentile is the score which a given percentage of scores equals or is less than. You do not necessarily have to report every percentage point and units of 10 might suffice for some purposes. Such a distribution would look something like Table 4.6. The table shows that 10% of scores are equal to 7 or less and 80% of scores are equal to 61 or less. Note that the 50th percentile corresponds to the median score.

Percentiles are commonly used in standardisation tables of psychological tests and measures. For these it is often very useful to be able to describe a person's standing compared with the set of individuals on which the test or measure was initially researched. Thus if a particular person's neuroticism score is described as being at the 90th percentile it means that they are more neurotic than about 90% of people. In other words, percentiles are a quick method of expressing a person's score relative to those of others.

Table 4.6 Example of percentiles

Percentile	Score
10th	7
20th	9
30th	14
40th	20
50th	39
60th	45
70th	50
80th	61
90th	70
100th	78

In order to calculate the percentiles for any data it is first necessary to produce a table of cumulative percentage frequencies. This table is then examined to find the score which cuts off, for example, the bottom 10%, the bottom 20%, the bottom 30%, etc. of scores. It should be obvious that calculating percentiles in this way is actually easier if there are a large number of scores so that the cut-off points can be found precisely. Generally speaking, percentiles are used in psychological tests and measures that have been standardised on large numbers of people.

Key points

- The most important concept in this chapter is that of the normal curve or normal distribution. It is worth extra effort to memorise the idea that the normal curve is a bell-shaped symmetrical curve.

- Be a little wary if you find that your scores on a variable are very *skewed* since this can lose precision in certain statistical analyses.

Computer analysis

The SPSS instruction book to this text is Dennis Howitt and Duncan Cramer (2008), *Introduction to SPSS in Psychology*, Harlow: Pearson. Chapter 4 in that book gives detailed step-by-step procedures for the statistics described in this chapter together with advice on how to report the results.

For further resources including data sets and questions, please refer to the CD accompanying this book.

5 Standard deviation and z-scores
The standard unit of measurement in statistics

Overview

- Standard deviation computationally is the square root of variance (Chapter 3).

- Conceptually standard deviation is distance along a frequency distribution of scores.

- Because the normal (bell-shaped) curve is a standard shape, it is possible to give the distribution as percentages of cases which lie between any two points on the frequency distribution. Tables are available to do this relatively simply.

- It is common to express scores as z-scores. A z-score for a particular score is simply the number of standard deviations that the score lies from the mean of the distribution. (A negative sign is used to indicate that the score lies below the mean.) It is also referred to as standardised scores.

Preparation Make sure you know the meaning of variables, scores, Σ and scales of measurement – especially nominal, interval and ratio (Chapter 1).

5.1 Introduction

Measurement ideally uses standard or universal units. It would be really stupid if, when we ask people how far it is to the nearest railway station, one person says 347 cow's lengths, another says 150 poodle jumps, and a third person says three times the distance between my doctor's house and my dentist's home. If you ask us how hot it was on midsummer's day you would be pretty annoyed if one of us said 27 degrees Howitt and the other said 530 degrees Cramer. We measure in standard units such as centimetres, degrees Celsius, kilograms, and so forth. The advantages of doing so are obvious: standard units of measurement allow us to communicate easily, precisely and effectively with other people.

It is much the same in statistics – the trouble is the perplexing variety of types of units possible because of the universality of statistics in many research disciplines. Some variables are measured in physical ways such as metres and kilograms. Others use more abstract units of measurement such as scores on an intelligence test or a personality inventory. Although it would be nice if statisticians had a standard unit of measurement, it is not intuitively obvious what this should be.

5.2 Theoretical background

Imagine a 30 centimetre rule – it will be marked in 1 centimetre units from 0 centimetres to 30 centimetres (Figure 5.1). The standard unit of measurement here is the centimetre. But you could have a different sort of rule in which instead of the scale being from 0 to 30 centimetres, the mid-point of the scale is 0 and the scale is marked as $-15, -14, -13, \ldots$, $-1, 0, +1, \ldots, +13, +14, +15$ centimetres. This rule is in essence marked in deviation units (Figure 5.2).

The two rules use the same unit of measurement (the centimetre) but the deviation rule is marked with 0 in the middle, not at the left-hand side. In other words, the mid-point of the scale is marked as 0 deviation (from the mid-point). The standard deviation is similar to this rule in so far as it is based on *distances or deviations* from the average or mid-point.

As it is the standard unit of measurement in statistics, it is a pity that statisticians chose to call it standard deviation rather than 'standard statistical unit'. The latter phrase would better describe what it is. In contrast to a lot of measurements such as metres and kilograms, the standard deviation corresponds to no single standard of measurement that can be defined in *absolute terms* against a physical entity locked in a vault somewhere.

The standard deviation of a set of scores is measured *relative* to all of the scores in that set. Put as simply as possible, *the standard deviation is the 'average' amount by which scores differ from the mean or average score.* Now this is an odd idea – basing your standard measure on a set of scores rather than on an absolute standard. Nevertheless, it is an important concept to grasp. Don't jump ahead at this stage – there are a couple of twists in the logic yet. Perhaps you are imagining that if the scores were 4, 6, 3 and 7 then the mean is 20 divided by 4 (the number of scores), or 5. Each of the four scores deviates from the average by a certain amount – for example, 7 deviates from the mean of 5 by just 2. The sum of the deviations of our four scores from the mean of 5 is $1 + 1 + 2 + 2$ which equals 6. Surely, then, the standard deviation is 6 divided by 4, which equals 1.5.

But this is *not* how statisticians work out the average deviation for their standard unit. Such an approach might seem logical but it turns out to be not very useful in practice.

Figure 5.1   A 30 centimetre rule

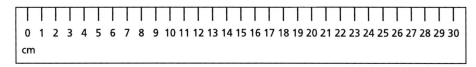

Figure 5.2   A 30 centimetre rule using deviation units

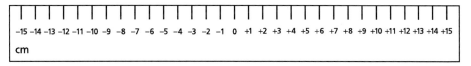

Instead *standard deviation uses a different type of average which most mortals would not even recognise as an average.*

The big difference is that standard deviation is calculated as the average *squared* deviation. What this implies is that instead of taking our four deviation scores $(1 + 1 + 2 + 2)$ we square each of them $(1^2 + 1^2 + 2^2 + 2^2)$ which gives $1 + 1 + 4 + 4 = 10$. If we divide this total deviation of 10 by the number of scores (4), this gives a value of 2.5. However, this is still not quite the end of the story since *we then have to calculate the square root of this peculiar average deviation from the mean.* Thus we take the 2.5 and work out its square root – that is, 1.58. In words, *the standard deviation is the square root of the average squared deviation from the mean.*

And that really is it – honest. It is a pity that one of the most important concepts in statistics is less than intuitively obvious, but there we are. To summarise:

1. The standard deviation is the standard unit of measurement in statistics.
2. The standard deviation is simply the 'average' amount that the scores on a variable deviate (or differ) from the mean of the set of scores. In essence, the standard deviation is the average deviation from the mean. Think of it like this since most of us will have little difficulty grasping it in these terms. Its peculiarities can be safely ignored for most purposes.
3. Although the standard deviation is an average, it is not the sort of average which most of us are used to. However, it is of greater use in statistical applications than any other way of calculating the average deviation from the mean.

The standard deviation gives greater numerical emphasis to scores which depart by larger amounts from the mean. The reason is that it involves *squared* deviations from the mean which give disproportionately more emphasis to larger deviations.

It should be stressed that the *standard deviation is not a unit-free measure.* If we measured a set of people's heights in centimetres, the standard deviation of their heights would also be a certain number of *centimetres.* If we measured 50 people's intelligences using an intelligence test, the standard deviation would be a certain number of IQ points. It might help you to remember this, although most people would say or write things like 'the standard deviation of height was 4.5' without mentioning the units of measurement.

CALCULATION 5.1

Standard deviation

The defining formula for standard deviation is as follows:

$$\text{standard deviation} = \sqrt{\frac{\Sigma(X - \bar{X})^2}{N}}$$

or the computationally quicker formula is:

$$\text{standard deviation} = \sqrt{\frac{\Sigma X^2 - \dfrac{(\Sigma X)^2}{N}}{N}}$$

Calculation 5.1 continued

Table 5.1   Steps in the calculation of the standard deviation

Scores (X) (age in years)	Scores squared (X^2)
20	400
25	625
19	361
35	1225
19	361
17	289
15	225
30	900
27	729
$\sum X = 207$	$\sum X^2 = 5115$

Table 5.1 lists the ages of nine students (N = number of scores = 9) and shows steps in calculating the standard deviation. Substituting these values in the standard deviation formula:

$$\text{standard deviation} = \sqrt{\frac{\sum X^2 - \frac{(\sum X)^2}{N}}{N}} = \sqrt{\frac{5115 - \frac{(207)^2}{9}}{9}}$$

$$= \sqrt{\frac{5115 - 4761}{9}}$$

$$= \sqrt{\frac{354}{9}} = \sqrt{39.333} = 6.27 \text{ years}$$

(You may have spotted that the standard deviation is simply the square root of the variance.)

Interpreting the results   Like variance, standard deviation is difficult to interpret without other information about the data. Standard deviation is just a sort of average deviation from the mean. Its size will depend on the scale of the measurement in question. The bigger the units of the scale, the bigger the standard deviation is likely to be.

Reporting the results   Usually standard deviation is routinely reported in tables which summarise a variable or a number of variables along with other statistics such as the mean and range. This is shown in Table 5.2.

Table 5.2   Illustrating the table for descriptive statistics

Variable	N	Mean	Range	Standard deviation
Age	9	23.00 years	20.00 years	6.27 years

The standard deviation is important in statistics for many reasons. The most important is that the *size* of the standard deviation is an indicator of how much variability there is in the scores for a particular variable. The bigger the standard deviation the more spread there is in the scores. However, this is merely to use standard deviation as a substitute for its close relative variance.

Estimated standard deviation

In this chapter the standard deviation is discussed as a descriptive statistic; that is, it is used like the mean and median, for example, to characterise important features of a set of scores. Be careful to distinguish this from the *estimated* standard deviation which is discussed in Chapter 11. Estimated standard deviation is your best guess as to the standard deviation of a population of scores based on information known about only a small subset or sample of scores from that population. Estimated standard deviation involves a modification to the standard deviation formula so that the estimate is better – the formula is modified to read $N - 1$ instead of just N.

The formula for the estimated standard deviation is:

$$\text{estimated standard deviation} = \sqrt{\frac{\sum X^2 - \frac{(\sum X)^2}{N}}{N - 1}}$$

If you wish, this formula could be used in all of your calculations of standard deviation. Some textbooks and some computer programs give you calculations based on the above formula in all circumstances. Since virtually all statistical analyses in psychology are based on samples and we normally wish to generalise from these samples to all cases then there is good justification for this practice. The downside is that if we are describing the data rather than generalising from them then the formula is theoretically a little imprecise.

5.3 Measuring the number of standard deviations – the z-score

Given that one of the aims of statisticians is to make life as simple as possible for themselves, they try to use the minimum number of concepts possible. Expressing standard statistical units in terms of standard deviations is just one step towards trying to express many measures in a consistent way. Another way of achieving consistency is to express all scores in terms of a *number* of standard deviations. That is, we can abandon the original units of measurements almost entirely if all scores are re-expressed as a number of standard deviations.

It is a bit like calculating all weights in terms of kilograms or all distances in terms of metres. So, for example, since there are 2.2 pounds in a kilogram, something that weighs 10 pounds converts to 4.5 kilograms. We simply divide the number of pounds weight by the number of pounds in a kilogram in order to express our weight in pounds in terms of our standard unit of weight, the kilogram.

It is very much like this in statistics. If we know that the size of the standard deviation is, say, 7, we know that a score which is 21 above the mean score is 21/7 or three standard deviations above the mean. A score which is 14 below the mean is 14/7 or two standard deviations below the mean. So, once the size of the standard deviation is known, all scores can be re-expressed in terms of the *number of standard deviations they are from the mean*. One big advantage of this is that unlike other standard units of measurement such as distance and weight, the *number* of standard deviations will apply no matter what the variable being measured is. Thus it is equally applicable if we are measuring time, anxiety, depression, height or any other variable. So *the number of standard deviations is a universal scale* of measurement. But note the stress on the *number* of standard deviations.

Despite sounding a bit space-age and ultra-modern, the *z-score* is nothing other than the *number* of standard deviations a particular score lies above or below the mean of the set of scores – precisely the concept just discussed. So in order to work out the *z*-score for a particular score (*X*) on a variable we also need to know the mean of the set of scores on that variable and the value of the standard deviation of that set of scores. Sometimes it is referred to as the *standard score* since it allows all scores to be expressed in a standard form.

CALCULATION 5.2

Converting a score into a z-score

To convert the age of a 32-year-old to a *z*-score, given that the mean of the set of ages is 40 years and the standard deviation of age is 6 years, just apply the following formula:

$$z\text{-score} = \frac{X - \bar{X}}{\text{SD}}$$

where *X* stands for a particular score, $\bar{X}$ is the mean of the set of scores, and SD stands for standard deviation.

The *z*-score of any age (e.g. 32) can be obtained as follows:

$$z\text{-score}_{[\text{of a 32-year-old}]} = \frac{32 - 40}{6} = \frac{-8}{6} = -1.33$$

The value of −1.33 means that:

1. A 32-year-old is 1.33 standard deviations from the mean age of 40 for this set of age scores.
2. The minus sign simply means that the 32-year-old is younger (lower) than the mean age for the set of age scores. A plus sign (or no sign) would mean that the person is older (higher) than the mean age of 40 years.

Interpreting the results   There is little to be added about interpreting the *z*-score since it is defined by the formula as the number of standard deviations a score is from the mean score. Generally speaking, the larger the *z*-score (either positive or negative) the more atypical a score is of the typical score in the data. A *z*-score of about 2 or more is fairly rare.

Reporting the results   As *z*-scores are scores they can be presented as you would any other score using tables or diagrams. Usually there is no point in reporting the mean of a set of *z*-scores since this will be 0.00 if calculated for all of the cases.

5.4   A use of *z*-scores

Z-scores, at first sight, deter a lot of students. They are an odd, abstract idea which needs a little time to master. In addition, they seem to achieve very little for students who do their statistics using computer programs. There is some truth in this but it overlooks the fact that standardised scores (very like *z*-scores) appear in many of the more advanced statistical techniques to be found later in this book. So if you master *z*-scores now, this will make your learning at later stages much easier.

So *z*-scores are merely scores expressed in terms of the *number* of standard statistical units of measurement (standard deviations) they are from the mean of the set of scores. One big advantage of using these standard units of measurement is that variables measured in terms of many different units of measurement can be compared with each other and even combined.

A good example of this comes from a student project (Szostak, 1995). The researcher was interested in the amount of anxiety that child tennis players exhibited and its effect on their performance (serving faults) in competitive situations as compared with practice. One consideration was the amount of commitment that parents demonstrated to their children's tennis. Rather than base this simply on the extent to which parents claimed to be involved, she asked parents the amount of money they spent on their child's tennis, the amount of time they spent on their child's tennis, and so forth:

1.   How much money do you spend *per week* on your child's *tennis coaching*?
2.   How much money do you spend *per year* on your child's *tennis equipment*?
3.   How much money do you spend *per year* on your child's *tennis clothing*?
4.   How many *miles per week* on average do you spend travelling to tennis events?
5.   How many *hours per week* on average do you spend watching your child *play tennis*?
6.   How many *LTA tournaments* does your child participate in *per year*?

This is quite straightforward information to collect but it causes difficulties in analysing the data. The student wanted to combine these six different measures of commitment to give an overall commitment score for each parent. However, the six items are based on radically different units of measurement – time, money and so forth. Her solution was simply to turn each parent's score on each of the questionnaire items into a *z*-score. This involves only the labour of working out the mean and standard deviation of the answers to each questionnaire and then turning each score into a *z*-score. These six *z*-scores are then added (including the + or − signs) to give a total score on the amount of commitment by each parent, which could be a positive or negative value since *z*-scores can be + or −.

This was an excellent strategy since this measure of parental commitment was the best predictor of a child performing poorly in competitive situations; the more parental commitment the worse the child does in real matches compared with practice.

There are plenty of other uses of the standard deviation in statistics, as we shall see.

5.5   The standard normal distribution

There is a remaining important use of standard deviation. Although it should now be obvious that there are some advantages in converting scores into standard units of measurement, you might get the impression that, in the end, the scores themselves on a variable contain information which the *z*-score does not fully capture. In particular, if one looks at a distribution of the original scores, it is possible to have a good idea of how a particular individual scores relative to other people. So, for example, if you know the distribution of

Figure 5.3 Distribution of weights in a set of children

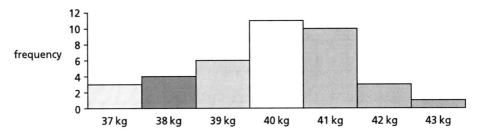

weights in a set of people, it should be possible to say something about the weight of a particular person relative to other people. A histogram giving the weights of 38 children in a school class allows us to compare a child with a weight of, say, 42 kilograms with the rest of the class (Figure 5.3).

We can see that a child of 42 kilograms is in the top four of the distribution – that is, in about the top 10% of the weight distribution. Counting the frequencies in the histogram tells us the percentage of the part of the distribution the child falls in. We can also work out that 34 out of 38 (about 90%) of the class are lighter than this particular child.

Surely this cannot be done if we work with standard deviations? In fact it is relatively straightforward to do so since there are ready-made tables to tell us precisely how a particular score (expressed as a *z*-score or number of standard deviations from the mean) compares with other scores. This is achieved by using a commonly available table which gives the frequency curve of *z*-scores assuming that this distribution is bell shaped or normal. This table is known as either the standard normal distribution or the *z*-distribution. To be frank, some versions of the table are rather complicated but we have opted for the simplest and most generally useful possible. Many statistical tables are known as *tables of significance* for reasons which will become more apparent later on.

Significance Table 5.1 gives the percentage number of scores which will be higher than a score with a given *z*-score. Basically this means that the table gives the proportion of the frequency distribution of *z*-scores which lie in the shaded portions in the example shown in Figure 5.4. The table assumes that the distribution of scores is normal or bell shaped.

Figure 5.4 The part of the z-distribution which is listed in Significance Table 5.1

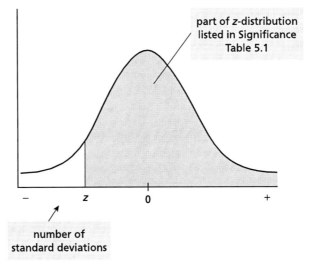

The table usually works sufficiently well even if the distribution departs somewhat from the normal shape.

CALCULATION 5.3

Using the table of the standard normal distribution

Significance Table 5.1 is easy to use. Imagine that you have the IQs of a set of 250 people. The mean ($\bar{X}$) of these IQs is 100 and you calculate that the standard deviation (SD) is 15. You could use this information to calculate the z-score of Darren Jones who scored 90 on the test:

$$z\text{-score} = \frac{X - \bar{X}}{SD} = \frac{90 - 100}{15}$$

$$= \frac{-10}{15} = -0.67 = -0.7 \text{ (to 1 decimal place)}$$

Significance Table 5.1   The standard normal z-distribution: this gives the percentage of z-scores which are higher than the tabled values

z-score	Percentage of scores higher than this particular z-score	z-score	Percentage of scores higher than this particular z-score
−4.00	99.997%	0.00	50.00%
−3.00	99.87%	+0.10	46.02%
−2.90	99.81%	+0.20	42.07%
−2.80	99.74%	+0.30	38.21%
−2.70	99.65%	+0.40	34.46%
−2.60	99.53%	+0.50	30.85%
−2.50	99.38%	+0.60	27.43%
−2.40	99.18%	+0.70	24.20%
−2.30	98.93%	+0.80	21.19%
−2.20	98.61%	+0.90	18.41%
−2.10	98.21%	+1.00	15.87%
−2.00	97.72%	+1.10	13.57%
−1.96	97.50%	+1.20	11.51%
Scores above this point are in the		+1.30	9.68%
extreme 5% of scores in either		+1.40	8.08%
direction from the mean (i.e. the		+1.50	6.68%
extreme 2.5% below the mean)		+1.60	5.48%
−1.90	97.13%	*Scores below this point are in the*	
−1.80	96.41%	*extreme 5% above the mean*	
−1.70	95.54%	+1.64	5.00%
−1.64	95.00%	+1.70	4.46%
Scores above this point are in the		+1.80	3.59%
extreme 5% below the mean		+1.90	2.87%

Calculation 5.3 continued

Significance Table 5.1   (*continued*)

z-score	Percentage of scores higher than this particular z-score	z-score	Percentage of scores higher than this particular z-score
−1.60	94.52%	*Scores below this point are in the*	
−1.50	93.32%	*extreme 5% of scores in either*	
−1.40	91.92%	*direction from the mean (i.e. the*	
−1.30	90.32%	*extreme 2.5% above the mean)*	
−1.20	88.49%	+1.96	2.50%
−1.10	86.43%	+2.00	2.28%
−1.00	84.13%	+2.10	1.79%
−0.90	81.59%	+2.20	1.39%
−0.80	78.81%	+2.30	1.07%
−0.70	75.80%	+2.40	0.82%
−0.60	72.57%	+2.50	0.62%
−0.50	69.15%	+2.60	0.47%
−0.40	65.54%	+2.70	0.35%
−0.30	61.79%	+2.80	0.26%
−0.20	57.93%	+2.90	0.19%
−0.10	53.98%	+3.00	0.13%
0.00	50.00%	+4.00	0.0003%

Taking a *z*-score of −0.7, Significance Table 5.1 tells us that 75.80% of people in the set would have IQs equal to or greater than Darren's. In other words, he is not particularly intelligent. If the *z*-score of Natalie Smith is +2.0 then this would mean that only 2.28% of scores are equal to or higher than Natalie's – she's very bright.

Of course, you could use the table to calculate the proportion of people with *lower* IQs than Darren and Natalie. Since the total amount of scores is 100%, we can calculate that there are 100% − 75.80% = 24.20% of people with IQs equal to or smaller than his. For Natalie, there are 100% − 2.28% = 97.72% of scores equal to or lower than hers.

■ More about Significance Table 5.1

Significance Table 5.1 is just about as simple as we could make it. It is not quite the same as similar tables in other books:

1. We have given negative as well as positive values of *z*-scores.
2. We have only given *z*-scores in intervals of 0.1 with a few exceptions.
3. We have given percentages – many other versions of the table give *proportions* out of 1. In order to convert the values in Significance Table 5.1 into proportions, simply divide the percentage by 100 and delete the % sign.
4. We have introduced a number of 'cut-off points' or zones into the table. These basically isolate extreme parts of the distribution of *z*-scores and identify those *z*-scores which come into the extreme 5% of the distribution. If you like, these are the exceptionally high and exceptionally low *z*-scores. The importance of this might not be obvious right now but will be clearer later on. The extreme zones are described as 'significant'.

We have indicated the extreme 5% in either direction (that is, the extreme 2.5% above and below the mean) as well as the extreme 5% in a particular direction.

5.6   An important feature of z-scores

By using z-scores the researcher is able to say an enormous amount about a distribution of scores extremely succinctly. If we present the following information:

- the mean of a distribution
- the standard deviation of the distribution
- that the distribution is roughly bell shaped or normal

then we can use this information to make very clear statements about the relative position of any score on the variable in question. In other words, rather than present an entire frequency distribution, these three pieces of information are virtually all that is required. Indeed, the third assumption is rarely mentioned since in most applications it makes very little difference.

Key points

- Do not despair if you have problems in understanding standard deviation; it is one of the most abstract ideas in statistics, but so fundamental that it cannot be avoided. It can take some time to absorb completely.

- Remember that the standard deviation is a sort of average deviation from the mean and you will not go far wrong.

- Remember that using z-scores is simply a way of putting variables on a standard unit of measurement irrespective of special characteristics of that variable. Standardised values are common in the more advanced statistical techniques so it is good to master them at an early stage.

- Remember that virtually any numerical score variable can be summarised using the standard deviation and that virtually any measurement can be expressed as a z-score. The main exception to its use is measurements which are in *nominal* categories like occupation or eye colour. Certainly if a score is *interval or ratio* in nature, standard deviation and z-scores are appropriate.

Computer analysis

The SPSS instruction book to this text is Dennis Howitt and Duncan Cramer (2008), *Introduction to SPSS in Psychology*, Harlow: Pearson. Chapter 5 in that book gives detailed step-by-step procedures for the statistics described in this chapter together with advice on how to report the results.

For further resources including data sets and questions, please refer to the CD accompanying this book.

Bivariate analysis 2: exploring relationships between variables

■ This chapter begins by explaining the fundamentals of bivariate relationship tests (chi-square and correlation coefficients – Spearman and Pearson).

■ It then demonstrates how to carry out these bivariate tests of relationships by hand and using SPSS.

INTRODUCTION

This chapter introduces you to tests of relationships between two (or more) variables. There are two major types of test of association introduced here. The first, χ^2 (**chi-square** – pronounced 'ky square') is a test of association for categorical data where we have frequency counts. **Correlation coefficients** (such as the Spearman and Pearson correlation coefficients), on the other hand, are designed to measure the relationship between pairs of continuous variables.

But what does it mean when we say two variables are related? Well, first it is important to stress that the search for relationships is not that different from the search for differences. If, for instance, we find that women do worse at tests of mechanical ability than men we would also expect to find a relationship (association) between men and scores on tests of mechanical ability. So, although we have split tests of difference from tests of association this is not a distinction cast in stone. In essence, tests of relationships are concerned with identifying patterns of relationships between two (or more) variables. If there is a relationship between two variables then the variation of scores in one variable is patterned and not randomly distributed in relation to the variation of scores in the other variable. So, for instance, we might expect to find a relationship (correlation) between social class and income: the higher one's social class, the higher one's income. So, income is not randomly distributed across social class (the likelihood of someone in a low social class having a high income is not the same as someone in a high social class). Instead, there is a pattern between the two variables that we can measure: income increases the higher the social class (or decreases the lower the social class). This chapter is concerned with detailing some of those measures of relationships between variables and includes information on measures of association for categorical (χ^2) and continuous variables (Spearman and Pearson correlation coefficients).

The **chi-square test** is a test of association suitable for use with frequency data, that is, when data are in the form of counts. So, if we counted the number of students working (counts for 'working' versus 'not-working') and looked at the impact of this on examination success (in terms of 'pass' versus 'fail') then we would have appropriate data for a chi-square test. The test is not, however, suitable for use with continuous variables unless those continuous variables are turned into categorical variables. If, for instance, we measured our participants' ages by asking people to write a number on a questionnaire, we would have a continuous variable unsuitable for use in a chi-square test. We could, if we wished, convert age into a series of categories (18–21, 21–25, etc., or young, middle-aged, older) where each category includes the information about how many (frequency) people belong in that particular category. The problem with conversions of this kind is that we lose valuable information about our distribution of scores. In general, we want to maximise statistical power and therefore preserve as much information as possible about our data. We would therefore normally only convert a continuous variable into a categorical variable if it were necessary to test a particular hypothesis.

Theoretical background

The basis for calculating chi-square is really very simple. The easiest way of understanding this statistic is to look at some data (pass/fail rates in a test of mechanical ability separated for equal numbers of men and women) in a table:

	Men	Women	Totals
Pass	23	14	37
Fail	7	11	18
Totals	30	25	55

This table shows that 23 out of 30 men passed the test on mechanics and 14 out of 25 women passed the same test. Seven out of the 30 men failed and 11 out of 25 women failed. Therefore, the proportion of men passing the test (23 out of 30 or 77 per cent) is greater than the proportion of women passing the same test (14 out of 25 or 56 per cent). The chi-square test provides us with a way of determining how unlikely it is to get such a difference in proportions as that shown here. That is, is the difference in proportions significant and are the two variables (gender and success/failure in the test of mechanics) significantly related? Or, more accurately, does membership of one category (e.g. men) tend to be associated with membership of another category (e.g. pass)?

It is quite easy to work out what frequencies we should *expect* in each of the four cells if there was *no association* at all. Thirty-seven out of 55 people (67.27 per cent) pass the test in total and, if there were no association, we would expect this *proportion* of men and this *proportion* of women to pass the test. This is very easy to calculate: we simply multiply this proportion as a fraction ($37 \div 55 = 0.6727$) by the total number of men ($N = 30$) to calculate the expected frequency for men passing (and by the total number of women, $N = 25$, for the expected frequency of women passing).

Expected number of men passing the test = $0.6727 \times 30 = 20.18$
Expected number of women passing the test = $0.6727 \times 25 = 16.82$

We can use the same method to work out the expected frequencies for the other two cells in the table (men and women failing the test). The general formula for calculating the expected frequency of a cell is:

$$\text{Expected frequency } (E) = \frac{\text{row total} \times \text{column total}}{\text{overall total}}$$

The final table of expected frequencies, where there is no association, for these data is shown below:

	Men	Women	Totals
Pass	20.18	16.82	37
Fail	9.82	8.18	18
Totals	30	25	55

It is now simply a case of using the formula for chi-square (given in Box 12.1 below) to compare the **observed frequencies** (O) we obtained in our research with those **expected frequencies** (E) we have just calculated. If there is a sufficiently large difference between O and E we should find the value of chi-square larger and therefore significant.

It is important to note at this stage that chi-square is *only appropriate* when the observations made to generate the frequencies are *independent* of each other. That is, each observation must qualify for *one cell only* in the frequency table. It is not appropriate to use chi-square when you have a repeated measures design with pairs of scores.

Degrees of freedom

There are a few other important things that you should know about chi-square before you attempt to calculate this statistic. Firstly, although the example given above concerns a **2 × 2 contingency table** (a table of frequencies with two columns and two rows), chi-square can be calculated for larger frequency tables using exactly the same method. Expected cell frequencies are calculated and then compared against the observed distribution using the chi-square statistic.

The only extra information needed concerns the **degrees of freedom** (df) of the table being analysed. With a 2 × 2 table there is only one degree of freedom (this is because when one of the expected frequencies has been calculated the rest can be found by subtraction from the column and row totals – the totals being fixed). If you have a larger table you will need to use a formula for calculating degrees of freedom with chi-square:

$$df = (R - 1) \times (C - 1)$$

where R is the number of rows and C the number of columns.

Small samples

Finally, concerns have been raised over the use of chi-square with very small sample sizes. In general, the smaller the sample the worse the fit of the chi-square statistic to the continuous distribution against which it is measured. There are disagreements among statisticians about what counts as too small, however. The general guidance usually offered is to avoid using chi-square when more than 20 per cent of expected cells have values below 5. This would mean that we should not use chi-square on a 2 × 2 table if one or more of our cells had an *expected* (not observed) frequency below 5. However, if the total sample size is greater than 20 it seems to be accepted to use chi-square when one or two cells have expected frequencies below 5 (although the values should not be zero). If the sample size is below 20, however, there is a strong risk of a Type I error even if just one of the cells has an expected frequency below 5 and the chi-square statistic should not be used.

12.2   Calculating chi-square

The formula and instructions for calculating chi-square by hand are given in Box 12.1. Instructions for obtaining chi-square using SPSS are given in Box 12.2. Both examples use the same data but the calculation by hand will use data already displayed in a contingency table while the calculation using SPSS will use data entered normally case by case. Further information about interpreting the SPSS output is also given below.

Box 12.1

Stats box   Calculating a chi-square test of association

Formula for calculating a chi-square statistic

$$\chi^2 = \sum \frac{(O - E)^2}{E}$$

Worked example

Let us return to the data on the success (or not) of men and women passing the test on mechanics and use that data here. Steps 1 and 2 have already been completed for this data.

Step by step procedure

1   Arrange your data in a contingency table with row and column totals.

2   Calculate the expected frequency (*E*) for each cell in your table using the formula:

$$\text{Expected frequency (E)} = \frac{\text{row total} \times \text{column total}}{\text{overall total}}$$

3   Create another table for the expected frequencies or put them into your original table as below:

	Men	Women	Totals
Pass	23	14	37
	20.18	16.82	
Fail	7	11	18
	9.82	8.18	
Totals	30	25	55

4   Calculate the difference between *O* and *E* for each cell:

A $(O - E) = 23 - 20.18$ =   2.82
B $(O - E) = 14 - 16.82$ =   −2.82
C $(O - E) = 7 - 9.82$ =   −2.82
D $(O - E) = 11 - 8.18$ =   2.82

5   Square each of these values to obtain $(O - E)^2$ for each cell:

A $(O - E)^2 = 7.95$
B $(O - E)^2 = 7.95$
C $(O - E)^2 = 7.95$
D $(O - E)^2 = 7.95$

Box 12.1 *Continued*

6   Divide each of these values by the appropriate value of E for that cell:

         A $7.95 \div 20.18$ $= 0.39$
         B $7.95 \div 16.82$ $= 0.47$
         C $7.95 \div 9.82$ $= 0.81$
         D $7.95 \div 8.18$ $= 0.97$

7   Now it is simply a case of calculating chi-square using all three elements of the formula calculated above:

$$\chi^2 = 0.39 + 0.47 + 0.81 + 0.97 = 2.64 \text{ with 1 df}$$

8   Look up the value of chi-square for 1 df in the appropriate table (in the Appendix). Chi-square = 3.84 for 1 df. Our value is below this so there is not a significant association between gender and passing the test on mechanics.

9   Report your findings:

     There was not a significant association between observed and expected frequencies for gender and performance (pass/fail) on the test of mechanics given (χ^2 2.64, df = 1, ns).

Note: some writers suggest the use of Yates's correction when calculating χ^2 with 2 × 2 contingency tables because of a danger of overestimating the value of χ^2 in this case. This correction very simply requires us to subtract 0.5 from the value of $(O - E)$ for each cell before squaring the value for all four cells. It is probably safest to use this correction when calculating χ^2 for 2 × 2 tables. The χ^2 formula with Yates's correction is given below:

$$\chi^2 = \sum \frac{[(O - E) - 0.5]^2}{E}$$

Box 12.2

Command box   **Computing a chi-square test of association**

1   Your data (RMBChiSquare.sav, available from the book's website) should be entered normally, with cases (each person) as rows and variables (gender and pass/fail on the test) as columns and not as a contingency table.

2   Click **Descriptive Statistics** on the top menu bar.

3   Click on **Crosstabs**. This will bring up a dialogue box (see Fig. 12.1). It is called 'crosstabs' because we are cross-tabulating our data (putting it in a table to compare cells).

Box 12.2 *Continued*

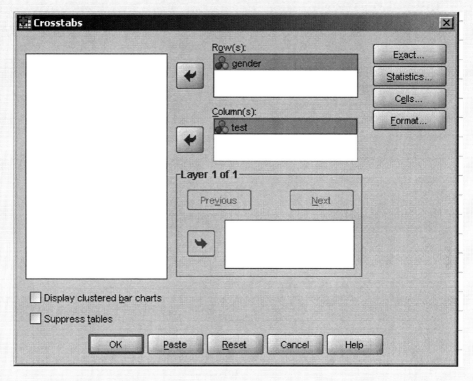

Figure 12.1 Chi-square test dialogue box

4   Move your row and column variables ('gender' and 'test') into the **Row** and **Column** boxes respectively using the **Variable Picker** button.

5   Click on **Statistics** to bring up another dialogue box where you can choose **Chi-square** by clicking the box next to the name. Click **Continue** to return to the previous dialogue box.

6   If you want to see row and column frequencies (and percentages) you will need to click on **Cells** and then click on the boxes next to **Observed**, **Expected** and **Row**, **Column** and **Total** percentages, if you wish, in this dialogue box (see Fig. 12.2). Then click **Continue** to return to the previous dialogue box.

7   Click **OK** to run your test. The results will appear in the output viewer window as usual.

Interpreting your SPSS output

SPSS produces three output tables (Figs 12.3–12.5). The first table simply shows the number of cases used in the test (all 55 in this case as there was no missing data). The second table (Fig. 12.3) is a contingency table which shows the

Case Processing Summary

	Cases					
	Valid		Missing		Total	
	N	Percent	N	Percent	N	Percent
gender * test	55	100.0%	0	.0%	55	100.0%

Figure 12.2 Case processing output table

gender * test Crosstabulation

			test		
			1	2	Total
gender	1	Count	23	7	30
		Expected Count	20.2	9.8	30.0
		% within gender	76.7%	23.3%	100.0%
		% within test	62.2%	38.9%	54.5%
		% of Total	41.8%	12.7%	54.5%
	2	Count	14	11	25
		Expected Count	16.8	8.2	25.0
		% within gender	56.0%	44.0%	100.0%
		% within test	37.8%	61.1%	45.5%
		% of Total	25.5%	20.0%	45.5%
	Total	Count	37	18	55
		Expected Count	37.0	18.0	55.0
		% within gender	67.3%	32.7%	100.0%
		% within test	100.0%	100.0%	100.0%
		% of Total	67.3%	32.7%	100.0%

Figure 12.3 Cross-tabulation output table

observed and expected frequencies (because we selected this option using **Cells**). The third table (Fig. 12.4) gives the chi-square statistic, the degrees of freedom and significance level as the first line ('Pearson Chi-Square'). So, the chi-square value is 2.65 (to two decimal places), df = 1 and $p = 0.10$ (to two decimal places) and so is non-significant. The line beneath this gives the value of chi-square when Yates's correction is applied (as you can see, the value of chi-square is lower and so the chances of significance less). This is the line we should use when reporting our data with a 2 × 2 table (i.e. two variables). The other line worthy of attention is the one reporting **Fisher's Exact Test**. This test is an alternative to chi-square (which does the same thing) that should be used if you have a 2 × 2 table with small expected frequencies (below 5). SPSS also includes information about the number of cells with frequencies below 5 underneath this table, and

Chi-Square Tests

	Value	df	Asymp. Sig. (2-sided)	Exact Sig. (2-sided)	Exact Sig. (1-sided)
Pearson Chi-Square	2.645[a]	1	.104		
Continuity Correction[b]	1.790	1	.181		
Likelihood Ratio	2.652	1	.103		
Fisher's Exact Test				.150	.091
Linear-by-Linear Association	2.597	1	.107		
N of Valid Cases	55				

a. 0 cells (.0%) have expected count less than 5. The minimum expected count is 8.18.

b. Computed only for a 2x2 table

Figure 12.4 Chi-square statistics output table

this information should be used to make the decision between reporting the chi-square or Fisher's exact test statistics (with a 2 × 2 table). Details of how to report chi-square results are given in Box 12.1.

12.3 Introducing correlation coefficients

The notion of correlation has already been introduced at the beginning of this chapter and in previous chapters (when discussing scattergrams, for instance) so will not need much further discussion here. Two ways of calculating correlation coefficients are covered here. The first is **Spearman's Rho**, or rank-order correlation coefficient (normally just called 'Spearman's correlation coefficient'), which is suitable for non-parametric data. The second is **Pearson's Product–Moment Correlation Coefficient** (normally just called 'Pearson's correlation coefficient'), which is suitable for parametric data and is generally considered more powerful.

Theoretical background

A **correlation coefficient** (such as Pearson's or Spearman's) is a *descriptive* measure of the relatedness of two variables. We can, however, test correlation coefficients for significance by comparing them against tables of critical values. The strength of a correlation coefficient is expressed on a scale from –1 to +1 where –1 indicates a perfect negative correlation and +1 a perfect positive correlation. A value of 0 means there is no relationship between the two variables. Generally, correlation coefficients above 0.8 (positive and negative) are thought to represent strong relationships between variables. A correlation simply tells us about the pattern of the relationship between the two variables. A *positive* correlation tells us that as one variable increases (income, for instance) so does the other (age, for instance). A *negative* correlation, on the other hand, tells us that as one variable increases (age, for instance) the other variable decreases (memory test scores, for instance). The sign indicates the direction of the relationship while the number indicates the strength.

An important concept with correlation is the **coefficient of determination**. This is a measure of the amount of variation in one variable that is accounted for by the other. The coefficient of determination is simply the square of Pearson's correlation coefficient (r) multiplied by 100 (to give us the percentage of variation accounted for) and is therefore known as r^2. If we have a large correlation coefficient of 0.8, for instance, we can say that one variable accounts for $(0.8 \times 0.8) = 0.64 \times 100 = 64$ per cent of the variation in the other. A slightly lower correlation that may still be significant, of 0.6, means that only 36 per cent of the variance in one variable is accounted for by the other (as we are only talking about correlation and not causality it does not matter which way round we put our variables). In other words, 64 per cent of the variance in one variable is due to variables other than the one we measured! We therefore have to be cautious when interpreting correlation coefficients. Their absolute size matters: significance is not everything here! A small or moderate correlation coefficient may well be significant (especially with large sample sizes) but only explain a tiny amount of the variance.

It is generally a good idea to plot a scattergram (see Chapter 10) of the variables under investigation before computing a correlation coefficient. A scattergram enables us to visually inspect the relationship between two variables and check that the relationship is **linear**. The correlation coefficients being described here determine the strength of linear relationships. It is possible, however, to get relationships between variables that are not linear. Curvilinear relationships (see Fig. 12.5) are not unknown in psychology. If we used a linear technique with such data our results would be spurious (we are most likely not to find a relationship when one really does exist).

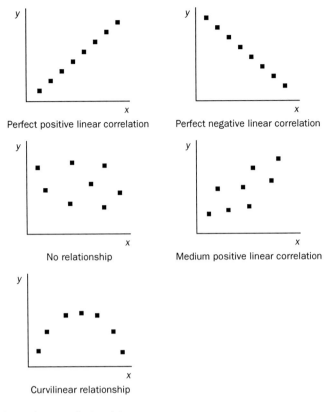

Figure 12.5 Linear and non-linear relationships

12.4   Calculating correlation coefficients

The formula and instructions for calculating a Spearman correlation coefficient by hand are given in Box 12.3. The formula and instructions for calculating a Pearson correlation coefficient by hand are given in Box 12.4. Instructions for obtaining both correlation coefficients using SPSS are given in Box 12.5. All examples of the correlation tests given here (the two calculations by hand and the one using SPSS) will use the same data (detailed in Box 12.3). Further information about interpreting the SPSS output is also given below.

Box 12.3

Stats box   **Calculating a Spearman correlation coefficient**

Formula for calculating a Spearman correlation coefficient

$$\rho = 1 - \frac{6 \sum d^2}{N(N^2 - 1)}$$

Box 12.3 *Continued*

Worked example

We have collected scores on a standardised test of creativity for maths and music students and, on the basis of previous research, want to know if there is a relationship between the scores.

Data

Maths	Music
2	4
4	1
5	4
7	6
8	7
9	7
5	6
8	6
9	9
7	8

Step by step procedure

1   Begin by setting out the columns of scores you need to calculate the component parts of the formula (ranks for each group of scores *separately*, difference between ranks and squares of these difference scores):

Rank A	Rank B	d	d^2
1	2.5	−1.5	2.25
2	1	1	1
3.5	2.5	1	1
5.5	5	0.5	0.25
7.5	7.5	0	0
9.5	7.5	2	4
3.5	5	−1.5	2.25
7.5	5	2.5	6.25
9.5	10	−0.5	0.25
5.5	9	−3.5	12.25

2   Calculate Σd^2 from your data = 29.5.

3   Simply insert these numbers into the formula:

$$\rho = 1 - \frac{6 \times 29.5}{10(100 - 1)}$$

4   Spearman's ρ (rho) therefore equals 0.82 and indicates a strong positive correlation between maths and music students on the test of creativity.

Box 12.3 *Continued*

5   This value can be compared against those in the table of critical values (see the Appendix) to assess its significance. The critical values for ρ at $p < 0.05$ and $p < 0.01$ are 0.648 and 0.794 respectively. Our value is above both of these values and is therefore significant at $p < 0.01$.

6   Report your findings:

There is a statistically significant positive correlation between maths and music students on the test of creativity ($\rho = 0.82$, $p < 0.01$).

Note: both the Spearman and Pearson correlation coefficients can be calculated only for *pairs of scores*.

Box 12.4

Stats box   Calculating a Pearson correlation coefficient

Formula for calculating a Pearson correlation coefficient

$$r = \frac{N\sum(XY) - \sum X \sum Y}{\sqrt{[N\sum X^2 - (\sum X)^2][N\sum Y^2 - (\sum Y)^2]}}$$

There are variations on this formula so you may see it written differently. This is clearly a little more complex than the formulae for the Spearman correlation coefficient. However, do not worry too much about formulae such as this: it really is quite straightforward if you break it down into its component parts.

Worked example

We will use the same data here as we did for the Spearman correlation coefficient (ρ) and see what result we get.

Step by step procedure

1   Begin by setting out your columns in order to calculate the elements of the formula you need (XY, which just means $X \times Y$, and X^2 and Y^2, where X represents the scores in group A – maths students – and Y the scores in group B – music students):

XY	X^2	Y^2
8	4	16
4	16	1
20	25	16
42	49	36
56	64	49
63	81	49
30	25	36
48	64	36
81	81	81
56	49	64

Box 12.4 *Continued*

2 Use these scores to calculate the other elements of the formula needed:

ΣX = 64
ΣY = 58
ΣXY = 408
ΣX^2 = 458
ΣY^2 = 384

3 Now insert these figures into your formula and get working on that calculator:

$$r = \frac{(10 \times 408) - (64 \times 58)}{\sqrt{[(10 \times 458) - (64 \times 64)] \times [(10 \times 384) - (58 \times 58)]}}$$

4 Pearson's *r* therefore equals 0.77 (to two decimal places) and indicates a fairly strong correlation between maths and music students on the test of creativity.

5 This value can be compared against those in the table of critical values (see the Appendix) to assess its significance. The critical values for *r* at $p < 0.05$ and $p < 0.01$ are 0.632 and 0.765 respectively. Our value is above both of these values and is therefore significant at $p < 0.01$.

6 Report your findings:

There is a statistically significant positive correlation between maths and music students on the test of creativity ($r = 0.77$, $p < 0.01$).

Note: both the Spearman and Pearson correlation coefficients can only be calculated for *pairs of scores*.

Box 12.5

Command box	Computing Spearman and Pearson correlation coefficients

1 Your data (RMBCorLatDat.sav, available from the book's website) should be entered normally.

2 Click on **Analyze** on the top menu bar.

3 Click on **Correlate** and then click on **Bivariate**. This will bring up a dialogue box (see Fig. 12.6) where you can specify which variables you want to correlate with each other using the **Variable Picker** button to move them into the **Variables** box. Note you can include more than two variables in the Variables box (it will just calculate a series of bivariate correlations on your variables).

Box 12.5 *Continued*

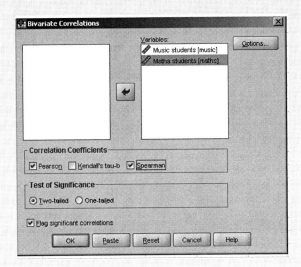

Figure 12.6 Correlation dialogue box

4   Select whether you want a **Pearso<u>n</u>** or **Spearman** (or both!) correlation coefficient by clicking in the box next to their name in the **Correlation Coefficients** section.

5   Click **OK** to run your command. Your results will appear in the output viewer window as usual.

Interpreting your SPSS output

SPSS produces one table for each correlation coefficient (so you will have only one table in your output if you only selected Pearson or Spearman). Here, we selected both so you could see the output from both tests (see Figs. 12.7 and 12.8). The first table (Fig. 12.7) shows the result of the Pearson calculation. The Pearson correlation coefficient ($r = 0.767$) is given along with its significance ($p = 0.01$). The second table (Fig. 12.8) shows the result of the Spearman calculation. The Spearman correlation coefficient ($p = 0.816$) is given along with its significance ($p = 0.004$). Both tables also include N (the number of cases in the data set). Details on how to report your findings are given in the two statistics boxes on calculating correlations by hand.

Correlations

		Music students	Maths students
Music students	Pearson Correlation	1.000	.767**
	Sig. (2-tailed)		.010
	N	10.000	10
Maths students	Pearson Correlation	.767**	1.000
	Sig. (2-tailed)	.010	
	N	10	10.000

**. Correlation is significant at the 0.01 level (2-tailed).

Figure 12.7 Pearson correlation coefficient output

Correlations

			Music students	Maths students
Spearman's rho	Music students	Correlation Coefficient	1.000	.816**
		Sig. (2-tailed)	.	.004
		N	10	10
	Maths students	Correlation Coefficient	.816**	1.000
		Sig. (2-tailed)	.004	.
		N	10	10

**. Correlation is significant at the 0.01 level (2-tailed).

Figure 12.8 Spearman correlation coefficient output

15 Probability

Overview

- Although probability theory is at the heart of statistics, in practice the researcher needs to know relatively little of this.

- The addition rule basically suggests that the probability of, say, any of three categories occurring is the sum of the three individual probabilities for those categories.

- The multiplication rule suggests that the probability of different events occurring in a particular sequence is the product of the individual probabilities.

Preparation   General familiarity with previous chapters.

15.1 Introduction

From time to time, researchers need to be able to calculate the probabilities associated with certain patterns of events. One of us remembers being a student in a class that carried out an experiment based on newspaper reports of a Russian study in which people appeared to be able to recognise colours through their finger tips. So we designed an experiment in which a blindfolded person felt different colours in random order. Most of us did not do very well but some in the class seemed excellent. The media somehow heard about the study and a particularly good identifier in our experiment quickly took part in a live TV demonstration of her skills. She was appallingly bad at the task this time.

The reason why she was bad on television was that she had no special skills in the first place. It had been merely a matter of chance that she had done well in the laboratory. On the television programme, chance was not on her side and she turned out to be as bad as the rest of us. Actually, this reflects a commonly referred to phenomenon called *regression to the mean*. Choose a person (or group) because of their especially high (or, alternatively, especially low) scores and they will tend to score closer to the mean on the next administration of the test or measurement. This is because the test or measure is to a degree unreliable and by choosing exceptional scores you have to an extent capitalised on chance factors. With a completely unreliable test or measure, the reversion towards the mean will be dramatic. In our colour experiment the student did badly on TV because she had been selected totally on the basis of a criterion that was fundamentally unreliable – that is, completely at random.

Similar problems occur in any investigation of individual paranormal or psychic powers. For example, a spiritual medium who addresses a crowd of 500 people is doing nothing spectacular if in Britain she claims to be speaking to a dead relative of someone and that relative is Mary or Martha or Margaret. The chances of someone in the 500 having such a relative are very high.

15.2   The principles of probability

When any of us use a test of significance we are utilising probability theory. This is because most statistical tests are based on it. Our working knowledge of probability in most branches of psychology does not have to be very great for us to function well. We have been using probability in previous chapters on significance testing when we talked about the 5% level of significance, the 1% level of significance and the 95% confidence intervals. Basically what we meant by a 5% level of significance is that a particular event (or outcome) would occur on five occasions out of 100. Although we have adopted the percentage system of reporting probabilities in this book, statisticians would normally not write of a 5% probability. Instead they would express it as being out of a *single* event rather than 100 events. Thus:

■   0.05 (or just .05) is an alternative way of writing 5%
■   0.10 (or .10) is an alternative way of writing 10%
■   1.00 is an alternative way of writing 100%.

The difficulty for some of us with this alternative, more formal, way of writing probability is that it leaves everything in decimals, which does not appeal to the less mathematically skilled. However, you should be aware of the alternative notation since it appears in many research reports. Furthermore, much computer output can give probabilities to several decimal places which can be confusing. For example, what does a probability of 0.000 01 mean? The answer is one chance in 100 000 or a 0.001% probability ($\frac{1}{100\,000} \times 100 = 0.001\%$).

There are two rules of probability with which psychologists ought to be familiar. They are the *addition rule* and the *multiplication rule*.

1.   The *addition rule* is quite straightforward. It merely states that for a number of mutually exclusive outcomes the sum of their probabilities adds up to 1.00. So if you have a set of 150 people of whom 100 are women and 50 are men, the probability of picking a woman at random is 100/150 or 0.667. The probability of picking a man at random is 50/150 or 0.333. However, the probability of picking either a man or a woman at random is 0.667 + 0.333 or 1.00. In other words, it is certain that you will pick either a man or a woman. The assumption is that the categories or outcomes are mutually exclusive, meaning that a person cannot be in both the man and woman categories. Being a man excludes that person from also being a woman. In statistical probability theory, one of the two possible outcomes is usually denoted p and the other is denoted q, so $p + q = 1.00$. Outcomes that are not mutually exclusive include, for example, the categories man and young since a person could be a man and young.

2. The *multiplication rule* is about a set of events. It can be illustrated by our set of 150 men and women in which 100 are women and 50 are men. Again the assumption is that the categories or outcomes are mutually exclusive. We could ask how likely it is that the first five people that we pick at random will all be women, given that the probability of choosing a woman on a single occasion is 0.667. The answer is that we multiply the probability associated with the first person being a woman by the probability that the second person will be a woman by the probability that the third person will be a woman by the probability that the fourth person will be a woman by the probability that the fifth person will be a woman:

$$\text{Probability of all five being women} = p \times p \times p \times p \times p$$

$$= 0.667 \times 0.667 \times 0.667 \times 0.667 \times 0.667$$

$$= 0.13$$

Therefore there is a 13% probability (0.13) that we will choose a sample of five women at random. That is not a particularly rare outcome. However, picking a sample of all men from our set of men and women is much rarer:

$$\text{Probability of all five being men} = q \times q \times q \times q \times q$$

$$= 0.333 \times 0.333 \times 0.333 \times 0.333 \times 0.333$$

$$= 0.004$$

Therefore there is a 0.4% probability (0.004) of choosing all men.

The multiplication rule as stated here assumes that once a person is selected for inclusion in the sample, he or she is replaced in the population and possibly selected again. This is called random sampling with replacement. However, normally we do not do this in psychological research, though if the population is big then not replacing the individual back into the population has negligible influence on the outcome. Virtually all statistical analyses assume replacement but it does not matter that people are usually not selected more than once for a study in psychological research.

15.3 Implications

Such theoretical considerations concerning probability theory have a number of implications for research. They ought to be carefully noted.

1. *Repeated significance testing* within the same study. It is tempting to carry out several statistical tests on data. Usually we find that a portion of these tests are statistically significant at the 5% level whereas a number are not. Indeed, even if there were absolutely no trends in the population, we would expect, by chance, 5% of our comparisons to be significant at the 5% level. This is the meaning of statistical significance, after all. The more statistical comparisons we make on our data the more significant findings we would expect. If we did 20 comparisons we would expect one significant finding even if there are no trends in the population. In order to cope with this, the correct procedure is to make the statistical significance more stringent the more tests of significance we do. So if we did two tests then our significance level per test should be 5%/2 or 2.5%; if we did four comparisons our significance level would be 5%/4 or

1.25% significance per test. In other words, we simply divide the 5% significance level by the number of tests we are doing. Although this is the proper thing to do, few psychological reports actually do it. However, the consequence of not doing this is to find more significant findings than you should.

2. *Significance testing across different studies.* An application of the multiplication rule in assessing the value of replicating research shows the dramatic increase in significance that this can achieve. Replication means the essential repeating of a study at a later date and possibly in radically different circumstances such as other locations. Imagine that the significance level achieved in the original study is 5% ($p = 0.05$). If one finds the same significance level in the replication the probability of two studies producing this level of significance by chance is $p \times p$ or $0.05 \times 0.05 = 0.0025$ or 0.25%. This considerably enhances our confidence that the findings of the research are not the result of chance factors but reflect significant trends.

CALCULATION 15.1

The addition rule

A psychologist wishes to calculate the chance expectations of marks on a multiple choice test of general knowledge. Since a person could get some answers correct simply by sticking a pin into the answer paper, there has to be a minimum score below which the individual is doing no better than chance. If each question has four response alternatives then one would expect that by chance a person could get one in four or one-quarter of the answers correct. That is intuitively obvious. But what if some questions have three alternative answers and others have four alternative answers? This is not quite so obvious but we simply apply the law of addition and add together the probabilities of being correct for all of the questions on the paper. This entails adding together probabilities of 0.33 and 0.25 since there are three or four alternative answers. So if there are 10 questions with three alternative answers and five questions with four alternative answers, the number of answers correct by chance is $(10 \times 0.33) + (5 \times 0.25) = 3.3 + 1.25 = 4.55$.

CALCULATION 15.2

The multiplication rule

A psychologist studies a pair of male twins who have been brought up separately and who have never met. The psychologist is surprised to find that the twins are alike on seven out of ten different characteristics, as presented below. The probability of their characteristics occurring in the general population is given in brackets:

1. They both marry women younger than themselves (0.9).
2. They both marry brunettes (0.7).
3. They both drive (0.7).

Calculation 15.2 continued

4.   They both swim (0.6).
5.   They have spent time in hospital (0.8).
6.   They both take foreign holidays (0.5).
7.   They both part their hair on the left (0.9).

However, they are different in the following ways:

8.   One attends church (0.4) and the other does not.
9.   One has a doctorate (0.03) and the other does not.
10.   One smokes (0.3) and the other does not.

The similarities between the two men are impressive if it is exceptional for two randomly selected men to be similar on each of the items. The probabilities of each of the outcomes are presented in brackets above. These probabilities are the proportions of men in the general population demonstrating these characteristics. For many of the characteristics it seems quite likely that they will be similar. So two men taken at random from the general population are most likely to marry a younger woman. Since the probability of marrying a younger woman is 0.9, the probability of any two men marrying younger women is $0.9 \times 0.9 = 0.81$. The probability of two men taken at random both being drivers is $0.7 \times 0.7 = 0.49$. In fact the ten characteristics listed above are shared by randomly selected pairs of men with the following probabilities:

1. $0.9 \times 0.9 = 0.81$
2. $0.7 \times 0.7 = 0.49$
3. $0.7 \times 0.7 = 0.49$
4. $0.6 \times 0.6 = 0.36$
5. $0.8 \times 0.8 = 0.64$
6. $0.5 \times 0.5 = 0.25$
7. $0.9 \times 0.9 = 0.81$
8. $0.4 \times 0.4 = 0.16$
9. $0.03 \times 0.03 = 0.0009$
10. $0.3 \times 0.3 = 0.09$

The sum of these probabilities is 4.10. Clearly the pair of twins are more alike than we might expect on the basis of chance. However, it might be that we would get a different answer if instead of taking the general population of men, we took men of the same age as the twins.

 Key points

■   Although probability theory is of crucial importance for mathematical statisticians, psychologists generally rely on an intuitive approach to the topic. This may be laziness on their part, but we have kept the coverage of probability to a minimum given the scope of this book. It can also be very deterring to anyone not too mathematically inclined. If you need to know more, especially if you need to estimate precisely the likelihood of a particular pattern or sequence of events occurring, we suggest that you consult books such as Kerlinger (1986) for more complete accounts of mathematical probability theory.

- However, it is important to avoid basic mistakes such as repeated significance testing on the same data without adjusting your significance levels to allow for the multitude of tests. This is not necessary for tests designed for multiple testing such as those for the analysis of variance, some of which we discuss later (Chapter 23), as the adjustment is built in.

For further resources including data sets and questions, please refer to the CD accompanying this book.

16 Reporting significance levels succinctly

Overview

- A glance at reports in psychology journals suggests that relatively little space is devoted to reporting the outcomes of statistical analysis.

- Usually, authors report their findings using very succinct methods which occupy very little space.

- Normally the test statistic, the sample size (or degrees of freedom), significance level and if it is a one-tailed test are reported.

- It is recommended that students adopt this succinct style of reporting for their research as it will result in a more professional-looking product.

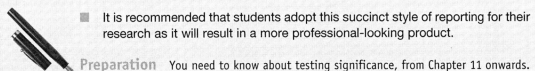

Preparation   You need to know about testing significance, from Chapter 11 onwards.

16.1 Introduction

So far, the reporting of statistical significance in this book has been a relatively clumsy and long-winded affair. In contrast, a glance at any psychology journal will suggest that precious little space is devoted to reporting significance. Detailed expositions of the statistical significance of your analyses have no place in professional reports. Researchers can make life much simpler for themselves by adopting the standard style of reporting statistical significance. Clarity is one great benefit; another is the loss of wordiness.

Although the standard approach to reporting statistical significance does vary slightly, there is little difficulty with this. At a minimum, the following should be mentioned when reporting statistical significance:

1. The statistical distribution used (e.g. F, chi-square, r, z, t, etc.).
2. The degrees of freedom (df). Alternatively, for some statistical techniques you may report the sample size (N).
3. The value of the calculation (e.g. the value of your z-score or your chi-square).
4. The probability or significance level. Sometimes 'not significant', 'not sig.' or 'ns' is used.

5. If you have a one-tailed hypothesis then this should be also mentioned. Otherwise a two-tailed hypothesis is assumed. You can also state that you are using a two-tailed test. This is most useful when you have several analyses and some are one-tailed and others are two-tailed.

16.2 Shortened forms

In research reports, comments such as the following are to be found:

■ The hypothesis that drunks slur their words was supported ($t = 2.88$, degrees of freedom = 97, $p < 0.01$).
■ There was a trend for drunks to slur their words more than sober people ($t = 2.88$, df = 97, significance = 1%).
■ The null hypothesis that drunks do not slur their words more than sober people was rejected ($t = 2.88$, degrees of freedom = 97, $p = 0.01$).
■ The analysis supported the hypothesis since drunks tended to slur their words the most often ($t (97) = 2.88$, $p = 0.01$, two-tailed test).
■ The hypothesis that drunks slur their words was accepted ($t (97) = 2.88$, $p = 0.005$, 1-tail).

All of the above say more or less the same thing. The symbol t indicates that the t-test was used. The symbol $<$ indicates that your probability level is smaller than the given value. Thus $p < 0.01$ could mean that the probability is, say, 0.008 or 0.005. That is, the test is statistically significant at better than the reported level of 0.01. Sometimes, the degrees of freedom are put in brackets after the symbol for the statistical test used, as in $t (97) = 2.88$. In all of the above examples, the hypothesis was supported and the null hypothesis rejected.

The following are examples of what might be written if the hypothesis was not supported by your data:

■ The hypothesis that drunks slur their words was rejected ($t = 0.56$, degrees of freedom = 97, $p > 0.05$).
■ Drunks and sober people did not differ in their average rates of slurring their speech ($t = 0.56$, df = 97, not significant).
■ The hypothesis that drunks slur their words was rejected in favour of the null hypothesis ($t = 0.56$, df = 97, $p > 0.05$, not significant).

The last three statements mean much the same. The symbol $>$ means that your probability is greater than the listed value. It is used to indicate that your calculation is not statistically significant at the stated level.

Notice throughout this chapter that the reported significance levels are not standardised on the 5% level of significance. It is possible, especially with computers, to obtain much more exact values of probability than the critical values used in tables of significance. While there is nothing at all technically wrong with using the more precise values if you have them to hand, there is one objection. Statistical significance can become a holy grail in statistics, supporting the view 'the smaller the probability the better'. Although significance is important, the size of the trends in your data is even more crucial. A significant result with a strong trend is the ideal which is not obtained simply by exploring the minutiae of probability.

One thing causes a lot of confusion in the significance levels given by computers. Sometimes values like $p < 0.0000$ are listed. All that this means is that the probability level for the statistical test is less than 0.0001. In other words the significance level might be, say, 0.000 03 or 0.000 000 4. These are very significant findings, statistically speaking. We would recommend that you report them slightly differently in your writings. Values such as 0.0001 or 0.001 are clearer to some readers. So change your final 0 in the string of zeros to 1.

16.3 Examples from the published literature

Example 1

> ... *a post hoc comparison was carried out between means of the adult molesters' and adult control groups' ratings using Student's* t-*test. A significant (*t *(49) = 2.96, p < 0.001) difference was found between the two groups.*
>
> (Johnston and Johnston, 1986, p. 643)

The above excerpt is fairly typical of the ways in which psychologists summarise the results of their research. To the practised eye, it is not too difficult to decipher. However, some difficulties can be caused to the novice statistician. A little patience at first will help a lot. The extract contains the following major pieces of information:

1. The statistical test used was the *t*-test. The authors mention it by name but it is also identified by the *t* mentioned in the brackets. However, the phrase 'Student's *t*-test' might be confusing. Student was the pen-name of a researcher at the Guinness Brewery who invented the *t*-test. It is quite redundant nowadays – the name Student, not Guinness!
2. The degrees of freedom are the (49) contained in the brackets. If you check the original paper you will find that the combined sample size is 51. It should be obvious, then, that this is an unrelated or uncorrelated *t*-test since the degrees of freedom are clearly $N - 2$ in this case.
3. The value of the *t*-test is 2.96.
4. The difference between the two groups is statistically significant at the 0.001 or 0.1% level of probability. This is shown by $p < 0.001$ in the above excerpt.
5. *Post hoc* merely means that the researchers decided to do the test after the data had been collected. They had not planned it prior to collecting the data.
6. No mention is made of whether this is a one-tailed or a two-tailed test so we would assume that it is a two-tailed significance level.

Obviously, there are a variety of ways of writing up the findings of any analysis. The following is a different way of saying much the same thing:

> ... a post hoc comparison between the means of the adult molesters' and adult control groups' ratings was significant ($t = 2.96$, df $= 49$, $p < 0.001$).

Example 2

> *The relationship of gender of perpetrators and victims was examined. Perpetrators of female victims were more often male (13 900 of 24 947, 55.8%) while perpetrators of males were more often female (10 977 of 21 373, 51.4%,* χ^2 *(1) = 235.18,* p *< 0.001).*
>
> (Rosenthal, 1988, p. 267)

The interpretation of this is as follows:

1. The chi-square test was used. χ is the Greek symbol for chi, so chi-square can be written as χ^2.
2. The value of chi-square is 235.18.
3. It is statistically very significant as the probability level is less than 0.001 or less than 0.1%.
4. Chi-square is usually regarded as a directionless test. That is, the significance level reported is for a two-tailed test unless stated otherwise.
5. Although the significance level in this study seems impressive, just look at the sample sizes involved – over 46 000 children in total. The actual trends are relatively small – 55.8% versus 51.4%. This is a good example of when not to get excited about statistically significant findings.

An alternative way of saying much the same thing is:

> Female victims were offended against by males in 55.8% of cases ($N = 24\,947$). For male victims, 51.4% of offenders were female ($N = 21\,373$). Thus victims were more likely to be offended against by a member of the opposite sex (chi-square = 235.18, degrees of freedom = 1, $p < 0.1\%$).

Example 3

A 2 × 2 analysis of variance (ANOVA) with anger and sex of target as factors was conducted on the BP2 (after anger manipulation) scores. This analysis yielded a significant effect for anger, F (1, 116) = 43.76, p < 0.004, with angered subjects revealing a larger increase in arousal (M = 6.01) than the nonangered subjects (M = 0.01).

(Donnerstein, 1980, p. 273)

This should be readily deciphered as:

1. A two-way analysis of variance with two different levels of each independent variable. One of the independent variables is anger (angered and non-angered conditions are the categories). The other independent variable is the sex of the target of aggression. Something called BP2 (whatever that may be – it turns out to be blood pressure) is the dependent variable. (We cover two-way analysis of variance in Chapter 22.)
2. The mean BP2 score for the angered condition was 6.01 and the mean for the non-angered condition was 0.01. The author is using M as the symbol of the sample mean.
3. The test of significance is the F-ratio test. We know this because this is an analysis of variance but also because the statistic is stated to be F.
4. The value of F, the variance ratio, equals 43.76.
5. There are 1 and 116 degrees of freedom for the F-ratio for the main effect of the variable anger. The 1 degree of freedom is because there are two different levels of the variable anger (df = $c - 1$ or the number of columns of data minus one). The 116 degrees of freedom means that there must have been 120 participants in the experiment. The degrees of freedom for a main effect is N – number of cells = $120 - (2 \times 2) = 120 - 4 = 116$. All of this is clarified in Chapter 22.
6. The difference between the angered and non-angered conditions is statistically significant at the 0.4% level.

A slightly different style of describing these findings is:

> Blood pressure following the anger manipulation was included as the dependent variable on a 2 × 2 analysis of variance. The two independent variables were sex of the target of aggression and anger. There was a significant main effect for anger ($F = 43.76$, df = 1, 116, $p < 0.4\%$). The greater mean increase in blood pressure was for the angered group (6.01) compared to the non-angered group (0.01).

Key points

- Remember that the important pieces of information to report are:
  - the symbol for the statistic (t, T, r, etc.)
  - the value of the statistic for your analysis – two decimal places are enough
  - an indication of the degrees of freedom or the sample size involved (df = . . . , $N = . . .$)
  - the probability or significance level
  - whether a one-tailed test was used.

- Sometimes you will see symbols for statistical techniques that you have never heard of. Do not panic since it is usually possible to work out the sense of what is going on. Certainly if you have details of the sort described in this chapter, you know that a test of significance is involved.

- Using the approaches described in this chapter creates a good impression and ensures that you include pertinent information. However, standardise on one of the variants in your report. Eventually if you submit papers to a journal for consideration, you should check out that journal's method of reporting significance.

- Some statistical tests are regarded as being directionless. That is, their use always implies a two-tailed test. This is true of chi-square and the analysis of variance. These tests can only be one-tailed if the degrees of freedom equal one. Otherwise, the test is two-tailed. Even when the degrees of freedom equal one, only use a one-tailed test if you are satisfied that you have reached the basic requirements of one-tailed testing (see Chapter 17).

Computer analysis

The SPSS instruction book to this text is Dennis Howitt and Duncan Cramer (2008), *Introduction to SPSS in Psychology*, Harlow: Pearson. This book gives detailed step-by-step procedures for the statistics described in this chapter including significance levels. It also provides examples on how to report the results.

For further resources including data sets and questions, please refer to the CD accompanying this book.

17 One-tailed versus two-tailed significance testing

Overview

- Hypotheses which do not or cannot stipulate the direction of the relationship between variables are called *non-directional*. So far we have only dealt with non-directional tests of hypotheses. These are also known as two-tailed tests.

- Some hypotheses stipulate the direction of the relationship between the variables – either a positive relation or a negative relation. These are known as directional hypotheses. They are also known as one-tailed tests.

- Directional tests for any given data result in more significant findings than non-directional tests when applied to the same data.

- However, there are considerable restrictions on when directional tests are allowable. Without very carefully planning, it is wise to deal with one's data as if it were non-directional. Most student research is likely to fail to meet the requirements of one-tail testing.

Preparation   Revise the null hypothesis and alternative hypothesis (Chapter 10) and significance testing.

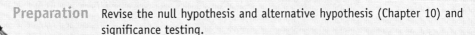

17.1   Introduction

Sometimes researchers are so confident about the likely outcome of their research that they make pretty strong predictions about the relationship between their independent and dependent variables. So, for example, rather than say that the *independent variable* age is correlated with verbal ability, the researcher predicts that the *independent variable* age is *positively* correlated with the *dependent variable* verbal ability. In other words, it is predicted that the older participants in the research will have better verbal skills. Equally the researcher might predict a *negative* relationship between the independent and dependent variables.

It is conventional in psychological statistics to treat such *directional* predictions differently from *non-directional* predictions. Normally psychologists speak of a directional prediction being one-tailed whereas a non-directional prediction is two-tailed. The crucial point is that if you have a directional prediction (one-tailed test) the critical values of the significance test become slightly different.

In order to carry out a one-tailed test you need to be satisfied that you have met the criteria for one-tailed testing. These, as we will see, are rather stringent. In our experience, many one-tailed hypotheses put forward by students are little more than hunches and certainly not based on the required strong past-research or strong theory. In these circumstances it is unwise and wrong to carry out one-tailed testing. It would be best to regard the alternative hypothesis as non-directional and choose two-tailed significance testing exactly as we have done so far in this book. One-tailed testing is a contentious issue and you may be confronted with different points of view; some authorities reject it although it is fairly commonplace in psychological research.

17.2 Theoretical considerations

If we take a directional alternative hypothesis (such as that intelligence correlates positively with level of education) then it is necessary to revise our understanding of the null hypothesis somewhat. (The same is true if the directional alternative hypothesis suggests a negative relationship between the two variables.) In the case of the positively worded alternative hypothesis, the null hypothesis is:

> Intelligence does not correlate *positively* with level of education.

Our previous style of null hypothesis would have left out the word *positively*. There are two different circumstances which support the null hypothesis that intelligence does not correlate *positively* with level of education:

> If intelligence *does not correlate* at all with level of education, *or*
> If intelligence correlates *negatively* with level of education.

That is, it is only research which shows a *positive* correlation between intelligence and education which supports the directional hypothesis – if we found an extreme negative correlation between intelligence and education this would lead to the rejection of the alternative hypothesis just as would zero or near-zero relationships. Because, in a sense, the dice is loaded against the directional alternative hypothesis, it is conventional to argue that we should not use the extremes of the sampling distribution in both directions for our test of significance for the directional hypothesis. Instead we should take the extreme samples in the positive direction (if it is positively worded) or the extreme samples in the negative direction (if it is negatively worded). In other words, our extreme 5% of samples which we define as significant should all be from one side of the sampling distribution, not 2.5% on each side as we would have done previously (see Figure 17.1 overleaf).

Because the 5% of extreme samples, which are defined as significant, are all on the same side of the distribution, you need a smaller value of your significance test to be in that extreme 5%. Part of the attraction of directional or one-tailed significance tests of this sort is that basically you can get the same level of significance with a smaller sample or smaller trend than would be required for a two-tailed test. Essentially the probability level can be halved – what would be significant at the 5% level with a two-tailed test is significant at the 2.5% level with a one-tailed test.

Figure 17.1   Areas of statistical significance for two-tailed and one-tailed tests

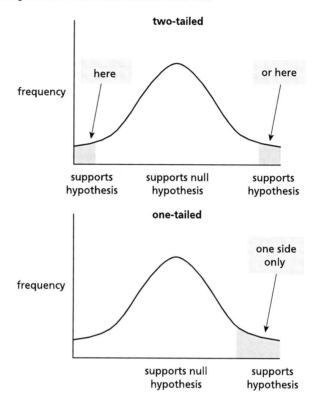

There is a big proviso to this. If you predicted a positive relationship but found what would normally be a significant negative relationship, with a one-tailed test you ought to ignore that negative relationship – it merely supports the null hypothesis. The temptation is, however, to ignore your original directional alternative hypothesis and pretend that you had not predicted the direction. Given that significant results are at a premium in psychology and are much more likely to get published, it is not surprising that psychologists seeking to publish their research might be tempted to 'adjust' their hypotheses slightly.

It is noteworthy that the research literature contains very few tests of significance of directional hypotheses which are rejected when the trend in the data is strongly (and significantly with a two-tailed test) in the opposite direction to that predicted. The only example we know of was written by one of us.

17.3   Further requirements

There are a number of other rules which are supposed to be followed if one is to use a directional hypothesis. These include:

1. The prediction is based on strong and well-researched theory and not on a whim or intuition.

2. The prediction is based on previous similar research demonstrating consistent trends in the predicted direction.

3. One should make the above predictions in advance of any information about the trends in the data about which the prediction is to be made. That is, for example, you do not look at your scattergrams and then predict the direction of the correlation between your variables. That would be manifestly cheating but a 'good' way otherwise of getting significant results with a one-tailed test when they would not quite reach significance with a two-tailed test.

There is another practical problem in the use of directional hypotheses. That is, if you have *more than two groups* of scores it is often very difficult to decide what the predicting trends between the groups would be. For this reason, many statistical techniques are commonly regarded as directionless when you have more than two groups of scores or subjects. This applies to techniques such as chi-square, the analysis of variance and other related tests.

Although this is clearly a controversial area, you will probably find that as a student you rarely if ever have sufficient justification for employing a one-tailed test. As you might have gathered, most of these criteria for selecting a one-tailed test are to a degree subjective which makes the use of one-tailed tests less objective than might be expected. We would recommend that you choose a two-tailed or directionless test unless there is a pressing and convincing reason to do otherwise. Otherwise the danger of loading things in favour of significant results is too great.

In addition to two-tailed critical values, the significance tables in the appendices give the one-tailed values where these are appropriate.

Key points

■ Routinely make your alternative hypotheses two-tailed or directionless. This is especially the case when the implications of your research are of practical or policy significance. However, this may not be ideal if you are testing theoretical predictions when the direction of the hypothesis might be important. Nevertheless, it is a moot point whether you should take advantage of the 'less stringent' significance requirements of a one-tailed test.

■ If you believe that the well-established theoretical or empirical basis for predicting the direction of the outcomes is strong enough, then still be a little cautious about employing one-tailed tests. In particular, do not formulate your hypothesis *after* collecting or viewing your data.

■ You cannot be faulted for using two-tailed tests since they are less likely to show significant relationships. Thus they are described as being statistically more conservative. Student research often does not arise out of previous research or theory. Often the research is initiated before earlier research and theory have been reviewed. In these circumstances one-tailed tests are not warranted.

For further resources including data sets and questions, please refer to the CD accompanying this book.

13 Writing up research

You have now completed a state-of-the-art, cutting-edge, incisive and comprehensive study (or at least, this is your belief). However, other people can only know of the brilliance of this research by being told about it in some way, usually through a written report, which will offer details on what you have done, why it was done and what the outcomes were. For an undergraduate, a large proportion of marks in a research module will probably be assigned to the final report, and success will depend almost entirely on the quality of the writing and presentation. It is therefore important to consider the way in which this work will be presented from the earliest stages through to the concluding comments; this is true whether the research was quantitative or qualitative and what follows will in large part be applicable to both approaches.

Ideally, a study should be written up as it progresses (it really is easier this way, rather than trying to remember what you did after the fact, which is the usual way for the majority of students). Mapping out the main points of the literature review as you do it will often serve as a guide in the formulation of hypotheses and will clarify design and methodological issues – points made right at the beginning of this book in Parts 1 and 2. Writing up the methodology section while it is still fresh in your mind will save you hours of work at a later stage, as will keeping a careful record of your references from the beginning (this goes for a bibliography as well, though note that a bibliography is quite different from a reference section: see section 13.6). The point here is that, if you are going to (or might) cite material in the body of your report, it must be properly referenced (see Box 13.15), with authors, year, journal title, etc. Noting this information at an early stage will avoid frantic scrabbling through scores of papers when it comes to writing up. One of the most common mutterings overheard in university libraries (from students and authors of textbooks alike) is, 'what did I do with that reference?'

Another area where it is important to keep track of what you are doing is in the results section – writing up your results as you conduct the analysis will identify any significant gaps while there is still sufficient time to fill them. Alternatively, this might also help you to recognise when further analysis is unnecessary: a common problem with many undergraduate reports is over-analysis of data, which creates needless work for both the student and the supervisor. However, even the most conscientious of researchers may have to make amendments to their report at the last minute, and it is only when discussions and conclusions have been written that the overall structure may be assessed (this is the reason why you should always write the abstract *last*). It is important to allow yourself the time to read your work critically before it has to be submitted, to reflect on its contents and to make any necessary changes. This is why you should make notes as you go along, and Box 13.1 should serve as a guide.

Box 13.1

Practicalities . . .

Keeping track

- File complete references of articles or books that you have read, with details of the main points of studies or theories.

- Write down the arguments behind your hypotheses – it is all too easy, during the course of a lengthy project, to lose sight of what the original aims were. Being able to return to some statement of intent will serve as a reminder as to why you are doing this. This may seem an odd point to make but students often experience periods of alarm when, bogged down by scores of questionnaires, rating scales and transcripts, they feel they have lost direction. This seems to become a particular problem at the data analysis stage and many supervisors are used to their students looking uncomfortable when asked why they carried out *this* analysis instead of *that*.

- Carefully record the means whereby you recruited participants, with details of the numbers agreeing or refusing to participate. This can become an important issue if you are hoping to generalise from your sample to a wider population – participant numbers and sampling procedures will be key limiting factors in how much you will be able to say here.

- Note any changes that you may have made to questionnaires or other instruments, and the arguments behind the changes. It is important to demonstrate how your research developed and one of the elements a supervisor will be interested in concerns your choice of, for example, questionnaire items: Why ask these questions? Why in this format? Why a Likert scale as opposed to a rating scale?

- Record details of pilot studies, and any modifications made as a result of those studies: as with the previous point, it is important to show how your research developed and how you ended up adopting a particular approach. Pilot studies often play a key role in determining the final structure and format of research; they should therefore be described in detail.

- Maintain a log of the exact procedures you employed, with appropriate justification. Much of the criticism levelled at undergraduate projects revolves around procedural problems – for example, not enough detail, or no explanation of why an approach was adopted.

- Keep track of coding procedures. Not only will you be expected to give an account of this in your report but, from a practical point of view, it is easy to forget which particular numerical values you used to denote responses on a multi-item questionnaire or to distinguish participants in a control group from those in an experimental group. To change a coding frame in the middle of a study can be fatal.

■ Keep a detailed record of all analyses carried out and why you did them. Apart from the obvious necessity of reporting this as part of your write-up, there is a risk of losing sight of what you are trying to do at this stage; wading through pages of SPSS output showing descriptive statistics, numerous *t*-tests and the odd analysis of variance can be confusing (what an understatement), not to mention a major contributor to the sense of panic which often strikes at the analysis stage of a research project. Faced with a tearful student wielding the results of umpteen correlations a supervisor will typically ask, "What was it you were trying to do?"

There are different ways to keep notes, although perhaps a diary or labbook format is the simplest; keeping up with reading, meetings with supervisors and notes needs a certain amount of self-discipline, and it is surprising how often one simply cannot remember such details at a later stage. You really will be saving yourself time and trouble if you keep an accurate running record of your research activities in some organised format. Relying on memory alone, or random scraps of paper, will not be effective; your supervisor will (or should) keep a diary of your progress and it is very much in your own interests to do the same.

13.3 The structure of a psychology report

The basic structure of your write-up should normally follow the familiar layout of a standard laboratory report, in that it should consist of the four major sections: Introduction, Method, Results, and Discussion, in that order, headed by a title and abstract and followed by a reference list and any appendices. Part of the reason for keeping to this conventional format is that the reader will know just where to find each piece of essential information about your research. You should therefore make sure that your report conforms to this layout as much as possible, and that relevant information is where it should be.

The report of a substantial research project is likely to be weightier than the average laboratory report. A common question from undergraduates is 'how long should the report be?' The answer, no matter how unsatisfactory, must be: *as long as it takes to report the research concisely, but clearly, accurately and completely.* Having said this, most student researchers will probably have some sort of length indication specified by their department or tutor (e.g., about 10,000 words). This is always a rough indication, since an assessor is not actually going to count the words (big surprise, especially to those of you who like to include a word count as part of submitted work), but any such limit is worth bearing in mind and a report should always endeavour to end up somewhere within the recommended range. One of the most annoying aspects of undergraduate reports for supervisors is unnecessary length – a product of over-writing and a sense that every concept, theory or piece of previous research must be explained in great detail, especially in the introduction. In most cases this is not necessary and a general overview of established theory is sufficient, except when a particular study or issue forms the basis for the current piece of research, in which case detail is essential. Box 13.2 offers a summary of how a report should be structured, while the sections which follow consider the elements of a typical report in detail.

Box 13.2

 A Closer Look At . . .

The structure of a typical project report

Title

Should be brief, clear, accurate; don't try to be funny or whimsical (10–12 words at most).

Abstract

Approximately 100–150 word summary. Say briefly what it's about, what was done and what was found. Write this last!

Introduction

What was this research all about? What relevant previous work was there? What did they find? Is there a central theory, or a debate about different theories? Was the present study the same (a replication) – if not, how was it different? In either case, what were you trying to do (aims)? And what did you expect to find (the hypotheses)?

Method

Four sub-headings, setting out the structure of the study, as follows:

Design	What sort of study was it (e.g., an experiment, a survey, a case-study)?
	Repeated measures design, independent groups, or a mixed design?
	What were the dependent variables (what was measured)?
	What were the independent variables (what varied across different participants)?
Participants	How many? Any *relevant* description.
Apparatus	What materials or equipment were used?
Procedure	Briefly describe what happened. Quote instructions given to the participants.

Results

A written presentation of summary or descriptive statistics, not individual participant data. For example, give the mean and standard deviation for the dependent variable for each different condition. If any graphs or tables help clarify the results, put them in here, but don't merely duplicate tabular data – figures are useful only if they clarify or highlight data in a manner not possible with tables. Report the statistics used, and say briefly whether or not the results supported the hypotheses.

Discussion

An examination of your results in light of your hypotheses or research questions, and in comparison with previous findings. What conclusions do your results point to? How do you interpret your findings? You could also suggest improvements or variations in the design, or further hypotheses which might be tested.

References

List only references actually cited earlier in the report. If it is important to mention other sources used, though not explicitly cited, these should be given in a separate bibliography.

Appendices

This is the location for the raw materials used in the study – stimuli, examples of question-naires and so on. Raw data and computer printouts are not recommended, unless there is a case for inclusion. Supervisors will normally inform you of their expectations here.

13.3.1 Title

This should be concise but informative, and should give a clear indication of what the project is about: for example, 'Individual differences in the perception of embedded figures', or 'Gender and age stereotypes of emotionality'. Readers should be able to tell from the title alone whether a report is of interest to them, or of relevance to their own research. A title that is too general may be at best uninformative and at worst misleading: for example, the title 'Gender and memory' gives no indication of which aspects of either gender or memory were investigated. If a report is likely to be placed on library access, or in other ways made available to a broader readership, it is important that the title contains the relevant keywords that any interested readers would be likely to use in their literature search (e.g., 'individual differences', 'perception' or 'embedded figures'). This is of particular importance today when, increasingly, researchers are using the Internet and other electronic databases to carry out keyword searches. Box 13.3 looks at common errors in titles.

Box 13.3

A Closer Look At . . .

Common errors in the title

Some authors try to apply snappy titles to their work, incorporating puns, innuendo or otherwise playing on words, presumably in the hopes of appealing to journal editors (or amusing supervisors enough to gain an extra few marks).
For example:

New treatment in substance abuse: Not to be sniffed at

Or

Altered states – dream on

Amusing as these may be, they don't actually offer much information about the studies and would be likely to be overlooked in the early stages of a literature review for this reason. And in case anyone is wondering, editors and supervisors would not be impressed.

13.3.2   Abstract

The abstract is a short summary of the main information contained in the project report as a whole. It should ideally be about 100 or 150 words in length, although some journals (and supervisors) now prefer structured abstracts. While the abstract is positioned at the beginning of the report, it is often the last part to be actually written – it will certainly be easier to write the abstract when the report is finished than the other way around. Normally the abstract should, very briefly, identify the problem studied; the hypotheses tested; the method employed, including the number and kind of participants; the results obtained; and the main conclusions drawn. Statistical details should usually be excluded, unless you have used a novel type of analysis, or have departed from the norm in any other important way (e.g., used a non-standard probability level). In short, an abstract should be like an extremely condensed version of the full report, providing key information from the introduction, method, results and discussion sections. Box 13.4 discusses common errors in abstracts.

Box 13.4

A Closer Look At . . .

Common errors in the abstract

In the search for brevity, some writers reduce the information content of an abstract to the point where it becomes impossible to judge the nature of a study without reading the entire report. This is a particularly common problem among undergraduate students, but it is not exclusive to them.

> A study on consumerism among a stratified sample failed to demonstrate significant differences between any of the comparison groups on any of the 15 differentiating behaviours. In all cases the null hypotheses were accepted.

An abstract of this nature is virtually useless – there is no real indication of what the study was about, which aspects of consumerism were being studied, or the type of participant used. Nor is there any indication as to what kind of statistical analysis was carried out in order to test the hypotheses, whatever they happened to be.

Equally unhelpful is the two-page abstract in which the writer is incapable of summarising the important elements of the study:

> In a study carried out over five days between April 1 and April 5, one hundred participants took part in a between-groups experiment on choice behaviour, with choice being determined as a preference for vegetarian versus non-vegetarian food in a canteen environment. The participants were initially drawn from a local population comprising primarily university undergraduates, all of whom lived within the campus area, except for a small group who commuted from a neighbouring district. Of these, the population was known to comprise 80% males and 20% females, with an age distribution roughly . . .
> Arghh!

This amount of detail, if extended to the rest of the study, would provide an abstract almost as long as the report itself, which is as counterproductive as the previous minimalist example.

BOX 13.5

Checklist . . .

The abstract

A good abstract should contain the following information:

- The research issue being explored – this would comprise the research question, or the theory being investigated in the study.
- The hypotheses being tested – the specific predictions which form the basis of the study.
- The design of the study – the way in which it has been set up to explore the hypotheses, expressed in the language of design (e.g., repeated measures, counterbalanced).
- The key (relevant) characteristics of the participants – for example, there is little point in offering detail on age in the abstract unless age influenced, or explained, the findings in some way.
- The key (relevant) characteristics of any apparatus used – for example, if findings can be explained only by reference to the specifics of apparatus, or if replication could not take place without this particular information.
- The outcome of the study – for example, whether the hypotheses are accepted or rejected, or the key findings.
- Conclusions, and a comment on any unusual features of the study, if appropriate.

Writing a good abstract (one that conveys key information clearly and accurately, without exceeding the length limit) is difficult, but it is important. Like the title, the abstract may be accessed by online search systems, so it should contain enough specific information to enable a researcher to find the work in the first place, and then to decide whether to read the whole thing. This is becoming increasingly important with the advent of modern databases since the abstract (and the title) will often be the first point of contact others will have with a researcher's work. It is therefore important to get it right (see Box 13.5).

13.3.3 Contents

If the purpose of a write-up is a final report rather than an article intended for publication (which, alas, is something few undergraduates actually consider), a list of contents could be provided, based on section or chapter headings. Also included here should be details of any appendices, and this is probably an appropriate point at which to remind you to number the pages – again, something often forgotten by keen (or late) students.

13.3.4 Introduction

This is the first major section of the report. A good introduction should provide the reader with the essential background to the project, starting out with a broad description of the particular research topic that is being dealt with, and moving on through a clear and accurate account of the previous research which has led up to the project. You should be able to show that your particular study is a natural development of this previous work, and that it adds something – even if that something is only that an effect is (or is not) replicated with a different sample. It is also important to show that you are aware of current or recent work which is relevant to the study, and that the important theoretical issues are understood.

There is no one correct way to begin an introduction, but it is probably a good idea to start off with a brief overview of the area of study to set the scene for what is to follow. For example, if a study concerns the relationship between exercise and psychological wellbeing, one could begin by describing the general assumptions made about this relationship, followed by a delineation of the aspects of exercise and wellbeing to be considered in further detail in the report. If a study concerns ways of coping with a particular illness, you could begin by describing the aspects of the illness which may be found stressful, followed by an outline of the model of stress and coping which you use as a framework for analysis. The introductory paragraphs should therefore outline, in a general way, what the study is about and which aspects of a given issue you are exploring.

The central part of an introduction should cover the relevant research which forms a background to the project. If the research is based on one major published study, describe this in some detail, including the number and type of participants used, the design of the original study, the measures taken, and the method of analysis. This amount of detail is necessary since, in your own study, you will probably be using a similar design, with similar types of people. If the aim is to refute or criticise a previous piece of research, you will still need this level of detail, if only to demonstrate how, for example, by using a different mode of analysis you generate completely different findings. Following on from this you should comment on the study which is serving as a platform for your own work, taking into account such issues as the adequacy of the sample, measures, design and analysis used, the extent to which the results may be generalised to other populations, and any theoretical implications of the results. You can then describe other studies in the area using this general framework, although unless they relate directly to the research issue, or provide a further foundation for what you are going to do, these should not be presented in anything like this amount of detail. In this way, the major areas of interest, related issues and matters pertaining to the particular approach you are taking, can be clarified as you proceed. Consequently, hypotheses or research questions when they are finally offered – usually in the concluding phase of the introduction – should not come as a surprise to the reader: every aspect of the hypotheses should have been mentioned at an earlier point in the introduction and should follow on naturally and logically from what has gone before. It is a common experience of supervisors to come to the aims, objectives and hypotheses section of a report and then to have to go back through the introductory discussion to try and find out where these hypotheses came from and what their rationale might happen to be. It is worth mentioning that this can be extremely irritating for a supervisor, so consider yourself warned. Box 13.6 lists common errors occurring in introductory text.

The introduction should normally lead towards an overview of what the study will actually do (but saving the details for the next section) and should conclude with a statement of the hypotheses. It is often useful to state these twice: first as a general prediction of outcomes (e.g., that exercise would be related to wellbeing); and then more precisely. For example:

> It was therefore hypothesised that significant differences in psychological wellbeing would be observed between the two conditions (exercise vs. non-exercise), such that participants in the exercise condition would gain higher scores on the measure of

A Closer Look At . . .

Common errors in the introduction section

- Writing an anecdotal, subjective background which is based more on personal opinion than a sound knowledge of the field.
- Trying to cover the entire history of research in the field: be selective, and review only that which is directly relevant to your own study. This is especially important in areas which have proved popular among researchers (imagine trying to review the last 50 years of research into personality and you will get the point).
- Explaining too much: you may assume some theoretical knowledge on the part of your reader. You should not have to define common terms – unless, of course, you are using them in a specialised way. (It is worth considering the nature of your readership here: a report for publication in a scientific journal will not have to spell out the characteristics of various measurement scales in questionnaire design. A presentation to undergraduates, on the other hand, might require that the structure of, for example, a Likert scale be explained.)
- Explaining too little: we are not all experts in your field, so write as if for the intelligent, interested, non-specialist. In practical terms a balance will have to be struck between this and the previous point.
- Failing to show how your review of the relevant literature leads up to, and provides a rationale for, your particular study.
- Failing to state just what it is that your study is seeking to accomplish. A frequent form of this error is failing to state your hypotheses at the end of the introduction.

wellbeing than would participants in the non-exercise condition. It was further hypothesised that this effect would be moderated by gender, such that differences between the two conditions would be greater for females than for males.

It is also useful at this stage to identify (as much for your own benefit as the reader's) the independent and dependent variables so that it is always clear what is being tested: the more precise your hypotheses, the more straightforward the analysis. (And the more likely you will be able to recover from the sense of panic common to the middle stages of a project, when there is a danger of losing sight of what it was you were trying to do.)

Pilot studies may also be mentioned in the introduction if they have contributed to the development of hypotheses or research questions. Otherwise, the convention is that details of pilot studies are given in the method section, especially where they relate to developing questionnaire items or strategies for data gathering.

13.3.5 Method

The method section is the next major part of a research write-up, in that it gives all the information about how the research was actually carried out. Its purpose is to present a detailed description of the conduct of the study in such a way that the reader can follow the natural timeline, or sequence of events, which characterised the study, from general introduction through specific hypotheses to actual testing and data gathering. This is an important section since it provides the opportunity to explain what you actually did. Most of the material covered in the introduction is concerned with theory and hypotheses. The method section is concerned with the concrete: Who participated? How were participants assigned to groups? What was measured? What checks were made on extraneous factors? These are typical questions posed by anyone reviewing or assessing a report and the answers should be readily available in this section, simply because of the detail offered by the researcher. From a practical point of view, the method section also provides a supervisor with insight into the extent to which a student has been careful and systematic in the conduct of a study. This is the section in which design flaws become highlighted and the limitations of the study underlined. Often, when criticising the findings of a study, a supervisor will return to the method section with comments such as, 'you cannot make this generalisation with such a small sample', or, 'by doing it this way you overlooked an important issue . . .' Frightening as this revelation must be to many undergraduate readers, it nonetheless makes the point that this part of a report is central to the way in which a piece of research will be evaluated. If a study is flawed it will show up here but, if the researcher understands enough about the issues and how they were tackled, the limitations outlined here will form the basis of much of the later discussion section in which the writer will attempt to justify the conclusions drawn, demonstrate that she understands why hypotheses were not supported, and be able to outline ways in which the issues might be more effectively explored.

A second reason for providing a detailed method is to allow replication of the study; perhaps the study has broken new ground in its field, or perhaps its findings are unexpected, or even suspect in some way. Or perhaps a researcher wants to know if particular effects can be reproduced under different circumstances, or by using different types of participant. Whatever the case, replication is possible only if sufficient detail is provided on the conduct of the original study. Now realistically, this will rarely be true of most undergraduate research – as we have previously stated, studies at this level are more often carried out for demonstration and experiential purposes than to genuinely extend our understanding of the human condition. Yet, as part of this process, an ability to produce replicable methodology is an important skill for anyone intending to pursue their interest in psychology beyond the graduate level.

Below, we discuss the major divisions or sub-sections which comprise a typical method section, and describe the ways in which this part of a report would be structured.

13.3.6   Design

This, the initial part of the method section, describes the formal structure of the study. It is usually brief and concise, but lacking in specific details about participants and procedure, and it is generally couched in the technical language of a research design (between-groups, repeated measures, counterbalanced, etc.). First, you must specify what kind of investigation you carried out (for example, an experiment, an observational study, a survey, a case study, and so on). You should then define the variables either measured or manipulated in the study, making the distinction between independent variables (or predictors) and dependent variables (or outcome measures). This ought to be a straightforward task, since these matters will have been sorted out in the early stages of a study. However, supervisors are often surprised at the confusions which appear over the description of variables present in a study, even in cases where the rest of the work is of a high standard. (If this is remains a problem, a review of Part 2 will be helpful.)

Box 13.7

A Closer Look At . . .

A typical design

In a 2 × 3 quasi-experimental design, male and female patients were randomly assigned to one of three exercise conditions. The dependent variable was post-operative recovery time, measured in days to a pre-determined level, and the between-groups independent variables were gender (male or female) and exercise regime (none, moderate and regular). Age was controlled for in the analysis.

This difficulty of correctly identifying variables can sometimes be aggravated in correlational studies where identification is sometimes less clear – variables are related or associated with one another but not always in an obvious cause-and-effect manner. However, you should usually be able to distinguish between the variables that you want to find out about (outcome), and the variables that you are just using to get there (predictors). You should also specify any important extraneous variables: that is, factors which under other circumstances might be considered independent variables in their own right, but which in this case might have to be controlled for. (Our discussion on the distinction between multiple regression and partial correlation in Part 5 is a useful guide to the issue of when a variable is extraneous or not.)

Another important design element is whether you have used repeated measures (within-subjects design), independent groups (between-groups design), or a combination of the two (mixed design). (See Part 2 for more detail.) This should be accurately reported, especially in experimental studies (note that correlational designs by definition use repeated measures). The factor levels which form the experimental conditions should be described if appropriate, as should the method by which the participants were assigned to groups. Box 13.7 provides an example of the information expected in a typical design.

A common mistake made by undergraduates is to confuse design and procedural matters. It must be remembered that the design of a study is the plan of campaign, formulated before the study proper is implemented. Consequently when decisions are made it is not always possible to know how many participants would actually respond to your questionnaire, or that your particular experimental manipulation would produce a revolt among one of your groups. This is why the design is a formal statement of intent, expressed in general terms and using the language of experimentation (if appropriate). If you are still in doubt about this, have another look at Part 2. Box 13.8 also illustrates this point.

If your project is at the more qualitative end of the spectrum, you should still try to give a formal and objective description of your project under this heading. Thus you should clarify the method (e.g., observation, or semi-structured interview), the main issues under consideration, corresponding to dependent variables (e.g., types of non-verbal behaviours, expressed sources of stress at work), other variables or factors corresponding to independent variables and covariates (e.g., gender, age, employment status), and time factors, such as the frequency of repeated observations.

The final element in this section is shown in Box 13.9, comprising a checklist of key points which you should review before you consider any other developments in your study. It is worth remembering that if you have come up with an inappropriate design, or if you are unclear about key design elements, everything which follows will be affected.

Box 13.8

A Closer Look At . . .

Common errors in the design section

Many people, and especially those new to the research report, readily confuse procedural elements with the design. By way of example, what follows is an outline of procedural matters rather than design:

> Eighty subjects were used in the study, 40 males and 40 females, of varying ages and backgrounds. Both groups were treated identically, being shown a video (see Appendix 1), prior to the experimental manipulation, in which the procedural details were explained (see Appendix 2). The manipulation itself comprised a small parts assembly exercise in which a number of rivets, washers and bolts were assembled in a pre-determined order and then inserted into a pegboard. On completion of the experiment each subject completed a questionnaire which rated various attitudinal factors on a 1–5 scale . . .

The author has not clarified the type of study (is it between-groups or within-subjects, or mixed?); the dependent variables (is the main dependent variable time taken to complete the task, or attitudinal scores, or both?); or the independent variables (presumably gender is an independent variable, but this is not clearly stated). The key point about a design is that it should serve almost as a schematic map or diagram of a study in which the major elements – and only those – are illustrated. Most of the details in our example are procedural.

13.3.7   Participants

Give *relevant* details of those who participated in your research, including the number of individuals who comprised your sample, their age and gender, and on what basis they were allocated to subgroups. Any participant profile characteristics which might have affected their responses or behaviour should be mentioned, and you should explain how these were dealt with (e.g., 'to control for possible gender effects, equal numbers of male and female participants were allocated to each of the groups'). You should also state how

Box 13.9

 *Checklist . . .*

The design section

Your design should contain the following information:

- The nature of the study (e.g., experiment, survey, case study).
- The structure of the design (e.g., repeated measures, between-groups).
- The independent and dependent variables.
- Extraneous variables and any controls used to reduce their effect.

Box 13.10

A Closer Look At . . .

A section on participants

Sixty undergraduate students (30 males, 30 females) participated in the study. All were members of the university participant panel, and all responded to a formal written request for participants placed on the appropriate notice board: the first 60 volunteers were recruited for the study. The median age of participants was 19 years (range 17–23 years). Participants were assigned to either the hedgehog group or the newt group on a quasi-random basis, such that equal numbers of males and females were included in each group. Given the nature of the task, the participants were screened to ensure that their eyesight was normal or corrected to normal.

the participants were obtained, and give refusal rates if appropriate. You should aim to give sufficient detail to enable you and the reader to decide the extent to which your participants were representative of the population. For example, if you recruited participants through a self-help group or through a newsletter, you may have distributed 100 questionnaires but had only 40 returns. This should be stated, since it may imply that your results are applicable only to a subsection of the target population. While this may be a limitation of your project it is not something to be hidden, or indeed to be ashamed of. In this case, the possible limitations of your results should be considered in the discussion element of your report. See Box 13.10.

13.3.8 Apparatus (or materials)

Give full details of all equipment, apparatus and materials used. Trade names and model numbers of pieces of equipment should be given. The full names of published tests should be given, with references. Details of pilot studies may be given here, if they confirmed the utility of apparatus or materials, or, alternatively, if they indicated the need for changes or alterations. If questionnaires or other test materials have been changed in any way, give full details and a rationale for the changes made. For example, you may have changed the wording of certain items from a questionnaire originating in the United States to make it more suitable for a UK population, or you may have omitted an item because it was unethical or irrelevant within the context of your project.

If you have used a fairly lengthy questionnaire or interview schedule, you may wish to give some representative examples of items in this section, and refer the reader to an appendix where the entire list can be found. If your questionnaire incorporates a number of different sections or subscales, make it clear what these are and how they are to be calculated. If you have written a computer programme for your study, give a careful explanation of what it actually does. The programme itself can be listed in full in an appendix.

You may have devised an interview schedule for your project. In this case, describe the main areas covered in the interview and indicate the sources of any particular questions or wording. Give the interview schedule in full in an appendix.

13.3.9   Procedure

Describe exactly what was done, and include verbal instructions given to participants. If instructions were provided in handouts or with test materials, include these in an appendix. Bear in mind that the function of this section is to give the reader sufficient detail to repeat the study (although we accept that rarely will anyone wish to replicate an undergraduate study, except under exceptional circumstances). And of course, we mustn't forget the key role of the procedure in assessment – for your supervisor, the procedure is an important element of your report.

Indicate the circumstances under which the participants responded or were tested (e.g., in a designated room on their own, in groups, in their own homes, in the library), the order in which test items were completed (e.g., whether the order was randomised or fixed, and if fixed, what the order was) and the approximate length of time required of participants. You should also clarify the extent to which participants were offered anonymity, the instructions participants were given with regard to terminating their involvement in the project, any payment offered, and debriefing or feedback procedures. If a consent form was used (and it ought to be) this should be referred to and an example of a blank form shown in an appendix. You may have given some of this information in earlier sections; however, it is important to provide a full and clear description of procedure in this section, even at the risk of repeating yourself.

The method is the second major section of the report, but is often the first to be written. The reason for this is that most of the technical details, the structure, and the practical details of the study have to be decided in advance. The method section is also the easiest to write, since you do not have to invent anything or be creative in any way: you are simply reporting factual information about your study.

13.3.10   Results

If you have conducted a quantitative study, this section should contain all the objective outcomes of your study: the factual results, as generated from analyses and without any attempt at discussion, inference or speculation. This should be presented in conventional text format, as in the rest of the report (that is, give the main results in writing, with appropriate t-values, F-ratios or whatever). The temptation to expand and speculate here is admittedly huge – after all, this represents the point at which you have finally learned whether or not your predictions have been justified, hypotheses upheld or theories supported. However, the discussion section is the place to argue about the implications, not the results section. (The names given to these different parts of a report, by the way, ought to be something of a give-away!)

First of all, present the descriptive statistics, which should summarise your data in a standard form. Then present the inferential statistics, which test whether your results can be distinguished from chance and hence whether your hypotheses have been rejected or upheld. It is not usually appropriate to report individual participants' raw data unless your study requires it (for example, a case study). Probably the easiest way to think of this is that the reader, having read through the introduction and focused on the aims and hypotheses, will now want to find out what you actually found – moving to the results ought to show, clearly and concisely, whether or not hypotheses were accepted, theories supported or indeed whether or not the experiment (if that's what it was) worked.

Descriptive statistics would normally consist of the means and standard deviations of your main outcome variables (which may be compared with any available published

Table 13.1 Mean error rate and standard deviations (SD) for three groups differentiated by cycling experience (novice, probationer, experienced).

	Mean errors	*SD*	*N*
Novice	35	2.76	15
Probationer	32	2.15	15
Experienced	17	0.27	15

norms), including not only global summary measures, but also those for any appropriate sub-groups or conditions. For example, you may wish to give separate means and standard deviations for males and females, or those in different age groups. However, if your main outcome variable is categorical rather than continuous, you should give percentages and numbers, as appropriate. The descriptive statistics can often be conveniently presented in a table (see Table 13.1), or alternatively in a figure (see Figure 13.1) if the nature of tabulated data is potentially misleading, or if there is so much of it that the information to be expressed is obscured. (It is worth noting, though, that tables and figures should be used as either-or alternatives – it is not appropriate to present the same data twice, once in each format. What would be the point?) The use of tables and figures in a report is discussed in detail in a later section, while Box 13.13 provides a summary of guidelines for the production of tables and figures.

If you are using a questionnaire or materials that other authors have used, compare your results with theirs at this stage. Thus you should be able to demonstrate that your sample has provided data which fall within an expected range (or not), and that these data are suitable for further statistical analysis. Both of these points may be raised in the discussion.

If your sample appears to be different from other samples in some important way (e.g., they have different profile characteristics, or they obtain markedly higher or lower measures on particular questionnaire items), you may still be able to carry out further analysis, but you should indicate the nature of the difference and show that steps (such as data transformation or recoding) have been taken to remedy the problem. The presentation of descriptive statistics is important, and forms the logical starting point of further analysis.

Figure 13.1 Mean error rates for three groups differentiated by cycling experience.

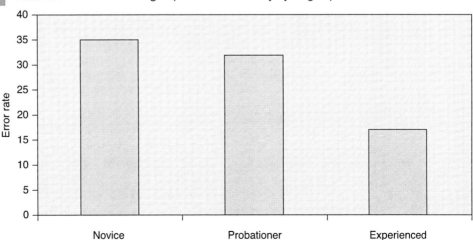

Moreover, as experienced researchers and reviewers are aware, inspection of descriptive statistics is often sufficient, on its own, to determine the outcome of a quantitative study – for instance, when two mean scores are close to one another it is often clear that no real difference exists between the groups, obviating the need for any further analysis. Indeed, many a supervisor will criticise a student for proceeding with a comprehensive and complex inferential analysis of data, when inspection of (and understanding of) the descriptive statistics would have clearly indicated that no effects were present. A useful thing for students to know! For this reason it is worth having a good look at these relatively straightforward statistics before moving on to the main analysis.

The results of the statistical analysis should then be presented in a clear and logical way. The most obvious approach is to deal with each hypothesis in turn, in the order given at the end of your introduction. The aim is to show clearly what your data say about each one, and then to state simply whether the evidence supports it or not. Generally speaking this requires you to report the appropriate significance test, giving the value of the statistic, the degrees of freedom and the associated probability. You should then help the reader by translating (briefly) what the test is telling you into a straightforward verbal statement, while avoiding the temptation to expand or speculate. For example, in a variant of our exercise and wellbeing study, psychological wellbeing scores were compared for two groups, one taking no exercise over a given period and one taking regular exercise. A one-way ANOVA was used to determine whether the two groups differed on wellbeing. (Note that we could have used an independent samples t-test.) The convention for statistical reporting of significance tests requires the following elements:

* state the test used
* state the variables being tested
* state the significance level applied to the test, or report the exact probability
* state the findings (in words)
* express the findings in terms of the statistic (t-value, F-ratio); the degrees of freedom; and the probability value, either as an exact probability, or greater than or less than a given alpha level
* state whether the statistic is significant
* translate the finding for the reader, and relate the finding to the hypothesis

In the present example, this could be expressed as follows:

> A one-way ANOVA was used to determine whether the scores of the two groups (exercise vs. non-exercise) differed significantly on wellbeing scores. A significant difference was found between the two groups: $F(1, 31) = 12.14, p < .05$, or $p = .002$. As can be seen from Table X, which displays the means and SDs of wellbeing scores for each group, those in the exercise group gained significantly higher wellbeing scores than did those in the non-exercise group. The hypothesis was therefore supported.

If you are examining differences between or among groups, remember that the reader will need to know the mean scores (and SDs) for each group; refer the reader to a table, or present the information at this point in the text. Without this information, the reader will not be able to understand your results. Note also that we have shown two versions of the statistical findings, one relating statistics to a pre-determined significance level, and one reporting the exact probability. Both are acceptable provided consistency is maintained over a number of tests in a report. See Box 13.11 for a comprehensive guide to the reporting of significance tests.

Box 13.11

How To . . .

Report the results of analyses

Correlation

At the .01 level of significance, a significant negative correlation was observed between cyclists' age and number of hedgehogs run over: r (29) = $-.43$, $p < .01$.

Partial correlation

A zero-order correlation analysis indicated that a significant positive relationship existed (at the 5% level) between sunspot activity and incidence of road rage: r (20) = .89, $p < .05$. However, a first-order partial correlation analysis indicated that this relationship was not significant when temperature was partialled out: $r_{xy.z}$ (17) = .32, $p > .05$. [x = the predictor (sunspot activity); y = the criterion (road rage); z = the variable partialled out (temperature).]

Simple regression

Exam performance was regressed on study time. A significant positive relationship was noted: r (11) = .93, $p = .002$. Exam performance and study time shared 84% of their variance ($r^2 = .84$). The regression equation was as follows: Estimated exam performance = 19.46 + 5.66 study time.

Multiple regression

The criterion variable, error rate, was regressed on the three predictors of age, extraversion, and experience (measured in months). The results were as follows: $R = .75$; F (3, 94) = 41.78, $p < .05$; $R^2 = .55$. Thus, 55% of the variance of error rate was explained by the three predictors. The regression equation was as follows: Estimated error rate = 5.69 − 0.05 age + 0.21 extraversion − 0.52 experience.

(Note: a table of beta coefficients, t-values and probabilities is necessary to demonstrate the relationships between the predictors and the criterion variable, and some reference to these relationships should be made in the text at this point.)

Independent t-test

No significant difference in blood pressure level was observed between the two groups at the .05 level: t (22) = 1.51, $p > .05$.

(Note that the same format is appropriate for paired t-tests.)

ANOVA

At the .05 level, a significant main effect of fishing experience was observed on the numbers of trout landed in competition: F (2, 99) = 14.52, $p < .05$. No main effect of lure was observed on the numbers of trout landed during competition: F (1, 99) = 1.77, $p > .05$. However, a significant Experience X Lure interaction was observed: F (2, 93) = 9.72, $p < .05$.

(Note: a table of means would be required to indicate the relationships among the variables. A figure would be required, or appropriate post hoc testing, to indicate the nature of the significant interaction.)

Chi-square

The association between gender and response to the dichotomous questionnaire item (Are you enjoying the book so far?) was not significant: χ^2(1, $N = 54$) = 2.75, $p > .05$.

Always bear in mind that you must clarify your results for the reader. It is tempting to use short-hand when describing certain variables, particularly in tables. Tables derived from computer printout usually bear the abbreviated labels used to code variables rather than the full variable name. If you do have to use shortened names in tables, provide a key underneath the table.

Table x.   Means and standard deviations (SD) for two variables: cholesterol levels in overweight cyclist group, and error rate.

Variable	Mean	SD
Ichygrp	7.53	0.09
Squish	16.39	0.22

Ichygrp – Incidence of cholesterol in the overweight cyclist group
Squish – Number of hedgehogs run over

Although the results section often contains a large amount of numerical and statistical information, it is nevertheless part of the text of your report and should be written in English. It is not acceptable simply to present a series of tables or diagrams without a clear accompanying text which explains in plain language what your illustrations show. Even less appropriate would be to base this section on computer printouts which are notoriously minimalist. Moreover, unless you have gone to the trouble of labelling your data during the initial data-entry stage, groups and sub-divisions in SPSS will be presented by their numerical code. One of the most common criticisms of the results section of a write-up is that tables and graphs are unclear. If you have lengthy or complex results, however, clarity is often greatly helped by including appropriate illustrative tables or figures. These can be a real help to the reader in understanding the overall pattern of your results, and therefore in following the argument. Sometimes, however, they can simply be confusing and counter-productive, or irrelevant and annoying. See Box 13.12 for a checklist relating to the results section.

Box 13.12

 *Checklist . . .*

The results section

- Have you presented descriptive statistics, and do these represent the data fairly and adequately?
- Do the results deal with each of your hypotheses?
- Are your results presented appropriately?
- Are all tables and figures correctly labelled?
- Is it possible to assess the outcome of the study by consulting the results alone, without the need to refer to other sections of the report?
- Have you included results that are not relevant to the research issue in general or the hypotheses in particular, or to which you do not refer again?

13.4 Tables and figures

Tables are easily produced by a word-processor, a spreadsheet package or even by the statistics package used for analysis. They usually consist of summary data (e.g., means and standard deviations, percentages, etc.), presented within a system of rows and columns representing various categories (e.g., different samples, categories within samples or experimental conditions). See Table 13.1 for an example.

Figures usually present the data in pictorial form (e.g., bar charts, histograms, scatterplots, etc.), and are either produced directly by your statistics package or indirectly by means of specialist software for diagrams and graphics. Increasingly, many integrated word-processing/spreadsheet/drawing packages offer this facility, bringing the opportunity to create effective illustrations within everyone's grasp. Generally speaking, the data contained in tabular form are precise (actual numerical values are used) whereas figures offer a less exact though often more immediate impression. Compare the earlier Figure 13.1 with Table 13.1.

All tables and figures must be numbered (e.g., Table 1, Figure 1) and should be given titles which are self-explanatory. Titles may appear above or below, but the location of titles should be consistent within a report. The reader should be able to understand what a table or figure is all about without digging through the text to find out. At the same time, the information displayed in tables or figures should not be mysteriously independent of the text: it *must* be discussed, explained or otherwise used in some relevant way. Common comments from supervisors with regard to tables and figures include the following: "What is this?" "What does this show?" "Why have you included this chart?"

The whole point of using figures and tables is to report, accurately and clearly, the outcome of a study. However, this section of any written report is often the main source of misleading, inaccurate and inappropriate information. Figure 13.2 shows a typical example. Here the researcher is guilty of two errors. On the one hand, there is simply too much information offered on the line graph and it becomes almost impossible to identify any trend or pattern in the data. On the other hand, there is no information on what each of the plotted lines is measuring: the legend for the graph is missing. Furthermore, this

Figure 13.2   Exam performance scores in five subjects across three degree programmes.

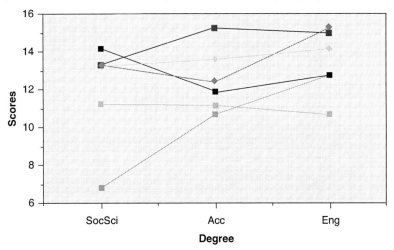

Figure 13.3   Mean scores for male and female participants on the measure of perception of discrimination against women in work.

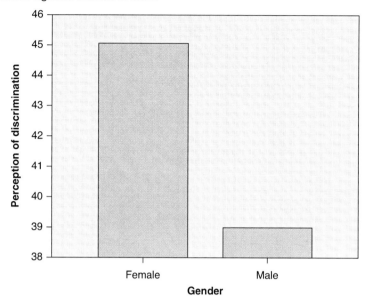

particular researcher seems to have lost the ability to count, as can be observed by closer inspection of the figure in question.

In the next example, Figure 13.3 demonstrates how a sneaky researcher can manipulate the vertical and horizontal axes of a figure to maximise an effect. Presenting data in this form suggests that there are indeed huge differences between males and females on a measure of attitudes – in this instance, perceptions of active discrimination against women in work.

Compare this with the final illustration in this section, Figure 13.4, in which the axes have been manipulated in a different but equally misleading way. The data are the same as for the previous figure, but the impression created is totally different, achieved by manipulating the vertical (*y*) axis.

This kind of manipulation is not recommended and the sophisticated reader is likely to pick up on such attempts to deceive quite quickly. If in any doubt how best to present data fairly and objectively, most current statistical software uses a recognised format for graphs which provides an acceptable standard. If still in doubt, there is an old adage beloved of statisticians long gone now, that the vertical axis should always be three-quarters the length of the horizontal! Combine this with axes showing true zero points and extending just beyond the highest data value and you have solved the problem, or at least attained consistency.

The question of when to use either of these features is a recurring one and students are always asking supervisors if they should use a graph or a table to describe some finding. At least they appreciate that it is an either-or event. Generally speaking most tutors would prefer a table because of its precision, and this tends to be the view of most journal editors also. A figure is appropriate when tabulated data become too complex to indicate trends, and a picture offers a quick, at a glance way of making a point. Similarly, when describing interactions – as in the two-way ANOVA case – a figure is often the only way such relationships can be expressed with any clarity. Figures are also useful when

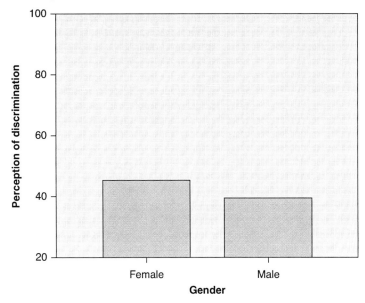

Figure 13.4 Mean scores for male and female participants on the measure of perception of discrimination against women in work.

presenting data to a statistically inexperienced readership; hence they are much favoured by newspapers. This is unlikely to be an issue for the student of psychology preparing work for a class assignment (hopefully). And finally, at the initial screening stage of data analysis, the use of figures offers an ideal overview of the shape of the data and can offer an early indication of departures from normality and other unusual occurrences.

This section concludes with a checklist in Box 13.13 to serve as a reminder of what tables and figures are supposed to be doing. Readers may also find a review of Part 4 useful.

Box 13.13

Checklist . . .

Tables and figures

Tables

- A table complements the content of the text. It should not duplicate it but should add something to the clarity of expression which is not possible within the text alone. Otherwise there is no need for a table.
- A table should be referred to in the text by its identifying number with key points noted.
- A table should be self-explanatory. If the reader has to refer to the text to understand what the table is showing or why it is there, the table has failed in its purpose.
- Tables should be numbered sequentially as they appear. Letter suffixes are not recommended. (Note, though, our discussion on suffixes in Part 4 concerning the use of tables within a textbook.)

▪ Tables should be identified by a title which is intelligible and supported by footnotes if abbreviations or special features are to be explained.

▪ The format of tables should be standardized. The APA (2001) guidelines encourage the use of horizontal lines to subdivide a table and discourage the use of vertical lines. See Table 1 for an illustration.

Figures

▪ Everything which offers a pictorial presentation is termed a figure. This includes photographs, drawings and charts, although in most undergraduate reports the chart is the most frequent form of figure.

▪ A figure complements the content of the text. It should add something to the clarity of expression which is not possible within the text alone or which would be unclear from a table. Otherwise there is no need for a figure.

▪ A figure should be referred to in the text by its identifying number with key points noted.

▪ A figure should be self-explanatory with the axes clearly labelled and scaled. If the reader has to refer to the text to understand what the figure is showing or why it is there, the figure has failed in its purpose.

▪ Figures should be numbered sequentially as they appear. As with tables, letter suffixes are not recommended.

▪ Figures should be identified by a title which is intelligible and supported by footnotes if abbreviations or special features are to be explained.

▪ The format of figures should be standardized within a report, especially if comparisons are to be drawn.

▪ Over-embellishment is to be discouraged. Figures should be simple and offer an immediate impression of the data. If figures need to be closely inspected to determine trends they have lost any advantage they might have over a table.

If these guidelines are followed, your figures and tables will be relevant and intelligible. For more information on this topic, refer to the APA (2001) guidelines.

13.5 Discussion

This is the section that probably demands the most of your creativity and intellect, where you try to make sense of it all, to relate your findings to previous research and explain what happened in your study – in particular, this is where the hypotheses are reviewed in the light of the results. The best guidance would be to start off by providing a summary of the main results of your study, indicating the implications of these results for your hypotheses. Then you can draw on the main points of your introduction: for example, you can indicate whether your results are consistent or inconsistent with the findings of other researchers, or whether they support one theory rather than another.

You have to present some explanations for your results – this may be easy if your results were entirely in the expected directions and all of your hypotheses were supported. It may be less straightforward (although more interesting) if your results were not consistent with the results of other researchers. Under these circumstances, you have to review all of the potentially relevant points made earlier in the report: you may have used a different participant pool, used a slightly different procedure, changed the test materials in some way, and all of these may have affected your results. You should not attempt to hide any such discrepancies; rather, the effects of discrepancies and variations should be highlighted, since they tell you something very important about the strength or robustness of any predicted effects. Moreover, being honest and 'up-front' like this indicates that you appreciate the limitations of your study, which in itself is commendable. More importantly, from an assessment point of view, if you don't do this your supervisor certainly will. One of the most irritating characteristics of tutors everywhere is their unerring knack of finding the flaws in the research of their students.

Overall, you should ensure that you cover all of the main points raised in your introduction. Thus if you mentioned the possibility of gender differences in the introduction, you should raise this issue again in your discussion, even if you were not able to examine gender differences (for example, because of limitations within the participant pool). One of the aims of the discussion is to highlight the limitations of your project and areas worthy of further investigation. You are not expected to conduct a study which covers every option; on the other hand, you are expected to discuss the strengths, weaknesses and limitations of your work in a clear and objective tone. (Remember the point made above about supervisors.) You should also consider ways in which your project might have been improved, and the direction of any future work which may be profitably undertaken in this area.

A very important point to note is that the failure to uphold your hypotheses does not mean that the study has 'failed', which is often the view of students new to research. To show that something is *not* the case can be as important as showing that it *is* the case: a null result does not mean that you have nothing to say. You should not, therefore, write your discussion of a null outcome in an apologetic way; yes, we all like to get a 'significant result', but the rejection of an hypothesis can be equally informative, and may lead to new ideas.

The converse of this is also true: rejecting a null hypothesis does not necessarily mean that a study has 'worked'. A truly huge sample, for instance, will allow you to demonstrate significance in almost anything, but to little point, and while admittedly this will not be an issue in most undergraduate research, small samples can be influenced by extreme scores, and deviations from normality can make interpretation of significance problematic.

The discussion should end with a paragraph or two of conclusions. It may be tempting at this stage to make rather sweeping statements. Remember the limitations of your study and try not to go beyond your own results. A useful checklist for the discussion section appears in Box 13.14.

13.6 References

The reference section of a report offers an alphabetical listing (by first author's surname) of all the sources mentioned or referred to in the main text of the report: journal articles, book chapters, commentaries and quotations – any material in fact to which you have made reference in the body of a report must be cited. An important point here, and one

Box 13.14

Checklist . . .

The discussion section

- Have you discussed all of the important issues raised in your introduction?
- Have ideas crept in to the discussion which are not really related to the study?
- Does the discussion concentrate purely on the findings, or does it consider broader issues?
- Conversely: does your discussion take sufficient note of the actual findings?
- Are there any findings which you have not discussed?
- Have you considered whether your data might support an explanation other than the one you prefer?
- Does the discussion point to original thinking?
- Are your conclusions clear?

which is a traditional source of confusion to many undergraduates, concerns the difference between a reference section and a bibliography. References, as already mentioned, relate to work actually cited. A bibliography, on the other hand, is a listing (again alphabetically, by first author) of any work which was consulted, browsed or which in some way contributed to the background, formulation and conduct of your study. For instance, in reviewing the type of research carried out in a particular area you might have read several journal articles and book reviews, none of which provided specific material to which you referred in your report. However, insofar as they did contribute to the overall foundations of your work, they would be listed in the bibliography – an opportunity for you to provide an overview of your own research into a topic. Note, however, that the inclusion of a bibliography is not always acceptable, and it is worth checking the guidelines offered by your own department or institution on this point.

The format for presenting references tends to vary slightly from publication to publication, but many psychology journals conform to formats favoured by the major journals and approved by both the APA and the BPS, the essence of which we have used in offering our own guidelines, as follows.

Citations in the text itself should be by author's surname and date only – which is the minimum information needed to correctly identify the full reference where it appears at the end of the report (see Box 13.15 for examples). Any other information, such as the title of the publication or the author's initial, is usually redundant here and serves only to distract. In multiple citations in the text (where you give a list of authors, in brackets, to support a point), reference your sources in alphabetical order (date order may also be acceptable). If you cite more than one article published by a single author in the same year, use the letters *a*, *b*, *c*, etc. after the date: for example, Boelen (1992a) and Boelen (1992b). The identifiers (*a, b, c*) are used in the order in which you cite them in your final reference list (and so in alphabetical order), and not in the order in which they were published in the particular year in question – they are *your* suffixes, not those of the author or publisher. And of course, the identifiers accompany the full reference in the reference section.

Box 13.15

How To . . .

Reference, in accord with APA (2001) guidelines

1. Journal articles

Single authorship

Likert, R. A. (1932). A technique for the measurement of attitudes. *Archives of Psychology, 140*, 55.

Joint authorship

Johnson, M. H., Karmiloff-Smith, A., & Patry, J. L. (1992). Can neural selectionism be applied to cognitive development and its disorders? *New Ideas in Psychology*, *10*, 35–46.

Note that (*a*) capital letters are not used in the titles of the articles except at the beginning of sections (or when proper names are used); (*b*) inverted commas are not used; (*c*) journal names are given in full; (*d*) journal names and volume numbers are italicised (or underlined, if you are not using a word-processor).

2. Books and chapters in books

Single authorship

Cohen, J. (1988). *Statistical power analysis for the behavioral sciences* (2nd ed.). Hillsdale, NJ: Erlbaum.

Joint authorship

Potter, J., & Wetherell, M. (1987). *Discourse and social psychology: Beyond attitudes and behaviour*. London: Sage.

Chapter

Burman, A. (1994). Interviewing. In P. Banister, E. Burman, I. Parker, M. Taylor, & C. Tindall (Eds.), *Qualitative methods in psychology: A research guide* (pp. 49–71). Buckingham: Open University Press.

Note that (*a*) capitals are not used in the titles except at the beginning of sections (although it is acceptable to use capitals for main words in book titles); (*b*) inverted commas are not used; (*c*) book titles are italicised (but not chapter titles); (*d*) page numbers are given if specifically referred to or quoted from in the text; (*e*) place of publication, then publishers, are cited last.

3. Citations in the text

In the text itself, sources are cited by surnames and date only. Citation can be direct or indirect:

Direct

Archer (1991) found higher testosterone levels in the more aggressive group.

Indirect

Higher testosterone levels were found in the more aggressive group (Archer, 1991).

Quotations are best avoided unless the full quotation given is of direct relevance to your own work. If you do quote verbatim from an author, give the page number as well as the author's name and date: e.g., 'Comparisons . . . revealed higher testosterone levels in the more aggressive group' (Archer, 1991, p. 21). If there are two authors, give both surnames using *and* for direct citation and *&* for indirect, e.g.,

Direct: Barry and Bateman (1992)

Indirect: (Barry & Bateman, 1992)

If there are more than two authors, give all the names the first time the source is cited (e.g., Johnson, Karmiloff-Smith, & Patry, 1992). For subsequent mentions, use *et al.* (e.g., Johnson et al., 1992).

4. Internet sources

The APA and BPS provide detailed guidelines on referencing material found on the Internet. Briefly, the aim of any reference is to provide the reader with sufficient information to track down the source. Since Internet sources can be updated, you should indicate the date on which you found or downloaded the material, and the source or URL.

Online periodical

Author, A., Author, B., & Author, C. (date). Title of article. *Title of periodical, volume*, start page–end page. Retrieved month, day, year, from source/URL.

Online document

Author, A. (date). Title of work. Retrieved month, day, year, from source/URL.

13.7 Appendices

These should include all test materials and examples of any stimuli used in the study. Any questionnaires developed by the researcher must be shown in full, although standardised instruments are not required. It can be assumed that the reader is familiar with the 16PF, or that detailed information on a particular test is readily available (through published test and administration manuals). Tables of norms should be given if they are relevant to the interpretation of the research findings. Note that most tutors and examiners will not welcome reams of computer output, even in an appendix, or raw data (although there is an understanding that they are available for inspection should it be required). If your study is qualitative in nature, however, you may wish to include interview transcripts and so on. Again, if in doubt, consult the typical format used in a standard journal (or ask your supervisor).

13.8 Presentation and style

Remember that presentation is important. Try to ensure that your work is free from spelling and grammatical errors. Check your work for errors before you hand it in. The style of writing should be plain and relatively formal, and you should use the past tense throughout and write in the third person; many novice researchers frequently use "I" and "we" in their writing ("we felt repeated measures were more appropriate"), but this tends to create an impression of informality and lack of scientific rigour. And, whether accurate or not, impressions do count. It is much better to place some distance between yourself and the report, as in: "It was found that/observed/noted" (except for a qualitative report in which the views of the author may be central).

13.9 Writing up qualitative research

Those of you who have conducted a qualitative study may feel uncertain as to how to present and write up your work. There is no one 'correct' way of writing up a qualitative study and many different formats can be used to impart the relevant details to the reader. However, the following discussion may help you when it comes to writing up your work.

13.9.1 The background to a qualitative report

The first point to make is that the aims of a qualitative study are likely to be different from those of a quantitative study, such that the aim is less likely to centre on an existing theory. For example, in grounded theory research, the researcher is unlikely to have posed any hypotheses at all, and the theory emerges after the study has been completed – which is, in fact, the point of this approach. An ethnographic study aims to describe cultures or groups with which the researcher was initially unfamiliar. It follows that research of this type cannot be theory-driven. In studies of this sort, the important points about theory are made in the discussion rather than in the introduction.

The second point we need to make here is that that there are a number of different techniques and traditions associated with qualitative research. Far from converging on an agreed set of procedures, these have tended to develop into distinct approaches to the conduct, analysis and presentation of research. This means that there is no one set of guiding principles, although a number of authors have published thoughtful and useful guidelines on this topic (see, for example, Elliott, Fischer, & Rennie, 1999; Finlay, 2002; Miles & Huberman, 1994; Smith, Jarman, & Osborn, 1999; Wetherell, Taylor, & Yates, 2001b). We can offer some general guidelines here, but bear in mind that what you are trying to do is to ensure that your reader understands and appreciates your study.

13.10 Guidelines on writing up qualitative research

The report on a qualitative study will normally take the form of a narrative or 'story', typically comprised of four sections. We deal with each of these in turn.

13.10.1 The introduction

This should cover the background to the study, the context and the nature of the research. You might first want to offer a rationale for the study: the reader will want to know what prompted the research, what it aimed to show or illustrate and why (the potential implications). Then you would present the context of the research, which would include any existing work in the area, or the factors that were likely to be relevant to the participants. Taking the study on the relationship between blood pressure and exercise as an example, your introduction should cover the basic issues, such as what is meant by high blood pressure, and the literature relating exercise to blood pressure. You would also want to consider the issue from the participants' point of view, such as the symptoms people commonly experience with high blood pressure, and the impact that the symptoms may have upon their lives, activities and subjective wellbeing. Then you need to present the nature of the research, with some justification for the approach taken. While some of this detail might be better suited for the method section, it will help the reader to learn something of the approach at this stage: for example, you might indicate that you have taken a phenomenological approach (and why you have done so), or that you have interviewed participants.

Given the central role of the researcher in a qualitative study, the researcher's thoughts, feelings, reflections and reactions are usually highly relevant. As we have said in Part 6, you need to think carefully about the extent to which you are willing or able to disclose personal information about yourself: you should not feel obliged to say anything in the report that you might later regret. On the other hand, if it is not too personal, it might be relevant to indicate any experience that relates to the topic at hand. So, you might indicate whether you have had experience of people with high blood pressure, and the nature of that experience. If your topic is one that is quite alien to you, or which affects people who are quite different from you, then you might make this point here. For example, if the topic affects middle-class white males, and you share none of those characteristics, it could be worth saying this. On a more pragmatic note, it sometimes makes more sense for the researcher to describe himself or herself as 'I' in the written report than as 'the researcher', but opinions vary on this point and we would advise you to check this up with your supervisor before submitting the final report.

13.10.2 The method

This is a major part of the report. Some researchers write up their work almost as a narrative, telling the story of the study from its inception, including details of key decisions in chronological order. This often makes good sense, particularly if things did not go according to plan. Generally speaking, the method section should cover the following points: the approach taken, with justification for this (and perhaps also justification for excluding other approaches); the recruitment of participants; the data collection methods used (in sufficient detail that the study could be repeated by the reader); how the study evolved or changed over the course of study; and what the researcher did to ensure that he or she represented the experiences of the participants. The issues concerning the approach taken must be considered in detail, demonstrating a clear understanding of any assumptions taken on board. Give examples if that helps the reader to understand exactly what happened and why. Remember that the reader (your supervisor and other markers) needs to follow the progress of the study, to understand what you did and why, and the reader also needs to be able to judge how well you carried out your study.

13.10.3 The results and discussion

In a qualitative report, it often makes sense to discuss the findings as you go along, rather than to have two separate sections. Again, the aim is to make it easy for your reader to follow what you have found. The first issue is generally that of analysis, unless you have covered this in the method section: explain carefully the procedures used to analyse the data, and the ways in which you drew up any themes, categories or topics. These themes and categories can then be used to structure your results, and you may find a table or diagram useful at this point. In your writing, sufficient original data should be provided to enable the reader to evaluate the interpretation. This brings us to the issue of quotation. Having decided on the themes or topics you are going to present, you may want to illustrate these with quotes from interview transcripts or the texts you were using. It is often tempting to include several quotes for each theme, but too many quotes can actually detract from the quality of your work. As a rule of thumb, two or three quotes for each theme should be sufficient. The best quotes do something in addition to illustrating a theme; for example, a good quote can also demonstrate an ambivalence or shift in the participant's perspective, it can illustrate a metaphor you have used and it can be used to demonstrate your analytical technique. Quotes are an important part of your 'evidence', and also part of your narrative, but they should illustrate rather than constitute your results/discussion sections. On a practical note, quotations are easier to read if they are indented (around 1.5 cm), and you should identify the participant with a number or pseudonym, depending on the conventions you are using.

13.10.4 Conclusions

In this final section of your report, you should review your study both in terms of its conduct and its findings. This may be the section where you present your theory, and if so, then you need to make some links with the existing literature. You should also review the quality of your study, and consider strengths, shortcomings and limitations (see Part 6, particularly section 12.16).

13.11 Giving a presentation of your study

There is an increasingly common expectation – if not a requirement – that undergraduates offer an oral presentation of their work to staff and fellow students at some stage during the conduct of a project. Timings vary, with some colleges and universities scheduling presentations before data collection begins, while others wait until the entire project is completed. Either way, presentations are now a familiar part of undergraduate life and they serve a variety of functions. At the most obvious level they provide the student with an opportunity to show off as it were – after all, a great deal of reading has probably gone into the development of a research project, only a fraction of which is ultimately used in the study proper. How satisfying to be able to demonstrate to your tutors that you have actually put considerable effort into your work (especially useful in those cases where presentations comprise an assessable component of a research methods module). Presentations also demonstrate the depth of your familiarity with a topic and tutors will often ask probing questions about issues which, even if they did not form a part of your study, you might be expected to know something about if your reading really was comprehensive.

If presentations occur at an intermediate stage then they serve the extremely useful function of generating constructive feedback, with an audience being given the chance to offer advice ('you need a larger sample for this type of analysis', or 'have you read . . . ?'). And of course, finally, having to prepare and give a presentation is now regarded as an important element of general research methods training – anyone hoping to pursue a career in the field will find that the presentation is an important way to disseminate information. A few guidelines on presentation techniques might come in useful.

A good starting point is to consider the purpose of the presentation. The aim is usually to describe, in the course of a 10-minute talk (sometimes longer), your study. During the presentation you must identify the research issue you have explored, outline the research background to the issue and provide a rationale for what you have done (or are about to do). The actual study must be described in sufficient detail that an audience can follow your design and procedure, and results (if appropriate) should be offered in a format which describes the outcome without confusion. Finally, you should be able to present your view of the implications of the study, and all in a manner which is interesting, informative and accurate. All in all, a pretty terrifying prospect!

In structure, a presentation should be like a trimmed-down version of a standard research report, comprising more or less the same major sections and sub-divisions. It will have a title, much like the report title, followed by a brief statement of what the study was about. This is not quite like an abstract since data and findings would not be offered at this stage, but more like an expanded explanation of the title, highlighting the general research area and stating the research questions ('an observational study in the area of . . . and exploring the specific issue of . . .').

A review of the background to the research is important, and this will take the form of a summarised version of the literature review found in the written report. Naturally, key studies would have to be mentioned, with their findings, along with any research which provided a rationale for the study, ending with a statement of the hypotheses explored.

An outline of the procedure would be offered next, with illustrations provided of questionnaires or stimuli. Data should be described in descriptive terms, followed by details of results. While most of the other sections would tend to be presented in general terms, this results section should be full and precise. It remains only to make concluding comments about the conduct of the study, how the findings relate to the research issue in general and the hypotheses in particular.

13.12 Practicalities: Giving a presentation

The previous section outlined the content of a typical presentation, but said little about how this material might be presented. This section attempts to offer some practical advice.

A key point to remember, when preparing for a presentation, is that an oral exposition of a piece of work differs from a text version. In the write-up you have ample opportunity to explain in detail the conduct of previous research in your field, to include the results of complex statistical analyses and to discuss at length your findings. In a presentation it is not possible to present such detailed material. For one thing, there are time constraints and, contrary to popular undergraduate belief, 10 minutes is not really that long; what you say has to be a much condensed version of your study, but one which nevertheless contains the essence of what you did. For another, while a reviewer or assessor can re-read the contents of a report, or follow up material in appendices, a presentation is a 'one-shot' affair – you have a single opportunity to say what you want, to make your points and show that you have done a good job. So how do you do this?

The starting point is your written report: if this is completed before presentations are given (as is the norm) then you already have all the information necessary for an oral version. You actually have too much information, so the report should be read carefully and important information extracted. Box 13.16 offers a summary of what is required.

The next stage is to decide how best to present the information gleaned from the full report: some undergraduates will simply write a summary, based on their notes, and the presentation comprises a rather tedious reading aloud of this summary. This is not a particularly effective method of giving a presentation – it tends to be dull, it doesn't allow the audience to focus on key elements and it can also be intimidating for the speaker; with no other source of stimulation the audience's entire attention is focused on the oral presentation itself.

Box 13.16

Practicalities . . .

Presenting research

The following is a suggested listing – with comments – of the major elements which should comprise an oral presentation. They appear in the typical order in which they would be introduced to an audience. They also represent the likely content of a series of slides or overheads which would be used as a basis for a presentation.

1. **A title for the presentation**, which will be based on the title of the study itself. Accompanying notes would expand on this title, identifying the research area in which your study was based, and outlining the research questions posed.

2. **An outline of key research in the area.** An overhead would display the authors of research, the date of the published work and the research findings – these might be in terms of mean scores for different groups, or a description of factors identified in the research: for example, 'Cattell (1969): 16 personality factors identified . . .' Accompanying notes would expand on the studies cited, explaining the findings in more detail and demonstrating how they formed a basis for your work.

3. **A statement of the aim of the study**, in general terms, and statements of the hypotheses being tested. Notes would expand on the aim, reminding the audience of how the stated aim has developed from previous research (or whatever), and each hypothesis would be explained in turn: what the basis for each hypothesised prediction was, and what the expected outcomes were.

4. **A description of procedural elements**, such as the sample characteristics (where relevant to the conduct and findings of the study), details of any apparatus used, including questionnaires and standardised test instruments. In the case of tests or questionnaires, examples of items, coding and scoring systems can be displayed. Full copies might also be distributed among the audience. Notes here would provide descriptive details of how samples were drawn, why certain characteristics were controlled for (e.g., extraneous variables) and how participants were assigned to groups, if appropriate; and whether or not the design was within-subjects or between-groups. Details would also be given on questionnaires, including pilot study data if appropriate. An explanation of the development of items would be given and the role and composition of sub-scales discussed. (Note: a lot of information is covered in this section and this might be represented in a number of slides. For instance, one might deal with participant characteristics, there might be two or more giving examples of test items and there might be an additional slide reviewing the findings of a pilot study.)

5. **A summary statement identifying independent and dependent variables and noting any extraneous factors.** Notes would briefly review the procedure, reminding how independent variables were manipulated and explaining how outcome measures were taken.

6. **Presentation of results.** Key findings would be illustrated, firstly in the form of summary statistics, and then in terms of analysis. These would include means, *t*-values, *F*-ratios and correlation coefficients, for example. Probability values would also be shown. Notes would indicate how the statistics were derived and what tests were carried out and any significant effects highlighted. Figures are often appropriate here for their visual impact.

7. **More results.** If additional analysis was carried out to further explore a finding, or you wish to highlight some unusual or worthy finding, this should be presented next. Notes would explain why additional analysis was necessary (e.g., 'it was noted that mean scores for males in the sample were higher than previous reported norms'), and any figures would be discussed.

8. **Hypotheses would be re-stated** and upheld or rejected in light of the results. Notes would expand upon the relationship between the findings and the predicted outcomes. Explanation would then extend to re-considering the entire research issue in view of the study just outlined. The presentation at this point is likely to return to the kind of general discussion of issues introduced at the very beginning.

A far better solution is to make use of some form of visual aid – overheads, slides and computer-generated screen graphics are all ideal and most departments will happily make facilities available for students. The advantages of this approach are considerable:

1. Key points of a study can be put on an overhead or slide allowing you to emphasise to your audience the important elements of the study. For instance, you might display the hypotheses as you explain procedural matters, making it easier for your audience to appreciate why you carried out your study *this* way, as opposed to *that* way.

2. Complex information can be presented more effectively in this format than by verbal explanation. Just imagine trying to explain the results of a multiple group comparison analysis verbally. A table or a graph projected onto a screen will describe at a glance what might take you several minutes to explain.

3. A series of slides tends to impose its own structure on a presentation, covering the logical sequence of activities which comprised the study (e.g., you will probably have, in order, slides displaying the title of the study, examples of previous work, statement of hypotheses, procedural matters, results, etc.). They also serve as *aides memoire*, reminders of what you need to talk about next, or which part of your notes to consult. Relying totally on notes, without this kind of external structure, can lead to confusion and loss of place, especially if the notes are extensive.

4. Using visual displays takes pressure off the presenter, especially useful for the nervous undergraduate who can panic quite freely in a corner while everyone's attention is focused on a projected image somewhere else.

Clearly there are advantages in using presentation aids, but be cautious. Firstly, the temptation to cover your slides with everything you want to say should be avoided at all costs. The purpose of these aids is to present key points and illustrations – any more than this and it would be as easy to provide each audience member with a text version of your talk. Legibility is another issue: if you've never used overheads before it's important to find out how big writing or font sizes need to be so that an audience can read them. And thirdly, organisation is important. There is nothing guaranteed better to destroy a nervous presenter's confidence than to discover their slides are in the wrong order, or that one is missing. Take it from two lecturers who know.

Material in support of overheads has to be considered. Previously it has been suggested that a slide can act as an *aide memoire*, triggering recall in the mind of the presenter and reminding him or her what to say next. In fact, only skilled presenters and lecturers are likely to be able to do this well and, unless a talk is well rehearsed, students are advised to use notes to accompany each overhead. Even experienced lecturers are often caught out by an overhead whose existence, never mind content, comes as a complete surprise to them, recognisable when a lecturer is caught staring blankly at a screen for some time.

Examples of test materials can also be made available to an audience, especially if a questionnaire has been custom-designed for a study. Even copies of standardised tests might be distributed if an audience includes fellow students who might not be familiar with specialised instruments.

To conclude this section on presentations, it is worth noting that giving a presentation is a skilled activity, and therefore requires practice to develop. Few undergraduates are going to be superb at this task but, with a bit of organisation and a lot of preparation, presentations can be made competent and interesting.

13.13 Assessment

Any study, no matter how elaborate and irrespective of its contribution to the fount of human knowledge, will ultimately be judged on the written exposition of the background, design, conduct and findings of the research. This is true whether the report is based on an undergraduate project, represents a submission to a periodical editor or is a published article in an international journal. In every case, a reader, tutor or reviewer is looking for the same kind of thing – evidence that the study has been well carried out, the data competently analysed and the research issue fully explored. A judgement here can only be based on the written report or article and, while your own research might not necessarily set the world of academia alight, if you have followed all the guidelines in this chapter, you will at least guarantee yourself a fair and objective hearing. Box 13.17 is the concluding illustration in this chapter and it offers a summary of the main points a reviewer or tutor will be looking for in a written report.

Box 13.17

 *Checklist . . .*

Typical assessment criteria

Originality

To what extent are the choice of topic and methdodology your own? Does the work show some originality in design or approach?

Initiative

Have you shown initiative in collecting data or in preparing test materials?

Introduction

How well have the research issues been identified and explained? Is the review of the literature relevant and thorough? Has the scope of the project been clearly presented? Are the hypotheses unambiguously stated, and is it clear how they relate to previous work? Is the rationale for the aims of the study and the specific hypotheses clear?

Design

Is the design of the project appropriate for the research question? Have issues concerning sampling and control been addressed? Have independent and dependent variables been correctly identified? Has this section been expressed in the appropriate language of design?

Participants

Were the participants representative of the population? Have their relevant characteristics been described? Are recruitment strategies presented? Are response and refusal rates recorded?

Apparatus/materials

Have the details of apparatus been recorded? Have the details of questionnaires, etc. been presented? Are justifications provided for the choice of materials, and for any changes made to published materials? In what ways do the materials provide data for analysis?

Procedure

Is it possible to understand exactly what procedures were followed in collecting data? Are these procedures appropriate? Could the study be replicated on the information provided?

Results

Are the results clearly presented? Is the analysis appropriate for the level of data? Does the analysis actually address the hypotheses or research questions under consideration?

Discussion

Are the results discussed with reference to the issues raised in the Introduction? Are the results discussed with reference to previous findings and relevant theory? Are any problems or limitations of the study fully understood and discussed?

References

Are all references given in full? Are they presented in a standard format?

Presentation

Is the project well presented? Is it free from spelling errors? Is it well written? Are arguments clearly and carefully presented?

(Note: the comments on initiative and originality, while relevant for any piece of research, are likely to be particular issues for undergraduate studies.)

Review

In this chapter, we have discussed the issues you need to think about when you are writing up your research. You should now be familiar with the following topics:

* the functions of each of the main sections of the report
* how to write an abstract
* what to put in the introduction section
* what to put in the methods section
* how best to present your results
* what to cover in the discussion section
* how to reference the work of other authors
* how to give an effective oral presentation of your work

Suggested further reading

American Psychological Association. (2001). *Publication manual of the American Psychological Association* (5th ed.). Washington, DC: American Psychological Association.

Cresswell, J. W. (1998). *Qualitative inquiry and research design: Choosing among five traditions.* Thousand Oaks, CA: Sage.

Day, R. A. (1989). *How to write and publish a scientific paper* (3rd ed.). Cambridge: Cambridge University Press.

Denzin, N. K., & Lincoln, Y. S. (Eds.). (1994). *Handbook of qualitative research.* Thousand Oaks, CA: Sage.

Howard, K., & Sharp. J. A. (1983). *The management of a student research project.* Aldershot, Hants: Gower.

Kantowitz, B. H., Roediger III, H. L., & Elmes, D. G. (1994). *Experimental psychology: Understanding psychological research* (5th ed.). St. Paul, MN: West Publishing.

Leedy, P. D., & Ormrod, J. E. (1989). *Practical research: Planning and design* (7th ed.). Upper Saddle River, NJ: Prentice Hall.

Miles, M. B., & Huberman, A. M. (1994). *Qualitative data analysis* (2nd ed.). Thousand Oaks, CA: Sage.

20 Data analysis
Grounded theory

Overview

- Grounded theory basically involves a number of techniques which enable researchers to effectively analyse 'rich' (detailed) qualitative data effectively.

- It reverses the classic hypothesis-testing approach to theory development (favoured by some quantitative researchers) by defining data collection as the primary stage and requiring that theory is closely linked to the entirety of the data.

- The researcher keeps close to the data when developing theoretical analyses – in this way the analysis is 'grounded' in the data rather than being based on speculative theory which is then tested using hypotheses derived from the theory.

- Grounded theory does not mean that there are theoretical concepts just waiting in the data to be discovered. It means that the theory is anchored in the data.

- In grounded theory, categories are developed and refined by the researcher in order to explain whatever the researcher regards as the significant features of the data.

20.1 Introduction

Sometimes qualitative data analysis is regarded as being an easy route to doing research. After all, it does not involve writing questionnaire items, planning experimental designs or even doing statistics. All of these tasks are difficult and, if they can be avoided, are best avoided. Or so the argument goes. Superficially, qualitative data analysis does seem to avoid most of the problems of quantification and statistical analysis. Carry out an unstructured interview or conduct a focus group or get a politician's speech off the Internet or something of the sort. Then record it using an audio recorder or video recorder, or just use the written text grabbed from the World Wide Web. Sounds like a piece of cake. You are probably familiar with the caricature of quantitative researchers as boffins in white coats in laboratories. The qualitative researcher may similarly be caricatured. The qualitative researcher is more like a manic newspaper reporter or television reporter who asks a few questions or takes a bit of video and then writes an article about it.

What is the difference between the qualitative researcher and the TV reporter with the tape recorder or camera crew? The answer to this question will take most of this chapter.

The book, *Discovery of Grounded Theory* (Glaser and Strauss, 1967), is still regarded as a major source on the topic of grounded theory. Historically, it was the first and most influential major publication arguing for this new conceptualisation of data analysis. Glaser and Strauss' approach was as much a reaction to the dominant sociology of the time as it was radically innovative. Basically, the book takes objection to the largely abstract sociological theory of the time which seemed divorced from any social or empirical reality. Indeed, empirical research was as atheoretical as the theoretical research was unempirical at the time. Grounded theory reversed many of the axioms of conventional research in an attempt to systematise many aspects of qualitative research. As such, it should be of interest to quantitative researchers since it highlights the characteristics of their methods.

However, many readers of this chapter will not yet have read any research that involves the use of grounded theory. So what are the characteristics of a grounded theory analysis? Ultimately the aim is to produce a set of categories into which the data fit closely and which amounts to a theoretical description of the data. Since the data are almost certain to be textual or spoken language then major features of most analyses can be anticipated. Like all forms of research, there are excellent grounded theory analyses, but also inadequate or mundane ones. A word of warning: to carry out a grounded theory analysis is a somewhat exacting task. Sometimes authors claim to have used grounded theory though perusal of their work reveals no signs of the rigours of the method. Sometimes the categories developed fit the data because they are so broad that anything in the data is bound to fit into one or other of the coding categories.

Like properly done qualitative data analyses in general, grounded theory approaches are time consuming, arguably because of the need for great familiarity with the data. Grounded theory employs a variety of techniques designed to ensure that researchers enter into the required intimate contact with their data as well as bringing into juxtaposition different aspects of the data. The approach has a lot of aficionados among the wide cross-section of qualitative research – though its use is far from universal.

Just to stress, grounded theory methods result in categories which encompass the data (text or speech almost invariably) as completely and unproblematically as the researcher can manage. In this context, theory and effective categorisation are virtually synonymous. This causes some confusion among those better versed in quantitative methods who tend to assume that theory means an elaborate conjecture system from which hypotheses are derived for testing. That is not what grounded theory provides – the categorisation system is basically the theory. Furthermore, researchers seeking a theory that yields precise predictions will be disappointed. While grounded theory may generalise to new sets of data, it is normally *in*capable of making predictions of a more precise sort. Charmaz (2000) explains:

> . . . *grounded theory methods consist of systematic inductive guidelines for collecting and analyzing data to build middle-range theoretical frameworks that explain the collected data. Throughout the research process, grounded theorists develop analytic interpretations of their data to focus further data collection, which they use in turn to inform and refine their developing theoretical analyses.*

[p. 509]

Several elements of this description of grounded theory warrant highlighting:

- Grounded theory consists of *guidelines* for conducting data collection, data analysis and theory building, which may lead to research which is closely integrated to social reality as represented in the data.

■ Grounded theory is *systematic*. In other words, the analysis of data to generate theory is not dependent on a stroke of genius or divine inspiration, but on perspiration and application of general principles or methods.

■ Grounded theory involves *inductive* guidelines rather than deductive processes. This is very different from what is often regarded as conventional theory building (sometimes described as the 'hypothetico-deductive method'). In the hypothetico-deductive method, theory is developed from which hypotheses are derived. In turn, these hypotheses may be put to an empirical test. Research is important because it allows researchers to test these hypotheses. The hypothetico-deductive method characterised psychology for much of its modern history. Without the link between theory building and hypothesis testing, quantitative research in psychology probably deserves the epithet of 'empiricism gone mad.' Particularly good examples of the hypothetico-deductive approach are to be found in the writings of psychologists such as Hans Eysenck (for example, Eysenck, 1980). However, grounded theory, itself, was not really a reaction against the hypothetico-deductive method but one against overly abstracted and untestable social theory.

■ Grounded theory requires that theory should develop out of an understanding of the complexity of the subject matter. Theories (that is, coding schemes) knit the complexity of the data into a coherent whole. Such theories may only be tested effectively in terms of the fit between the categories and the data, and by applying the categories to new data. In many ways this contrasts markedly with mainstream quantitative psychology. There is no requirement that the analysis fits all of the data closely – merely that there are statistically significant trends, irrespective of magnitude, which confirm the hypothesis derived from the theory.

■ The theory building process is a continuous one rather than a sequence of critical tests of the theory through testing hypotheses. In many ways, it is impossible to separate the different phases of the research into discrete components such as theory development, hypothesis testing, followed by refining the theory. The data collection phase, the transcription phase and the analysis phase all share the common intent of building theory by matching the analysis closely to the complexity of the topic of interest.

20.2 Development of grounded theory

Grounded theory is usually described as being a reaction against the dominant sociology of the twentieth century, specifically the Chicago School of Sociology. Some of the founders of this school specifically argued that human communities were made up of subpopulations, each of which operated almost on a natural science model – they were like ecological populations. For example, subpopulations showed a pattern whereby they began to invade a territory, eventually reaching dominance, and finally receding as another subpopulation became dominant. This was used to explain population changes in major and developing cities such as Chicago. Large scale social processes and not the experiences of individuals came to be the subject of study. The characteristics which are attributed to the Chicago School are redolent of a lot of psychology. In particular, the Chicago School sought to develop exact and standard measuring instruments to measure a small number of key variables that were readily quantified. In sociology, research in natural contexts began to be unimportant in the first half of twentieth century – the corresponding change in psychology was the increased importance of the psychological laboratory as a research base. In sociology, researchers undertook field research mainly in order to develop their measuring instruments. Once developed, they became the focus of interest themselves. So social processes are ignored in favour of broad measures such as social class and alienation, which are abstractions. The theorist and the researcher were often different people, so much so that much research became alienated from theory, that is, atheoretical (Charmaz, 1995).

Grounded theory methodology basically mirror-imaged or reversed features of the dominant sociology of the 1960s in a number of ways:

- Qualitative research came to be seen as a legitimate domain in its own right. It was not a preliminary or preparatory stage for refining one's research instruments prior to quantitative research.

- The division between research and theory was undermined by requiring that theory comes after or as part of the data collection and is tied to the data collected. Furthermore, data collection and their analysis were reconstrued as being virtually inseparable. That is, analysis of the data was encouraged early in the collection of data and this early analysis could be used to guide the later collection of data.

In order to achieve these ends, grounded theory had to demonstrate that quantitative research could be made rigorous, systematic and structured. The idea that quantitative data analysis is no more than a few superficial impressions of the researcher was no part of grounded theory. Equally, case studies are considered in themselves *not* to achieve the full potential of qualitative research.

Despite being the mirror image of mainstream research, grounded theory analysis does not share all of the features of other qualitative methods such as discourse analysis and ethnomethodology. In particular, some users of grounded theory reject *realism* (the idea that out there somewhere is a social reality which researchers will eventually uncover) whereas others accept it. Similarly, some grounded theorists aim for objective measures and theory development that does not depend on the researcher's subjectivity. Others regard this as a futile and inappropriate aim.

20.3 Data in grounded theory

Grounded theory is not primarily a means of collecting data but the means of data analysis. Consequently, grounded theory does not require any particular type of data although some types of data are better for it than others. So, for example, grounded theory can be applied to interviews, biographical data, media content, observations, conversations and so forth. All of these sources potentially may be introduced into any study. The key thing is, of course, that the data should be as richly detailed as possible, that is, not simple or simplified. Charmaz (1995, p. 33) suggests that richly detailed data involve 'full' or 'thick' written descriptions. So, by this criterion, much of the data collected by quantitative researchers in the so-called quantitative approach would be unsuitable. There is little that a grounded theory researcher could do with answers to a multiple-choice questionnaire or personality scale. Yes–no and similar response formats do not provide detailed data. The data for grounded theory analysis mostly consist of words, but this is typical of much data in psychology and related disciplines. As such, usually data are initially transcribed using a notation system such as Jefferson's (Chapter 19). Some lessons from grounded theory could be useful to all sorts of researchers. In particular, the need for richness of data, knowing one's data intimately and developing theory closely in line with the data would benefit a great deal of research.

20.4 How to do grounded theory analysis

Potter (1998) likens grounded theory to a sophisticated filing system. This filing system does not merely put things under headings but there is cross-referencing to a range of other categories. It is a bit like a library book that may be classified as a biography, but it may also be a political book. Keep this analogy in mind as otherwise the temptation is to believe that the data are only filed under one category in grounded theory analysis. There seems to be a general acceptance that grounded theory analysis has a number of key components. These are outlined below.

Comparison

Crucially, grounded theory development involves constant comparisons at all stages of the data collection and analysis process – without comparing categories with each other and with the data, categories cannot evolve and become more refined:

- People may be compared in terms of what they have said or done or how they have accounted for their actions or events, for example.
- Comparisons are made of what a person does or says in one context with what they do and say in another context.
- Comparisons are made of what someone has said or done at a particular time with a similar situation at a different time.
- Comparisons of the data with the category which the researcher suggests may account for the data.
- Comparisons are made of categories used in the analysis with other categories used in the analysis.

So, for example, it is a common criticism of quantitative research that the researcher forces observations into ill-fitting categories for the purpose of analysis; in grounded theory the categories are changed and adjusted to fit the data better. This is often referred to as the method of *constant comparisons*. Much of the following is based on Charmaz's (1995, 2000) recommendations about how to proceed.

Coding/naming

Grounded theory principles require that the researcher repeatedly examines the data closely. The lines of data will be numbered at some stage to aid comparison and reference. In the initial stage of the analysis, the day-to-day work involves coding or describing the data line-by-line. It is as straightforward as that – and as difficult. (Actually, there is no requirement that a line be the unit of analysis and a researcher may choose to operate at the level of the sentence or the paragraph, for example.) The line is examined and a description (it could be more than one) is provided by the researcher to describe what is happening in that line or what is 'represented' by that line. In other words, a name is being given to each line of data. These names or codings should be generated out of what is in that particular line of data. In many ways, describing this as coding is a little misleading, because it implies a pre-existing system which is not the case. Others describe the process in slightly different terms. For example, Potter (1997) describes the process as being one of giving labels to the key concepts that appear in the line or paragraph.

The point of the coding is that it keeps the researcher's feet firmly in the grounds of the data. Without coding, the researcher may be tempted to over-interpret the data by inappropriately attributing 'motives, fears or unresolved personal issues' (Charmaz, 1995, p. 37) to the participants. At the end of this stage, we are left with numerous codings or descriptions of the contents of many lines of text.

Categorisation

Quite clearly, the analyst has to try to organise these codings. Remember that codings are part of the analysis process and the first tentative steps in developing theory. These are the smallest formal units in the grounded theory analysis. While they may describe the data more-or-less well, by organising them we may increase the likelihood that we will be able to effectively revise them. This is a sort of reverse filtering process: we are starting with the smallest units of analysis and working back to the larger theoretical descriptions. So the next stage is to build the codings or namings of lines of data into categories. This is a basic strategy in many sorts of research. In quantitative research, there are statistical methods which are commonly used in categorising variables into groupings of variables (for example, factor analysis and cluster analysis). These statistical methods are not generally available to the grounded theorist, so the categorisation process relies on other methods. Once again, the process of constant comparison is crucial, of course. The analyst essentially has to compare as many of the codings with the other codings as possible. That is, is the coding for line 62 really the same as that for line 30 since both lines are described in very similar words? Is it possible to justify coding lines 88 and 109 in identical fashion since when these data lines are examined they appear to be very different?

The constant comparing goes beyond this. For example, does there seem to be a different pattern of codings for Mr X than for Mrs Y? That is, does the way that they talk about things seem to be different? We might not be surprised to find different patterns for Mr X and Mrs Y when we know that this is a couple attending relationship counselling or that one is the boss of a company and the other an employee. The data from a person at a particular point in time or in a particular context may be compared with data from the same person at a later point in time or in different contexts.

It need not stop there. Since the process is one of generating categories for the codings of the data which fit the data well and are coherent, one must also compare the categories with each other as they emerge or are developed. After all, it may become evident, for example, that two of the categories cannot be differentiated – or you may have given identical titles to categories which actually are radically different. The process of categorisation may be facilitated by putting the data or codings or both onto index cards which can be physically moved around on a desk or table in order to place similar items close together and dissimilar items further apart. In this way, relationships can begin to be identified in a more active visual way.

It is difficult to give a brief representative extract of grounded theory style codings. Table 20.1 reproduces a part of such codings from Charmaz (1995) which illustrates aspects of the process reasonably well. Take care though since Table 20.1 contains a very

Table 20.1   A modified extract of grounded theory coding based on Charmaz (1995, p. 39)

Interview transcript	Coding by researcher
If you have lupus, I mean one day it's my liver	Shifting symptoms
One day it's in my joints; one day it's in my head, and	Inconsistent days
It's like people really think you're a hypochondriac if you keep	Interpreting images of self
. . . It's like you don't want to say anything because people are going to start thinking	Avoiding disclosure

Source: Charmaz (1995)

short extract from just one out of nearly two hundred interviews conducted by her. It can be seen that the codings/categories are fairly close to the data in this example. It should be noted that her's are not the only codings which would work with the data.

Memo writing

None of the stages in grounded theory analysis are as distinct as they first appear. The process of analysis is not sequential, although explaining grounded theory analysis makes it appear so. It is a back-and-forward process. Memo writing describes the aspect of the research in which the data are explored rather than described and categorised. The memo may be just as one imagines – a notebook – in which the researcher notes suggestions as to how the categories may be linked together in the sense that they have relationships and interdependencies. But the memo does not have to be a purely textual thing. A diagram – perhaps a flow diagram – could be used in which the key concepts are placed in boxes and the links between them identified by annotated arrows. What do we mean by relationships and interdependencies? Imagine the case of male and female. They are conceptually distinct categories but they have interdependencies and relationships. One cannot understand the concept of male without the concept of female.

The memo should not be totally separated from the data. Within the memo one should include the most crucial and significant examples from the data which are indicative and typical of the more general examples. So the memo should be replete with illustrative instances as well as potentially ill-fitting or problematic instances of ideas, conceptualisations and relationships that are under development as part of the eventual grounded theory:

If you are at a loss about what to write about, look for the codes that you have used repeatedly in your data collection. Then start elaborating on these codes. Keep collecting data, keep coding and keep refining your ideas through writing more and further developed memos.

[Charmaz, 1995, p. 43]

In a sense, this advice should not be necessary with grounded theory since the processes of data collection, coding and categorisation of the codes are designed to make the researcher so familiar with their data that it is very obvious what the frequently occurring codings are. However, it is inevitable that those unaccustomed to qualitative analysis will have writing and thinking blocks much the same as a quantitative researcher may have problems writing questionnaire items or formulating hypotheses.

Sometimes the memo is regarded as an intermediary step between the data and the final written report. Though, as ever in grounded theory, in practice the distinction between the different stages is not rigid. Often the advice is to start memo writing just as soon as anything strikes one as interesting in the data, the coding or categorisation. The sooner the better would seem to be the general consensus. This is very different from the approach taken by quantitative researchers. Also bear in mind that the process of theory development in grounded theory is not conventional in that the use of a small number of parsimonious concepts is not a major aim. (This is essentially Occam's razor which is the logical principle that no more than the minimum number of concepts or assumptions are necessary. This is also referred to as the principle of parsimony.) Strauss and Corbin (1999) write of conceptual density which they describe as a richness of concept development and relationship identification. This is clearly intended to be very different from reducing the analysis to the very minimum number of concepts as is characteristic of much quantitative research.

Theoretical sampling

Theoretical sampling is about how to validate the ideas developed within the memo. If the ideas in the memo have validity then they should apply to some samples of data but not to others. The task of the researcher is partly to suggest which samples the categories apply to and which they should not apply to. This will help the researcher identify new sources of data which may be used to validate the analysis to that point. As a consequence of the analysis of such additional data, subsequent memo writing may be more closely grounded in the data which it is intended to explain.

Literature review

In conventional methodological terms, the literature review is largely carried out in advance of planning the detailed research. That is, the new research builds on the accumulated previous knowledge. In grounded theory, the literature review should be carried out after the memo writing process is over – signed, sealed and delivered. In this way, the grounded theory has its origins in the data collected *not* the previous research and theoretical studies. So why bother with the literature review? The best answer is that the literature review should be seen as part of the process of assessing the adequacy of the grounded theory analysis. If the new analysis fails to deal adequately with the older research then a reformulation may be necessary. On the other hand, it is feasible that the new analysis helps integrate past grounded theory analyses. In some respects this can be regarded as an extension of the grounded theory to other domains of applicability.

That is what some grounded theorists claim. Strauss and Corbin (1999) add that the grounded theory methodology may begin in existing grounded theory so long as they 'seem appropriate to the area of investigation' and then these grounded theories 'may be elaborated and modified as incoming data are meticulously played against them' (pp. 72–3).

20.5 Computer grounded theory analysis

A number of commercially available grounded theory analysis programs are available. Generically they are known as CAQDAS (Computer Assisted Qualitative Data Analysis software). NUD*IST was the market leader but it has been replaced by NVivo, which is very similar, and there are others. These programs may help with the following aspects of a grounded theory analysis:

■ There is a lot of paper work with grounded theory analysis. Line-numbered transcripts are produced, coding categories are developed, and there is much cutting and pasting of parts of the analysis in order to finely tune the categories to the data. There is almost inevitably a large amount of textual material to deal with – a single focus group, for example, might generate ten or twenty transcribed pages. Computers, as everyone knows, are excellent for cutting down on paper when drafting and shifting text around. That is, the computer may act as a sort of electronic office for grounded analyses.

■ One key method in grounded theory is searching for linkages between different aspects of the data. A computer program is eminently suitable for making, maintaining and changing linkages between parts of a document and between different documents.

■ Coding categories are developed but frequently need regular change, refinement and redefinition in order for them to fit the data better and further data that may be introduced perhaps to test the categories. Using computer programs, it is possible to recode the data more quickly, combine categories and the like.

Box 20.1 discusses computer-based support for grounded theory analysis.

Box 20.1 PRACTICAL ADVICE

Computers and qualitative data analysis: Computer Assisted Qualitative Analysis Software (CAQDAS)

Using computer programs for the analysis of qualitative data is something of a mixed blessing for students new to this form of analysis. The major drawback is the investment of time needed to learn the software. This is made more of a problem because no qualitative analysis program does all of the tasks that a qualitative analyst might require. Thus it is not like doing a quantitative analysis on a computer program such as SPSS where you can do something useful with just a few minutes of training or just by following a text. Furthermore, qualitative analysis software is much more of a tool to help the researcher whereas SPSS, certainly for simple analyses, does virtually all of the analysis. So think carefully before seeking computer programs to help with your qualitative analysis, especially if time is short as it usually is for student projects. There is little or nothing that can as yet be done by computers which cannot be done by a researcher using more mundane resources such as scissors, glue, index cards and the like. The only major drawback to such basic methods is that they become unwieldy with very substantial amounts of data. In these circumstances, a computer may be a major boon in that it keeps everything neat and tidy and much more readily accessible on future occasions.

There are two main stages for which computer programs may prove helpful: data entry and data analysis.

1. *Data entry* All students will have some word processing skills which may prove helpful for a qualitative analysis. The first major task after data has been collected is to transcribe it. This is probably best done by a word processing program such

→

Box 20.1 continued

as Microsoft's Word which is by far the most commonly used of all such programs. Not only is such a program the best way of getting a legible transcript of the data but it is also useful as a resource of text to be used in illustrating aspects of the analysis in the final research report. Word processing programs can be used for different sorts of transcription including Jefferson transcription (see Chapter 19) which utilises keyboard symbols universally available. Of course, the other big advantage of word processing programs is that they allow for easy text manipulation. For example, one can usually search for (find) strings of text quickly. More importantly, perhaps, one can copy-and-paste any amount of text into new locations or folders. In other words, key bits of text can be brought together to aid the analysis process simply by having the key aspects of the text next to each other.

Computers can aid data entry in another way. If the data to be entered is already in text form (e.g. magazine articles or newspaper reports) then it may be possible to scan the text directly into the computer using programs such as TextBridge. Alternatively, some may find it helpful to use voice recognition software to dictate such text into a computer as an alternative to typing. Of course, such programs are still error prone but then so is transcribing words from tape by hand. All transcripts require checking for accuracy no matter how they are produced.

In the case of discourse analysis or conversation analysis (see Chapters 22 and 23) features of the data such as pauses, voice inflections and so forth need to be recorded. So editing software such as CoolEdit (now known as Adobe Audition) are useful for these specialised transcription purposes. This program, for example, has the big advantage that it shows features of the sound in a sort of continuous graphical form which allows for the careful measurement of times of silences and so forth. There is a free-to-download computer program which helps one transcribe sound files. It is known as SoundScriber and can be obtained at http://www.lsa.umich.edu/eli/micase/soundscriber.html.

The downside is that by saving the researcher time the computer program reduces their familiarity with their data. This undermines one of the main strategies of qualitative analysis which is to encourage the researcher to repeatedly work through the analysis in ways which encourage greater familiarity.

2. *Data analysis* There are many different forms of analysis of qualitative data so no single program is available to cope with all of these. For example, some analyses simply involve counts of how frequently particular words or phrases (or types of words or phrases) occur in the data or how commonly they occur in close physical proximity. Such an analysis is not typical of what is done in psychology and, of course, it is really a type of quantitative analysis of qualitative data rather than a qualitative data analysis as such. The most common forms of qualitative analysis tend to involve the researcher labelling the textual data in some way (coding) and then linking the codings together to form broader categories which constitute the bedrock of the analysis.

The most famous of the computer programs helping the researcher handle grounded theory analyses is NUD*IST which was developed in the 1980s and NVivo which was developed a decade or so later but is closely related to NUD*IST. The researcher

Box 20.1 continued

transcribes their data (usually these will be interviews) and enters the transcription into one of these programs usually using RTF (Rich Text Format) files which Word can produce. The programs then allow you to take the text and code or label small pieces of it. Once this is complete the codes or labels can be grouped into categories (analogous to themes in Thematic analysis – Chapter 21). The software company which owns NVivo suggests that it is useful for researchers to deal with rich-text-data at a deep level of analysis. They identify some of the qualitative methods discussed in this book as being aided by NVivo such as grounded theory, conversation analysis, discourse analysis and phenomenology. The software package is available in a student version at a moderate price but you may find that a trial-download is sufficient for your purposes. This was available at the following address at the time of writing: http://www.qsrinternational.com/products/productoverview/product_overview.htm.

The system allows the user to go through the data coding the material a small amount at a time (the unit of analysis can be flexible) or one can develop some coding categories in a structured form before beginning to apply them to the data. In NVivo there is the concept of *nodes* which it defines as 'places where you store ideas and categories'. There are two important types of nodes in the program which are worth mentioning here:

1. *Free nodes*   These can most simply be seen as codings or brief verbal descriptions or distillations of a chunk of text. These are probably best used at the start of the analysis before the researcher has developed clear ideas about the data and the way the analysis is going.

2. *Tree nodes*   These are much more organised than the free nodes (and may be the consequence of joining together free nodes). They are in the form of a hierarchy with the parent node leading to the children nodes which may lead to the grand-children nodes. The hierarchy is given a numerical sequence such as 4 2 3 where the parent node is here given the address 4, one of the child nodes is given the address 2 and where the grandchild is given the address 3. Thus 4 2 3 uniquely identifies a particular location within the tree node. So, for example, a researcher may have as the parent node *problems at work*, one of the child nodes may be *interpersonal relationships* (another child node might be *redundancy*, for example), and one of the grandchild nodes might be *sexual harassment*.

These nodes are not fixed until the researcher is finally satisfied but can be changed, merged together or even removed should the researcher see fit. This is the typical process of checking and reviewing that makes qualitative research both flexible and time consuming.

NVivo has other useful features such as a 'modeller' which allows the researcher to link the ideas/concepts developed in the analysis together using connectors which the researcher labels. There is also a search tool which allows the researcher to isolate text with particular contents or which has been coded in a particular way.

An alternative to NUD*IST/NVivo is to use CDC EZ-Text which is free-to-download at http://www.cdc.gov/hiv/SOFTWARE/ez-text.htm if you want to access a qualitative analysis program without the expense of the commercial alternatives. EZ-Text is available for researchers to create and manage databases for semi-structured qualitative

Box 20.1 continued

interviews and then analyse the data. The user acts interactively with the computer during the process of developing a list of codes to be applied to the data (i.e. create a code-book) which can then be used to give specific codes to passages in the material. The researcher can also search the data for passages which meet the researcher's own pre-set requirements. In many respects, this is similar to NVivo.

There is no quick fix for learning any of these systems. There are training courses for NVivo, for example, lasting several days which suggests that the systems cannot be mastered quickly.

Example of a NVivo/NUD*IST analysis

Pitcher and her colleagues (2006) studied sex work by using focus group methodology (see Chapter 18) in which residents in a particular area talked together under the super-vision of a facilitator. NUD*IST was used to analyse the data originally. In order to demonstrate NVivo, we have taken a small section of their data and re-analysed it. This is shown in the screenshot (Figure 20.1). Of course, different researchers with different purposes may analyse the same qualitative data very differently. We have done the most basic coding by entering free nodes for the interview passage. This will give you some idea of how complex even this initial coding can be with NVivo – notice the pane

Figure 20.1   A screenshot of NVivo coding (from QSR International Pty Ltd)

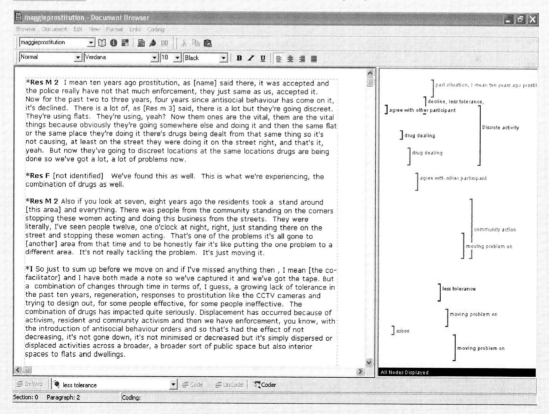

Box 20.1 continued

at the side of the screenshot where the sections coded are identified between horizontal square brackets. Also, notice how the sections coded can overlap. It is possible to give several distinct codings or free nodes to the same selection of text. Basically, the researcher highlights a section of text, chooses an existing coding for that section or adds a new coding by typing in the lower box, and then selects the code. Of course, this is just the start since the researcher may wish to revise the codings, put the codings (free nodes) into a tree node structure, identify all of the text with a particular coding and so forth.

We are grateful to Maggie O'Neil and Jane Pitcher for help with this box.

20.6 Evaluation of grounded theory

Potter (1998) points out that central to its virtues is that grounded theory:

> *. . . encourages a slow-motion reading of texts and transcripts that should avoid the common qualitative research trap of trawling a set of transcripts for quotes to illustrate preconceived ideas.*

[p. 127]

This is probably as much a weakness as a strength since the size of the task may well defeat the resources of novices and others. Certainly it is not always possible to be convinced that preconceived ideas do not dominate the analysis rather than the data leading the analysis.

There are a number of criticisms which seem to apply to grounded theory:

■ It encourages a pointless collection of data, that is, virtually anything textual or spoken could be subject to a grounded theory analysis. There are no clear criteria for deciding, in advance, what topics to research on the basis of their theoretical or practical relevance. Indeed, the procedures tend to encourage the delay of theoretical and other considerations until after the research has been initiated.

■ Potter (1998) suggests that 'The method is at its best where there is an issue that is tractable from a relatively common sense actor's perspective . . . the theoretical notions developed are close to the everyday notions of the participants' (p. 127). This means that commonsensical explanations are at a premium – explanations which go beyond common sense may be squeezed out. Potter puts it another way elsewhere '. . . how far is the grounding derived not from theorizing but from reproducing common sense theories as if they were analytic conclusions?' (Potter, 1998, p. 127). This may be fair criticism. The difficulty is that it applies to any form of research which gives voice to its participants. Ultimately, this tendency means that grounded theory may simply codify how ordinary people ordinarily understand the activities in which they engage.

■ There is a risk that grounded theory, which is generally founded on admirable ideals, is used to excuse inadequate qualitative analyses. It is a matter of faith that grounded theory will generate anything of significant value, yet at the same time, done properly, a grounded theory analysis may have involved a great deal of labour. Consequently, it is hard to put aside a research endeavour which may have generated little but cost a lot of time and effort. There are similar risks that grounded theory methods will be employed simply because the researcher has failed to focus on appropriate research questions so leaving them with few available analysis options. These risks are particularly high for student work.

■ Since talk and text are analysed line by line (and these are arbitrarily divided – they are not sentences, for example) then the researcher may be encouraged to focus on small units rather than the larger units of conversation as, for example, favoured by discourse analysts (Potter, 1998). Nevertheless, grounded theory is often mentioned by such analysts as part of their strategy or orientation.

So it is likely that grounded theory works best when dealing with issues that are amenable to common sense insights from participants. Medical illness and interpersonal relationships are such topics where the theoretical ideas that grounded theory may develop are close to the ways in which the participants think about these issues. This may enhance the practicality of grounded theory in terms of policy implementation. The categories used and the theoretical contribution are likely to be in terms which are relatively easy for the practitioner or policymaker to access.

20.7 Conclusion

Especially pertinent to psychologists is the question of whether grounded theory is really a sort of Trojan horse which has been cunningly brought into psychology, but is really the enemy of advancement in psychology. Particularly troubling is the following from Strauss and Corbin (1999):

> . . . *grounded theory researchers are interested in patterns of action and interaction between and among various types of social units (i.e., 'actors'). So they are not especially interested in creating theory about individual actors as such (unless perhaps they are psychologists or psychiatrists).*

[p. 81]

Researchers like Strauss and Corbin are actually willing to allow a place for quantitative data in grounded theory. So the question may be one of how closely psychological concepts could ever fit with grounded theory analysis which is much more about the social (interactive) than the psychological.

Key points

■ Grounded theory is an approach to analysing (usually textual) data designed to maximise the fit of emerging theory (categories) to the data and additional data of relevance.

■ The aim is to produce 'middle range' theories which are closely fitting qualitative descriptions (categories) rather than, say, cause-and-effect or predictive theories.

▓ Grounded theory is 'inductive' (that is, does not deduce outcomes from theoretical postulates). It is systematic in that an analysis of some sort will almost result from adopting the system. It is a continuous process of development of ideas – it does not depend on a critical test as in the case of classic psychological theory.

▓ Comparison is the key to the approach – all elements of the research and the analysis are constantly compared and contrasted.

▓ Coding (or naming or describing) is the process by which lines of the data are given a short description (or descriptions) to identify the nature of their content.

▓ Categorisation is the process by which the codings are amalgamated into categories. The process helps find categories which fit the codings in their entirety, not simply a few pragmatic ideas which only partially represent the codings.

▓ Memo writing is the process by which the researcher records their ideas about the analysis throughout the research process. The memo may include ideas about categorisation but it may extend to embrace the main themes of the final report.

▓ Computer programs are available which help the researcher organise the materials for the analysis and effectively alter the codings and categories.

▓ A grounded theory analysis may be extended to further critical samples of data which should be pertinent to the categories developed in the analysis. This is known as theoretical sampling.

▓ The theoretical product of grounded theory analysis is not intended to be the same as conventional psychological theorisation and so should not be judged on those terms.

Activity

Grounded theory involves the bringing of elements together to try to forge categories which unite them. So choose a favourite poem, song or any textual material, and write each sentence on a separate sheet of paper. Choose two at random. What unites these two sentences? Then choose another sentence. Can this be united with the previous two sentences? Continue the exercise until you cease coming up with new ideas. Then start again.

3

Reliability, validity, sampling and groups

- This chapter begins by explaining the concepts of reliability and validity.
- It then covers sampling, sampling bias and methods of sampling.
- Finally, this chapter will introduce you to the use of control and placebo groups in experimental research.

INTRODUCTION

As you saw in the previous chapter, psychological research requires us to be very precise in the ways we measure variables. Without precision we cannot guarantee the quality of the findings we produce. This chapter introduces you to some more technical issues in research. Two concepts that are central to any understanding of whether our findings are of worth or not are **reliability** and **validity**. These two watchwords are first introduced in this chapter, but covered in greater depth in Chapter 5 because they are central to the topic of questionnaire design. This chapter then covers the important, but sadly often neglected, topic of **replication**. We then move on to look at how we select participants for our studies, that is, how we **sample**. Finally, in this chapter we look at the benefits that can be gained through the use of **control** and **placebo groups**.

3.1   Reliability

Reliability concerns the stability of what we are measuring. That is, do we get the same result from our test (or study) on more than one occasion or was the result a freak instance (and therefore fairly meaningless if we are trying to say something general about human nature)? We want our results to be rigorous and this can be partly achieved through us gathering data that are reliable. So, for example, imagine we wish to produce a test of attitudes towards animal welfare. We give this test to our 'guinea pig', John, and he scores high (positive) on attitudes towards animal welfare. We then give John the same test on another occasion (several weeks later) and find he scores very low (negative) on attitudes towards animal welfare. So, what happened here? Well, very simply, our test is probably not reliable. We have tested it with the same person (so a comparable situation) on two occasions (this is a way of measuring **test–retest reliability**, which is discussed in Chapter 5) and found the test produced different results. This is not good enough if we are trying to produce a rigorous test of attitudes towards animal welfare. We want our measures to be reliable and provide similar results on different but comparable occasions.

3.2 Validity

Validity is another key element that should concern us when we are trying to carry out rigorous research. In short, validity is about whether a test (or measure of any kind) is really measuring the thing we intended it to measure. In chemistry or physics it is often the case that the item being measured exists in the world in a simple physical way (even if we need very sophisticated devices to see or measure it). However, psychological phenomena are not like these physical phenomena. Psychologists *assume* that people have 'attitudes' or 'personality traits' on the basis of our theories and evidence from studies of the way people behave in the world. However, we cannot ever really know if we are *really* measuring an attitude or personality trait in the same way as we know we are measuring wind speed or an electrical current since we cannot gather direct physical evidence for attitudes or personality traits.[1] In spite of this obvious limitation, psychologists have attempted to develop measures of psychological phenomena that are as valid as possible. Like reliability, there are several forms of validity that we should take into account when developing or testing measures of psychological phenomena. All types of validity have limitations, of course, and should be considered as ways of *increasing*, not proving, the *validity* of our measures. No measure is perfect, and there are no guarantees. These

---

[1] We will discuss this much more in Part 3 on qualitative approaches to data analysis. However, many qualitative approaches are not modelled on the natural sciences at all for the simple reason that (they argue) people's psychology is not like molecules or atoms in that it is not a measurable object extended in the world that is perpetually unchanging. Instead researchers from these perspectives argue that we can know about people (and their psychology) only in interactions between people or through language as that is the only information about our psychology that is publicly available to us all. We can never 'go inside' people's heads to find an attitude or personality trait (we could, of course, go inside to find some neurochemical pathways or anatomical structure). The other major factor that makes some researchers question an approach based on the natural sciences concerns human agency (the capacity, that we appear to have at least, to act in the world). Molecules and atoms do not make decisions and do not therefore have the potential to be different when placed in identical situations: human beings do and are often contradictory. We only need to observe other people to see this element of human nature in action.

issues are discussed in more detail in Chapter 5, in relation to questionnaires and psychometric tests. One type of validity is worth mentioning here, because it is relevant to psychological studies in general: ecological validity.

Ecological validity

Ecological validity is being increasingly examined in psychological studies. This is because a great deal of psychological research has been modelled on the natural sciences and therefore conducted in laboratories. Psychologists carry out rigorous studies in laboratories in an attempt to minimise the effect of extraneous variables. The worry with this approach is that these studies may lack ecological validity. That is, we may question whether the results gathered in a laboratory about some psychological phenomenon will generalise to other settings or places. Would our participants behave in the same way outside the laboratory as they do when subjected to a study within a laboratory setting? There is increasing concern that many of the findings produced through laboratory studies may lack ecological validity and therefore not reflect the natural behaviour of human beings at all. So, for instance, Asch's study of conformity, which we referred to in Chapter 1, was a laboratory-based study, which may have some limitations on account of its ecological validity. The participants were all strangers and were not given the opportunity to discuss their thoughts about the line lengths with each other. How often are you in a situation like that? We may seek to replicate Asch's study among an established group (such as friends in a lecture theatre) and allow people the possibility of discussion in an attempt to improve the ecological validity. What effect do you think this would have on the findings of the study? However, while many laboratory studies do suffer problems on account of a lack of ecological validity, it is important to be both realistic and thoughtful about the implications of this problem for research from this perspective. It is all too easy to criticise laboratory studies in this way but we do not think that this means all findings from laboratory-based research are just plain wrong! We have gained (and will continue to gain) considerable knowledge about human nature from laboratory-based research in spite of the limitations to this kind of work. All research in the social sciences suffers from some problems. What we need, if we wish to be good, effective and rigorous psychologists, is an awareness of these limitations and knowledge of how best to minimise their effects.

3.3 The role of replication in the social sciences

Replication is an important aspect of a traditional scientific approach to research in the social sciences. It is, however, often neglected because of the demand to produce new and novel findings. However, replication is important and worthy of attention. In order to establish the reliability and validity of research findings we need to be able to repeat a study exactly and find the same results as the original researcher. This is why you are instructed to produce research reports in a particular format (with all that detail). Other researchers need to be able to read a research report and carry out the same study themselves (that is, replicate it). As well as establishing whether findings are reliable and, to some extent, valid, replication also protects the discipline against fake (or fraudulent) findings. While this is uncommon, there are some notorious cases of psychologists inventing their results!

3.4   Populations and samples

Within a traditional scientific approach to psychology we often wish to generalise findings from a **sample** of people (a smaller subset) to the **population** from which they came. It is obviously impractical (if not impossible) in many cases to carry out research on every person within a particular population. We therefore need to be able to select a smaller number of participants for our research who are representative of the population as a whole. So, if we wish to carry out research on the phenomenon of the 'white van man' we cannot send a questionnaire (or interview) to every man who drives a white van in the United Kingdom (let alone every man who drives a white van in the rest of the world). What we need to do is select a smaller number of men who drive white vans as our sample. If our sample is a good one we would expect it to be representative of the population as a whole (all 'white van men'). The findings from our study of 'white van men' should tell us something about the whole population of 'white van men'. This is not as easy as it seems for we are always at risk of generating biased (or inaccurate) findings if our sample is not truly representative.

3.5   The problem of sampling bias

As mentioned above, we need our sample to be representative of the population from which it was drawn. If we studied only student samples in psychology we might well end up believing that most people stay up late, enjoy drinking and study hard. We need to be aware of the possibility of sampling bias when choosing who we are going to select from our population to study in our research. A great deal of research in the social sciences has been conducted with **convenience** samples (more on these below) which often comprise students. People who volunteer for social science research (and students in particular) have been found, in many ways, to be unrepresentative of the wider population. This is clearly a worry if we attempt to generalise our findings beyond our sample to the population. The principal way of minimising sampling bias is to employ one of the many sampling strategies recognised in the social sciences.

The first thing that is needed for all sampling to be effective is to clearly define the population of interest. All key variables that are used to define and mark the population of interest must be known and clearly defined. Once the population is clearly defined we then use an appropriate sampling strategy to draw our sample participants from the population of interest. Most of the strategies below (with the notable exception of convenience sampling) are ideals which are very difficult (if not impossible in some cases) to achieve in day-to-day real world research.

Random

This is generally considered to be the 'gold standard' for sampling. With **random sampling** each member of the population being studied has an equal chance of being selected for the sample. Furthermore, the selection of each participant from the population is independent of the selection of any other participant. There are a number of different methods for carrying out random sampling but it often involves potential participants being given a number (1 to N, where N is the total number of participants in the population). Then random number tables (or some other method of random number generation – e.g. through a calculator or computer) are used to generate numbers between 1 and N and those numbers selected become our sample participants. Random sampling is a particularly effective and unbiased method of sampling but, like all methods, cannot completely eliminate the sampling error that always occurs when we take a sample from a population (more of this in Chapter 6). Furthermore, random sampling is often an impossible ideal when we do not have access to the total population of interest.

Systematic

Systematic sampling is often used as a substitute for random sampling whereby we draw the sample from the population at fixed intervals from the list. So, if we had a list of addresses from the electoral roll for Sheffield we might decide to select every tenth address to make up our sample (which will receive our questionnaire). This approach is much simpler and easier to achieve than true random sampling. The main disadvantage of this approach is that there may exist some periodic function of our sample. If we decided to select the first ten members of a class of schoolchildren from a range of schools we might find that boys' names are always listed first. If this were the case our sample would probably consist of boys. Similarly, if we selected the first people to respond to a request for help with our research we might be selecting people who demonstrate particularly high levels of sociability or compliance. We must be careful with this approach to sampling that we do not accidentally introduce bias into our study (and it is easily done, for it is difficult to think of every possible factor that may influence our findings in advance of carrying out a study).

Stratified

Stratified sampling may be random or systematic and introduces an extra element into the process of sampling by ensuring that groups (or strata) within the population are each sampled randomly or to a particular level. We might, for instance, wish to carry out a survey of all first year students at the University of Imaginarytown about attitudes to a new university-wide compulsory course in IT and study skills. We cannot afford (in terms of time or money) to send a questionnaire to all first year students so we decide to randomly sample from the population (to a total of 10 per cent). However, we realise that simple random sampling may result in biased findings if, for instance, more students respond from the faculties of arts and humanities than from the faculties of science and engineering. This is where we might choose to use random stratified sampling. With this sampling technique we randomly sample from each faculty in the university until we have a final sample that reflects the proportions of students that we have in each faculty in the university. So, for instance, if we have 1000 students in the faculty of science and 500 in engineering we would want (if we were sampling 10 per cent of all university students) to randomly sample 100 students from the science faculty and 50 from the engineering faculty. This would mean that our final sample would be randomly generated in proportion to the number of students in each university faculty. Of course, university faculty is just one example of how we might stratify a sample. We might choose to stratify according to sex or age, social class and so on (the list is endless).

Cluster

There are times when we may wish to sample entire groups of people rather than individuals for our research. One common example of this is when psychologists carry out research in educational settings (especially schools). It is often most appropriate to sample entire classes from schools (for a variety of practical and ethical reasons). Sampling of natural groups (such as classes of students or schoolchildren) rather than individuals is called **cluster sampling**. Like the previous methods of sampling, care needs to be taken when sampling clusters to make sure those clusters are representative of the population. At the simplest level a researcher may just sample one cluster (a class of schoolchildren from one school). Here there is considerable danger in generalising from one's results to other classes and schools in the area and beyond. At the other extreme a researcher may randomly sample classes across age ranges and stratified by geographical region from the entire population of schools in the United Kingdom.

Stage

Stage sampling entails breaking down the sampling process into a number of stages. So, for instance, we may (in stage one) randomly sample a number of classes of children from schools in the United Kingdom. Then (in stage two) we may randomly sample a number of children from those classes that we have sampled. This approach would be called multi-stage cluster sampling (and you could even throw in a 'random' there if you liked and have 'multi-stage random cluster sampling'). Multi-stage designs are often particularly useful in very large studies. It is often (practically) impossible to randomly sample individuals from very large populations (for instance, all children from all schools in the United Kingdom). But if we wish to have a large sample that is representative of a very large population (such as all children in school in the United Kingdom) then multi-stage sampling may be the answer. So, for instance, if we wish to generate a sample of children that is representative of all children in school in the United Kingdom (a very ambitious thing to do!) we could begin by getting lists of all schools in the United Kingdom. We could then randomly sample from this list of schools (stage one), taking care to stratify our sample appropriately (e.g. by geographical region). Then we could contact those schools and get lists of all classes and randomly sample from those class lists (stage two) – again using appropriate stratification techniques. And finally in stage three we could get lists of children who belong to those classes and randomly sample from them. This would provide us with a random sample that (to a certain extent at least) would be representative of the total population of schoolchildren in the United Kingdom. We should point out that this particular example is not terribly realistic (as various aspects of the research process would intervene along the way to make things much more difficult and messy). Furthermore, this grand random multi-stage sampling strategy would be enormously expensive in terms of both time and resources.

Opportunity (or convenience)

This is, unfortunately, one of the commonest sampling strategies used by researchers in the social sciences today. Very simply, it entails us recruiting participants in any way possible (or convenient). So, we may recruit students in lecture theatres or people from the office block across the road. We may advertise and take all those that volunteer. This approach is clearly not ideal as we have little idea about whether our sample is representative of the population of interest to us in our research. However, **opportunity** sampling may be the only approach possible in some circumstances and we may have to tolerate the potential biases that ensue from this strategy. A lot of research in the social sciences is poorly funded (if funded at all) and conducted under extreme time pressure and may therefore necessitate a simple recruitment strategy. We might only have the resources available to recruit students in lecture theatres to our research. This may still be acceptable if we believe this strategy will introduce minimal (or irrelevant) bias to our findings. What we need to do if we use this approach is be sceptical of our findings and keep a careful watch on whether they seem to be valid and reliable.

Snowball

Snowball sampling is a very common sampling strategy that is often no more than convenience sampling under another name. However, there are times when snowball sampling is an appropriate (sometimes necessary) and strategic form of sampling. With this sampling technique the researcher will make contact with a small number of potential participants whom they wish to recruit to the research study. They will then use these initial contacts to recruit further participants (by recruiting friends and then friends of friends until the sample is sufficiently large). This strategy may be the most appropriate sampling strategy with some research studies. For instance, if you wish to study street gangs or drug users, access to these populations will be particularly difficult unless you are already a member of the group, and it is highly unlikely that you will be able to recruit many participants using the usual sampling strategies. However, if you can establish contact with just one or two gang members (or drug users) you can then use snowball sampling to recruit a sufficiently large sample. You would ask your initial participant to recruit fellow gang members (or drug users) to the study on your behalf. You can then ask this second set of participants to recruit some of their friends and so on until you have a large enough sample for your study.

The obvious problem with snowball sampling is that members of the sample are unlikely to be representative of the population. However, this depends on what we consider the population in our study. If we are interested only in the experience of a particular gang or members within this gang then it may be appropriate to recruit using a snowball strategy. This is more often the case with qualitative research concerned with understanding the experience of a (often small) number of people.

3.7   Sample sizes

So, the sixty-four million dollar question – does size really matter? Well, in general yes, the larger the sample size the better. This is simply because larger samples have less sampling error (we will return to sampling error in Part 2 – for now, take it on trust that the larger the sample size, the greater the precision of the sample in representing the population from which it was drawn). However, with all research there is a trade-off between size of sample and time and cost. With small sample sizes (50, 100, 150) precision increases significantly as the sample size increases and it is worth making every attempt to recruit as many participants as practically possible. However, once a sample gets above 1000 or so then there is less to be gained from significant increases in size. Sample error (and therefore precision) will continue to increase above 1000 but at a less rapid rate than below this figure. It is also important to remember that it is *absolute*, rather than *relative*, sample size that is important. Therefore, a national sample of 1000 children in the United Kingdom is as valid a sample as a national sample of 1000 children in the United States, despite the much larger population of children in the United States.

There are a number of additional factors that should be borne in mind when attempting to decide on the most appropriate sample size for your study. Firstly, it is important to consider the *kind of analysis* that will be conducted on your data, for this will have an impact on the size of sample needed. Students commonly forget to consider this factor in calculating their sample size and then run into problems when the time comes for them to analyse their data. Very simply, you need larger samples the larger the number of variables you plan to include in your study. This is sometimes referred to as the ratio of cases to IVs. There is no simple figure we can give you, for the ratio of cases to IVs will vary depending on which statistical technique you use to analyse your data. Various writers have provided formulae for calculating these ratios and the minimum sample size needed for different forms of analysis. This is beyond the scope of this text but worth checking out if you are carrying out your own research and need to know the minimum sample size for particular forms of statistical analysis (see the Further reading at the end of this chapter for more details).

Another factor that needs to be taken into consideration when calculating what sample size is needed is the likely response rate for the study. You will often see or hear mention of response rates in social survey research. In any research you will find people deciding not to respond to your request for them to participate. So, whether you send out 1000 unsolicited questionnaires or stand on a street corner asking every passer-by to come into the laboratory, a number of people will not complete the questionnaire or will refuse to take part in your experiment. It is important to know how many people have refused to take part, for a very high refusal rate may produce concerns about the **representativeness** of your sample. Are you recruiting only a particular type of person? How can you trust your findings if you do not have data on 90 per cent of those you sent the questionnaire to or asked to take part? We therefore try to maximise the response rate (the proportion of those contacted that agreed to take part). However, not everyone we contact may be suitable for our study or able to take part, so we tend to calculate the percentage response rate as follows:

$$\frac{\text{Number of questionnaires completed and returned (or people agreeing to take part)}}{\text{Number of questionnaires sent (or people approached)} - \text{unsuitable or uncontactable members of the sample}} \times 100$$

So, for instance, if we sent out 1000 questionnaires and had 100 returned correctly completed, 10 returned but not completed correctly and 10 returned because the addressee was not known then we have a response rate of $[100/(1000{-}10{-}10)] \times 100$, or 10.2 per cent. This is obviously a very low response rate but it is not uncommon to have low response rates (around 25 per cent) with unsolicited self-completion questionnaires sent by post. As well as trying to maximise our response rate (more on this in Chapter 5) we may need to try to predict the response rate if we wish to recruit a particular number of participants to our study. So, if we are sending out an unsolicited self-completion questionnaire and we need a sample size of 500 for our analysis, then, if we expect a return rate of 25 per cent, we need to distribute 2000 questionnaires.

The final factor that will be briefly mentioned here that may impact on the size of sample needed concerns the heterogeneity of the population from which we draw our sample. When a population is very heterogeneous, such as a national population of schoolchildren, then we are going to need a larger sample from this population than if the population is fairly homogeneous. Conversely, if our sample is very similar and demonstrates little variation (homogeneous across a number of characteristics of interest) then we will have less need to recruit a larger sample. It is also worth adding a note of caution about very large samples. Very large samples increase the likelihood of getting significant results (for a variety of statistical reasons). Good, you may think. Well, not necessarily, as the results may be significant but of no importance or practical consequence. This issue is discussed further in Chapter 11. So, while size does matter, it is not everything!

3.8   Control and placebo groups

In experimental (and some quasi-experimental) research we may need to recruit participants and assign them to one of two groups: **experimental** or **control**. We do this so that we can make comparisons between two (or more) groups of participants. The **experimental group** would be that which was given some intervention or programme (whether a new drug, education programme or psychological intervention) while the **control group** would be a matched (on appropriate characteristics, such as age, social class, etc.) group who did not receive the intervention. It is important to predict accurately which variables are likely to be important when matching participants. These variables are often demographic characteristics (such as age, sex, ethnicity and social class) but may also be psychological variables (such as attitudes or personality traits). When we sample for experimental research of this kind we often recruit matched pairs of participants so that we can then randomly allocate them to either the experimental or control groups.

A variation on the control group is the placebo group. We may employ a placebo group if we are worried about the possibility of a **placebo effect**. This is where a person (or group of people) responds to some stimulus as if it were having an expected effect when in fact it should have no effect at all. The classic example of this, which is tried and tested, is when we assign participants to two groups and give one group alcohol and another group (the placebo group) a liquid that we tell them is alcohol (but in fact contains no alcohol at all). What you find is that the placebo group who received a pretend alcoholic drink act as if they have consumed alcohol. So, we employ placebo groups in many situations (such as trials for new drugs) in order to minimise the expectation effects. We will address the issue of experimental and control groups further in Chapter 6.

Further reading

Robson, C. (2002). *Real World Research*, 2nd edn. Oxford: Blackwell.

Contains further information on reliability and validity and, most notably, sampling strategies not covered here that are rarely, but occasionally, used in the social sciences.

Tabachnik, B. G. & Fidell, L. S. (2006). *Using Multivariate Statistics*, 5th edn. New York: HarperCollins.

This is an advanced text! We do not recommend it at the introductory level of your studies. We have included it here because it contains useful information on how to calculate the minimum sample sizes for statistical tests.

3 Experimental research designs

Key Issues

Chapter 3 introduces what is often regarded as the cornerstone of psychological research, experimental design. The essential elements of true experimentation are discussed in detail, and comparisons are made with quasi and non-experimental designs. In particular we contrast the classic between-groups and repeated measures approaches, outlining the advantages and disadvantages of each. We also offer advice on the sometimes tricky procedures of counterbalancing. We end the chapter with an introduction to more complex designs involving many factors.

- experimentation
- between-groups designs
- within-subjects designs
- repetition effects and how to deal with them
- quasi-experimental design
- factorial designs
- randomised control designs
- mixed designs

3.1 Introduction to experimental research

In Part 1 the purpose of research was discussed in terms of describing, explaining and predicting something about the psychological world we live in. The methods available to us for doing this are many and varied and we discuss these in some detail in Part 3. However, whether or not the approach is survey, questionnaire-based, observation or interview, most of the methods used in our research will share a number of important elements and adhere to a common language of design. The exception here is qualitative research which, as we have previously stated, possesses certain unique characteristics requiring different treatment, and these issues are discussed in Part 6. However, for much of the work carried out by undergraduates – whether survey, observation or whatever – the general approach will be quantitative and usually experimental in nature.

By experimental we refer not so much to the rigid, laboratory-based work of the cognitive psychologist, but to the more general set of procedures (this does not of course exclude laboratory research) whereby individuals are manipulated into different groups, groups are compared on some factor and relationships among variables are explored. In most cases, as far as design elements and technical language are concerned, it does not matter whether we are using surveys, interviews or, indeed, experiments; the components of our research are the same: there will be independent variables and dependent variables, there will be causes and there will be effects, there will be predictors and there will be outcomes, there will be extraneous variables and there will be controls. In this respect it could be argued that most psychological research is, at the very least, quasi-experimental in nature, in that it follows a common set of rules. These rules, and the language associated with them, form the basis of this chapter.

3.2   Experimental design

In most (though not all) instances, the research process aims to explore whether or not a relationship exists between or among variables. Does changing the presentation rate of stimulus words affect the accuracy of recall, for instance; do the different genders express different attitudes in response to a persuasive communication; does performance on a problem-solving task vary with a measure of self-perceived ability? Specifically, the aim in all these examples is to demonstrate that the relationship between the independent and dependent variable is causal. To achieve this we adopt an experimental design.

We have already remarked that experimental design does not just mean laboratory research but rather refers to any type of study which incorporates a number of key characteristics. Chief among these are the measures taken to control for the possible effects of extraneous variables, factors which might obscure or interfere with the relationship between an independent and a dependent variable. The most important of these is the way in which participants are assigned to different groups, or experimental conditions.

The purpose of an experiment is to demonstrate that a particular experimental manipulation or intervention results in a predicted outcome. For example, we might set up a study to demonstrate that exposing participants to a list of subliminally embedded food objects in an otherwise innocuous visual presentation will result in high scores on a hunger index. However, this on its own is not enough to prove a causal link between the independent and the dependent variable, since there could be many explanations for high scores in this scenario. In order to argue a causal case with any conviction we are required to demonstrate that, not only does the presence of the experimental treatment (the embedded subliminal images) result in high scores on the response measure, but that its absence fails to produce the predicted behaviour. Only then can we claim to have demonstrated a cause-and-effect relationship. The basic experimental design therefore usually involves a comparison between two groups on some **outcome** measure – an experimental group in which a treatment or intervention is present, and a control group in which the treatment is absent. The expectation is that (if a cause-and-effect relationship really exists) an effect will be observed in the treatment condition and be absent in the non-treatment condition.

The presence or absence of an effect, while an essential requirement of experimental design, is only meaningful providing we can demonstrate that the effect was due to variation in the independent variable, and not some other extraneous factor. The obvious culprit in the scenario we are describing is the fact that we have two different groups in our study. Who is to say that a difference in some measure between the two groups is determined by the independent variable, as opposed to the fact that the groups possess different characteristics? We have different people in each group, after all, and participant differences remain one of the key confounding factors in any study. The solution is to strive for equivalence between the groups, and the procedures whereby this can be attained are discussed in the next section.

3.3 Between-groups designs (independent groups designs)

As we have seen, the most basic kind of research design involves two groups being compared on some outcome measure, with any observed differences between the groups evaluated for statistical significance (hence, a **between-groups design**). Typically, in the case of a conventional experiment, one group is exposed to some kind of experimental procedure (a treatment), and the second group is not, so as to serve as a comparison with the treatment group. This comparison group is then termed the **control group**, and the group receiving the treatment is termed the **experimental group**. The assumption is that, if both groups were equivalent prior to the experiment, yet demonstrated differences after the experiment, then the change must have been due to the experimental treatment.

There are three methods for ensuring equivalence in the between-groups design: matching, expanding the design and randomisation. Matching we discussed in Chapter 2, and while there are certain circumstances in which this will be an appropriate solution to the problem of different groups, it will be recalled that obtaining a perfect match between two groups of participants is almost impossible and places considerable demands on a participant pool (meaning that in order to eliminate or omit non-matches, numbers in the groups may become very small). In fact, the matching of participant characteristics across groups is rarely done and in the event that a particular variable is identified as a potential extraneous factor, the preference in these circumstances is often to expand the design to incorporate this factor as an additional independent variable. An example of this approach has been illustrated previously (see Box 2.4) and is further discussed in the section on factorial design.

The third technique for establishing equivalence, randomisation, is by far the most common in an experimental design, and usually the most preferred. The assumption is that, if we start with a population which is homogeneous (in which everyone is more or less the same as everyone else, in the most general terms) and randomly draw from it two samples, then on any measure we care to take we would expect both groups to be roughly similar. A requirement for this is that at the point of drawing from the population, each individual could be placed into either group, with an equal probability, and that this placement is random. What this does is create two groups which are clearly not identical (how could they be, with different members in each?) but which are probabilistically equivalent. It is this notion of probability which is important here, since if any individual could just as easily be in one group as in the other, then it follows that both groups must be (more or less) the same, or equivalent. Consequently it is assumed that if both groups were compared on some measure prior to any form of treatment or intervention, they would exhibit similar scores; if differences are evident after manipulation, we can reasonably assume that they are the result of the manipulation. It would of course be possible to actually take a measure from both groups as a **pre-test**, to assure ourselves of their initial similarity, and sometimes a design will require this, but it is not always necessary, since the randomisation process is seen as sufficient to ensure equivalence. Consequently, most designs of this type are termed **post-test**, since the only measure taken is after the experimental manipulation or treatment has occurred.

In design terminology this particular scenario is known as a **post-test randomised between-groups experimental design**. It forms the basis of much psychological research and because of the extent to which extraneous variables can be controlled – including unpredictable ones – any proposition of a causal relationship between independent and dependent variables is said to possess **internal validity**. Moreover, an experiment which conforms to this design, in which assignment to groups is randomised, is known as a **true experiment**.

There remains a final point to be made on the subject of between-groups designs. So far we have been considering the two-group case, and all our discussions and examples have involved this particular scenario. The reasons for this have hopefully been made clear – the two-group design, in which measures taken from a treatment group are compared with those from a control group, is regarded as the classic experimental position; adopting a control versus treatment approach which incorporates appropriate measures for dealing with extraneous variables provides us with the most economical method for demonstrating cause-and-effect relationships. Moreover, as will be noted in Parts 4 and 5, a number of statistical techniques have been developed specifically for this particular type of design, and a considerable proportion of psychological research conforms to this approach.

The astute reader, however, will have deduced that not all research settings will fit comfortably into this two-group structure – in a study exploring the relationship between learning style and word recall we may well compare a mnemonic group to a rote learning group, but there are many different mnemonic styles and our interest might be in exploring possible differences among them, as well as comparing them against a control condition. The procedure here is quite straightforward and merely requires that we expand the number of groups in our study to include all the conditions. Hence, for this example, we might have a control group learning words by rote, an experimental group learning words in terms of what they rhyme with, a second experimental group learning words in terms of their meaning and a third learning by association. As with the two-group case, a number of statistical techniques exist to analyse data from many-group designs, all of which are fully covered in the later parts on statistical procedure. The following sections consider variations on the experimental theme and the examples in Box 3.1 provide illustrations of the different research designs.

Box 3.1

A Closer Look At . . .

Different experimental designs

Research setting

Participants are drawn from a population and randomly assigned to a control group and an experimental group. The experimental group is trained in a word-association mnemonic prior to the presentation of a list of common nouns. The control group is presented with the word list without training. Subsequent recall of the presentation words is compared between the groups.

Research design

Post-test randomised between-groups experimental design with two conditions, A (mnemonic) and B (rote) of a single independent variable (learning strategy).

Research setting

Participants are drawn from a population and randomly assigned to a control group and two experimental groups. The experimental groups are trained in either a word-association or a rhyming mnemonic prior to the presentation of a list of common nouns. The control group is presented with the word list without training. Subsequent recall of the presentation words is compared among the groups.

Research design

Post-test randomised between-groups experimental design with three conditions, A (mnemonic 1), B (mnemonic 2) and C (control) of a single independent variable (learning strategy).

Research setting

In a study on dual processing theory (Paivio, 1971), a research sample is presented with a list of common nouns comprising equal numbers of concrete and abstract stimuli. Subsequent recall of concrete and abstract words is examined in terms of the prediction that different encoding systems will be used to process the different classes of stimuli.

Research design

Within-subjects design with two repeated measures, A (concrete) and B (abstract) on a single independent variable (type of stimulus).

Research setting

In a study on the 'availability heuristic' (Tversky & Kahneman, 1974), a sample drawn at random from an undergraduate population completes a 'fear of crime' questionnaire. The participants are subsequently presented with information on local crime statistics before responding again to the questionnaire. Responses are compared for the before- and after-presentation conditions.

Research design

A pre-test, post-test within-subjects design with two conditions, A (control; pre-presentation test), B (treatment, post-presentation test) on a single independent variable (presentation).

Research setting

In a study investigating the role of experience on error rate on a co-ordination motor task, a sample of novice cyclists is drawn from the cycling community. Error rates on a standard route are noted at novice level, after six months' cycling experience, and after one year, and the rates compared.

Research design

A post-test within-subjects design with three conditions, A (novice), B (six months) and C (one year) on a single independent variable (experience). (Note, there is no provision for a control group in this type of design, so a pre-test condition is unnecessary.)

Research setting

In an experiment exploring the effect of music on problem solving, a sample drawn at random from a population completes a number of problem-solving trials in silence and while listening to preferred music. To control for possible **order effects**, half of the participants complete the task in the silence condition first, while the other half experience the music condition first.

Research design

A partially counterbalanced, pre-test–post-test within-subjects design with two conditions, A (absence) and B (presence) on a single independent variable of music.

Box 3.2

Practicalities . . .

Achieving equivalence

The between-groups experimental design with two conditions is the classic technique for demonstrating the existence of a cause-and-effect relationship; typically one group of participants is exposed to some experimental treatment while a second group is not, and comparisons are made between the two. The key element of this approach is the equivalence of the groups, achieved through a process of random assignment. In practical terms this can create problems for you, the researcher – selecting a large sample from a population, then tossing a coin to decide which group each individual should be assigned to will probably result in unbalanced groups. (In 20 tosses of a coin, for instance, it would not be impossible to obtain 15 heads and 5 tails.) More useful, and practical, would be to use one of the many computer packages to generate random numbers. In Table 3.1, participants identified by case numbers 1 to 12 were allocated to groups 0 or 1 by drawing a random sample of exactly 6 from the total number of cases. This was achieved in SPSS in the Data menu, under the Select Cases command. Similar functions are available in Minitab and other packages.

Table 3.1   Participants randomly assigned to two groups, through a random sampling procedure in SPSS.

Case	Group
1.00	1
2.00	0
3.00	0
4.00	1
5.00	0
6.00	0
7.00	1
8.00	1
9.00	1
10.00	1
11.00	0
12.00	0

3.4 Within-subjects designs (repeated measures designs)

The major alternative to the between-groups design is the **within-subjects design**. Here, each participant experiences each condition of an independent variable, with measurements of some outcome taken on each occasion. As in the between-groups situation, comparisons are still made between the conditions, the difference being that now the same participants appear in each group or level. Consequently, all the requirements for an experimental design are met – there is a condition in which a treatment or intervention is present, and there is a condition in which it is absent (repeated measures are taken from the group, both before and after some treatment is applied); the 'groups' are equivalent (in that the same people are in each condition) minimising the possible confounding effects of extraneous variables. In a memory study, for example, a group of participants might be required to recall lists of common nouns under different conditions of interference; during the interval between initial learning of one particular list and recall, participants might experience a passive activity, such as watching television (the control condition). In a repetition, the same participants learn a different set of common nouns with a more active, problem-solving activity taking place between initial learning and recall (the experimental condition). Participants would then be compared on their recall under each of the conditions. Comparisons are not being made between different sets of participants, but within the same participants across different conditions.

The major advantage in using a within-subjects design, and one of the reasons many researchers opt for the approach whenever possible, is that it almost entirely eliminates the problem of individual variability which represents the main drawback of between-groups designs. Recall that, when different participants comprise the different categories of an independent variable, any observed differences on a corresponding dependent variable, while possibly due to the experimental factor under investigation, could be equally due to different people being in each group. Even if variation in an outcome measure is not directly caused by variation among participants, such individual differences will often interfere with or possibly dilute a true relationship between independent and dependent variables.

A further advantage of the within-subjects approach is that participant numbers are much reduced – even the most basic of between-groups studies requires a minimum of two groups, whereas a similar study using the within-subjects procedure needs only one. The same individuals are used for each condition, making the approach especially useful in situations where there are only a few available participants. In undergraduate research, where competition for a limited participant pool is often fierce, a willingness to accept smaller sample sizes might be a distinct advantage, although this must be balanced against the fact that participants may well be exposed to a more lengthy procedure involving repeated measures.

In addition to the arguments for using **repeated measures designs**, there are some instances in which no other method is feasible. **Longitudinal** research, for instance, in which a number of variables expected to change over time are measured, really could not be attempted in any other way. The alternative **cross-sectional** approach which uses different groups of participants of different ages, all measured at a single point in time, while more immediate will most likely exhibit huge variability due, not simply to individual differences, but also to the widely different age groups used. Comparing a group of 20-year-olds with a group of 60-year-olds goes beyond mere age differences, incorporating considerable changes in culture, society and experience which will have a huge impact on almost any measurable variable. A longitudinal approach, using repeated measures, can follow the changes and developments taking place within the same group over a number of years – today's 17-year-old participant is the 7-year-old we observed 10 years ago.

Other situations in which the within-subjects design is to be preferred are those in which the relationships between an independent and a dependent variable are believed to be real, consistent but very slight and possibly difficult to demonstrate. Under such circumstances a between-groups design with all its attendant sources of participant variability would probably completely obscure such effects. The only way of demonstrating a causal link between an independent and a dependent variable when an effect size is small is by eliminating extraneous factors as far as is possible. The within-subjects design is a good solution here.

By and large, many between-groups studies can be redesigned to take advantage of the within-subjects approach, reducing the need for large participant pools and controlling for a good deal of undesirable variability. A major exception is when the independent variable providing the basis for comparison in a study is of the participant profile variety (typical of most quasi-experimental research; see the section which follows). These are characteristics like age, gender, class and personality type – key descriptive aspects of an individual which place them into some mutually exclusive category. Consequently, when independent variables take this form the only possible design is between-groups. Within-subjects designs are really only possible when the independent variables involve either treatment or temporal differences.

Despite the generally positive regard many researchers have for the within-subjects approach to research, the procedure is not without its own problems. The main drawback is the simple fact that *it is* the same people who experience all the conditions within a variable, allowing for the very real possibility that experience of one treatment will influence measurements on another. The most obvious **repetition effect** is a practice phenomenon – in studies involving performance, if the same participants are used in a before and after design (i.e., participants are tested in the no-treatment condition, and then re-tested after some intervention), it is likely that an improvement in task performance is partially due to the participants simply getting better at the task. If it is the case that exposure to repeated treatments, irrespective of order, results in a generalised practice effect, there is little the researcher can do, other than resort to a between-groups design, swapping the practice problem for the individual differences problem. As ever, the choice as to which design will be the most appropriate comes down to a matter of judgement on the part of the researcher, and a decision as to which effect will prove the more serious.

The type of repetition effect most difficult to deal with is that which is unpredictable – experience of one treatment might improve performance in another condition, as in a practice effect, but not in a third; or prior experiences might inhibit performance at a later stage. Furthermore, the order in which treatments are experienced might produce differing effects. The solution to this problem is to manipulate the order in which participants experience conditions, such that while one individual might be presented with treatments in the order A, B, C, another would undergo the treatments in the order B, A, C and so on. This process, known as **counterbalancing**, serves to reduce the influence of any one particular repetition effect by restricting the number of participants to whom it would apply.

There are various ways in which counterbalancing can be performed. The most complete and effective method is termed, not surprisingly, complete counterbalancing. Here, every possible order of treatments is presented to participants repetitively until everyone has experienced all combinations. While this is the most effective method for dealing with a mixture of known and unknown repetition effects – the effect of any one order is balanced against every other order – there is an obvious drawback. The more conditions there are in an independent variable, the more combinations of different orders are possible and, as the number of conditions increase, so the counterbalancing procedure becomes rapidly impractical, not to mention exhausting for your participants. Box 3.3 illustrates the problem. Realistically, this version of complete counterbalancing is only practical for up to four conditions, after which the procedure begins to place considerable demands on participants. More useful, certainly in an undergraduate context, would be a counterbalancing procedure in which the number of combination treatments is reduced, while at the same time trying to ensure that repetition effects are minimised. Unlike the previous procedure, each participant encounters each treatment only once, but in a different order from the next participant, and so on. An obvious advantage of this approach is that, in a study involving a number of conditions, there is a good chance that the researcher will still be alive at the end of it (death by old age or following a revolt by participants is minimised). The disadvantage is that any interaction effects between individual participants and order of treatment presentation cannot be controlled for. This is a serious problem which should not be overlooked if we are taking the trouble to counterbalance in the first place. There are ways round this of course, but the procedures are potentially complex and there are several models for producing an effective counterbalancing design. Procedures also exist for partial counterbalancing in which only some of all possible orders are tested. Such procedures, though, go beyond the introductory nature of this book and moreover, few undergraduates will have either the time or resources to operate at this level of complexity with possibly the majority of supervisors steering their protégés towards something more economical. However, in the event that your own work *is* more complex than a basic two-treatment, or even three-condition repeated measures design, we recommend the Shaughnessy and Zechmeister (1994) text, which offers an acceptable discussion on advanced counterbalancing techniques. Alternatively, the Christensen (2004) text provides a number of counterbalancing illustrations which should cover most of the designs likely to be considered by undergraduate researchers. Finally, in Box 3.3 we offer some practical guidance on counterbalancing which you may find useful.

By way of a concluding comment, it will have become apparent that the basic two-condition within-subjects design can be readily developed to incorporate many conditions, in much the same way that the basic between-groups experiment can be expanded

---

Box 3.3

How To . . .

Balance repetition effects in a within-subjects design

In a within-subjects study, when participants experience a series of conditions, with measurements being taken on each repetition, the order in which they encounter each condition can influence the outcome measure. This is not a mere practice effect, but a more complicated experimental or order effect. To control for this we can vary the order in which participants experience each condition; if we allow for all possible ways in which the order of presentation can vary, this will balance out the effects of any particular permutation. However, this procedure can generate its own set of problems:

Consider two studies investigating the recall of lists of common nouns under different conditions of learning. In the first study, two conditions are present: a control condition in which participants attempt to memorise a word list by rote, and an experimental condition in which they are required to make use of a mnemonic technique, such as considering each word on the list in terms of what it rhymes with. The following design is implemented:

A completely counterbalanced within-subjects design with two conditions, A (control) and B (rhyme), on an independent variable (learning style).

Participants in this experiment experience repetitions of the experimental treatments as shown:

All participants	Order 1	A, B
All participants	Order 2	B, A

In a more complex study, a second mnemonic approach is added, one in which partici-pants are required to consider the meaning of each word. The design becomes:

A completely counterbalanced within-subjects design with three conditions, A (control), B (rhyme) and C (meaning) on an independent variable (learning style).

All participants	Order 1	A, B, C
All participants	Order 2	B, A, C
All participants	Order 3	C, A, B
All participants	Order 4	C, B, A
All participants	Order 5	A, C, B
All participants	Order 6	B, C, A

Clearly things are getting out of hand – even with only three conditions, which is far from excessive, we require 6 different presentation orders to counterbalance all possible order effects. Just one more learning condition (another mnemonic system) and our experiment would require 24 separate presentations to allow for all the different permutations. With five conditions our experiment becomes so cumbersome as to be almost impractical. (Five conditions would generate 120 different permutations to allow for all possible order combinations.) In addition to this problem the demands on participant time, patience and co-operation will quickly become intolerable. The only solution, when faced with this kind of prospect, is to adopt one of the methods of incomplete counterbalancing. In the mem-ory example above, for instance, it would be permissible still to cover all possible order combinations, but with each individual experiencing only some, but not all permutations:

Participants 1–5	Order 1	A, B, C
Participants 6–10	Order 2	B, A, C
Participants 11–15	Order 3	C, A, B
Etc.		

This particular solution, and variants of it, will reduce the demands on the individual, but often at the cost of requiring a larger sample so that enough participants are experiencing each of the permutations. Alternatively, if neither complete nor incomplete counterbalanc-ing is seen as acceptable in a particular study, it would be necessary to consider adopting a partial counterbalanced design in which only a selection of all possible orders is adopted. Alternatively, changing to a between-groups design is a possibility although this will give rise to its own set of problems, as outlined in the section on between-groups approaches.

to a many-groups situation. Certainly a large number of studies will conform to the stan-dard *treatment present/treatment absent* situation (or before/after, as it is commonly called in within-subjects research), but there will be many cases in which we wish to compare several measures, or conditions of an independent variable. By way of example, a medical study may aim to explore the effects of exercise on resting blood pressure among a sample of hypertensive patients. There are various ways in which this could be done – a between-groups design would make use of two different groups of patients, one taking exercise and one not. However, if we feel that there will be several other factors which contribute to high blood pressure and that a between-groups design will allow for too many uncontrolled extraneous variables, we could opt for a within-subjects design. A basic structure might be a before-and-after design in which measures are taken from a single sample before and then after commencement of an exercise regime. In the event though that there is evidence of a long-term or cumulative effect of exercise, we would want to take measurements a number of times during the course of an exercise regime – say, after a month, then at three-month intervals over the space of a year. As might be anticipated, statistical techniques exist for such expanded repeated measures designs and if you feel sufficiently brave, a look at Part 5 and our treatment of the repeated measures ANOVA provides an example.

3.5   Non-equivalent-groups (quasi-experimental) design

In a **quasi-experiment** the same general principles of experimental design apply, in that the aim is to demonstrate a relationship, hopefully causal, between an independent and dependent variable. In this instance, however, rather than adopting a randomising procedure to assign individuals into one group or another, the researcher makes use of groups which already exist. For instance, a study might be concerned with differences between males and females on some opinion measure, in the lifestyles of different occupational groups, or in the coping strategies of one type of personality as opposed to another. In a variant of the quasi-experiment, groups being compared need not always be of the nominal categorical type – a variable measured on an interval or ratio scale can readily be used to create the different conditions of an independent variable by use of a cut-off score. This is a common technique in undergraduate research and is often found in studies comparing different personality types on some dependent measure. Here, a score on an extraversion scale (for example, as measured on Eysenck's EPQ[1]) might be compared to the mean or median value of a group of participants, with participants with scores above the mean assigned to an extravert group, and those with scores below the mean assigned to an introvert group. There are many such examples in which **cut-off assignment** can be used as a means of generating comparison groups and as an approach it is recognised as a useful design for demonstrating causal relationships, though not as good as the fully randomised experimental design.

In the language of research design, the different groups which are being compared represent the different categories of an independent variable. They could be the male and female components of a gender variable; or they could be an experienced versus inexperienced category of a skill variable in the cycling example we have been using (based on some cut-off value). Other frequently used terms for the components of an independent variable are **conditions** (the gender variable comprises two conditions – male and female) and **levels** (in one of our cycling examples there are two levels of skill – experienced and inexperienced, while in others we have added the third level of novice). In psychological research which adopts the quasi-experimental stance, the assumption is that the different groups to which people belong are sufficient to account for differences in a range of dependent measures. In true experimentation, on the other hand, the underlying assumption is that the two (or more) groups should be essentially similar (equivalent) at the outset, in

[1]Eysenck's Personality Questionnaire (Eysenck & Eysenck, 1975).

terms of some dependent variable we are interested in observing or measuring, but that this will change following the researcher's manipulations.

Another difference between the two approaches is that while true experimentation usually takes place in the laboratory, quasi-experimentation tends to be more 'real world' in context. As such it is the kind of design often favoured by social psychologists and it is used exclusively in survey research, since the opportunity to randomly assign participants to different conditions is limited in the real world. However, the key issue here is the demonstration of causality. It will be recalled that the main strength of the true experiment lies in the confidence with which we can argue a causal relationship between an independent and a dependent variable. This is due primarily to the fact that the randomisation procedure ensures equality (almost) between comparison groups at the outset of a study. In quasi-experimental research, though, the use of pre-existing or naturally occurring groups requires that our groups are different in significant ways at the outset. (If we devise a study to compare males and females on some measure we do so in the belief that the fact of their gender makes them different.) The problem is that if such groups are **non-equivalent** in one way, there is reason to assume they might be non-equivalent in others, differences that can act as extraneous variables on some outcome measure. This means that attempts to argue causality when comparing naturally occurring (and therefore non-equivalent) groups are more problematic.

A final note on terminology is that the term *quasi-experiment* is found most often in the broad area of social science research, which incorporates, among others, the fields of sociology, social policy, economics and politics. In psychological research the preference is usually for the more informative term, *non-equivalent-groups design. Quasi* means nearly or similar to, whereas *non-equivalence* explains the particular way in which a study is nearly (or not quite) an experiment.

3.6 Factorial designs

There are many variants on the basic experimental model, one of the most frequently employed being the factorial design. Recall that the simple experimental design – involving equivalent or non-equivalent groups – is attempting to examine a relationship between an independent variable and a dependent variable. Recall also that one of the confounding factors in any design is the effect of other variables present in a study. In previous discussions we have chosen to regard such additional variables as extraneous factors whose effects have to be controlled for. An alternative position would be to regard all such variables as potentially influential and we expand our study to include them as independent variables in their own right; hence the term **factorial research**, research which investigates the effects of several variables, or factors, on some outcome measure.

When we adopt a multi-factor approach to psychological research we design studies which have two or more independent variables, each of which can have two or more conditions. Not only are we looking for differences between the conditions of each individual factor, but we are also interested in possible interactions among the factors themselves. This type of study is termed a *factorial design*, and is carried out as follows.

Let's return for a moment to our hypothetical study of hedgehog-fearing cyclists. In this example it has been argued (not unreasonably) that performance on the task would be largely a function of level of skill – with performance measured in the number of errors made, or poor hedgehogs run over. Previously, while it was accepted that other factors might also have an impact on performance, these additional elements were treated largely as nuisance variables to be eliminated or controlled. However, should we decide that these other factors are important in their own right, and that, far from having their effects minimised, they should themselves be regarded as causal factors, then we have moved to a many-independent variable study. In a variant of our hedgehog example, assume that we have identified two main factors likely to cause variability in performance – skill level (novice or expert) and terrain (easy or difficult). A study set up on this basis would be termed a 2 × 2 (two by two) factorial design – there are two factors or independent variables in the study, both of which comprise two levels. Had we identified three levels of skill and two levels of terrain, this would give us a 3 × 2 factorial design. Moreover, if we proposed the existence of a third independent variable, such as gender (male or female), then we would have a 3 × 2 × 2 design.

If all of this sounds unnecessarily complicated, it is because factorial designs don't consider just the isolated or **main effects** of variables. If this were all we were interested in there would be nothing to prevent us carrying out a series of isolated studies in which each variable was considered on its own: we would perform one study in which performance is measured for skilled and novice cyclists, and a second study in which performance is measured for easy and difficult terrains. What we would miss with this approach is the possibility of an **interaction** – for example, that skill level on its own might not dictate performance, but that its impact depends on the type of terrain. Box 3.4 illustrates how the two factors might interact.

Box 3.4

A Closer Look At . . .

A factorial design with interactions

From inspection of the graph in Figure 3.1, the results of our study on cycling show that while skill level is a key determinant of performance, its effects depend on the second factor, terrain. When the ground is easy, experienced and novice riders produce similar numbers of errors. It is only with difficult terrain that the effects of skill level can be observed – skill level and terrain are interacting factors.

Figure 3.1 Errors on a performance task by terrain and skill level.

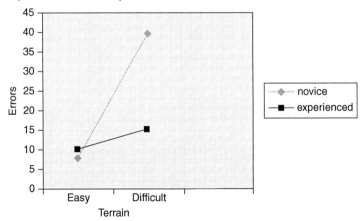

The great advantage of this type of study is that, not only can we observe the main effect of each independent variable on its own, but also, because every possible combination of conditions is considered, any interaction effects can be seen as well. This opportunity to explore interactions is of immense importance since, as we have observed, events in our social world are often the outcome of a large number of interacting factors – and to fully appreciate such events we must have access to these interactions.

An important consideration with factorial designs is the issue of causality. In the previous discussion on experimental design the point was made that only the equivalent-groups design permitted a strong causal argument: the random assignment of participants to groups offered the greatest control over the effects of extraneous variables and it is the preferred model for the researcher. It was noted, though, that some studies will make use of pre-existing or naturally occurring groups, requiring a modification to the basic experimental design to one which is quasi-experimental, or based on non-equivalent groups. The approach is valid and sometimes it is the only design which fits a particular context, although the drawback is the relative weakness of the causal argument. Because group membership has not been manipulated by a process of random assignment, there is a greater likelihood of confounding factors. Factorial designs which make use of non-equivalent groups suffer from the same limitations and the interpretation of both main and interaction effects must be made with caution.

3.7 Randomised controlled designs revisited

We have previously remarked that research in the medical field has adopted the classical experimental paradigm as its preferred model. Known as the randomised controlled trial (RCT), the approach relies on the assumption of equivalence when a control group and a treatment group are compared on some clinical measure, or in terms of response to an intervention. However, the basic two-group comparison study represents only one variety of the RCT, and it will be the case that some medical research will attempt to explore the effects of more than one factor on some outcome measure. For example, different patient groups might be compared on the efficacy of two different pain-relief drugs, each of which can be administered in different strengths, in what is obviously a factorial design. We mention this to make the point that there are certain fundamentals in research and that what we might term sound practice will be present in many disciplines, although terminology will vary. The RCT in the field of medicine is a case in point.

3.8 Mixed designs

Inevitably, in the design of a study involving more than one independent variable – a factorial design – factors might not always fall into just one class and we will have a mixture of equivalent group factors and non-equivalent group factors. Alternatively, the investigation of a topic might not be possible with a between-groups design on its own and there may be a requirement for an element of repeated measures as well. When a particular design involves some combination of the different design elements it is known as a **mixed design**, and there are several types.

* A common mixed design is one which combines equivalent and non-equivalent groups. Members of a group of skilled cyclists and a group of novice cyclists might be randomly

Table 3.2 The number of errors made by skilled and novice cyclists over two different types of terrain.

	Skilled	Novice	Totals
Easy	5	10	15
Difficult	5	50	55
Totals	10	60	

assigned to one of two terrains, varying in degree of difficulty; male and female undergraduates might be randomly assigned to either a control or an experimental group in a memory study, and so on. However, the same reservations about causality mentioned previously will also apply here: individuals who differ by virtue of their gender or skill level are likely to differ in other ways as well, and caution is required when arguing causality. This will apply to both main effects and interaction effects.

In the example shown in Table 3.2, if we observe a difference in total errors between the easy and difficult terrains, we can be confident that differences in terrain determined differences in errors, since the assignment to each condition was random (making the groups probabilistically equivalent). However, the same cannot be said of total error differences in the skilled and novice conditions, since these groups existed already and are therefore not equivalent. Differences here may well be due to any number of unknown factors and observed differences must be interpreted cautiously. The same is true of any observed differences among the interacting cells, or sub-groups, when any of them involve some element of non-equivalence.

⦿ A second type of mixed factorial design is one in which both between-groups and within-subjects elements are present. A medical researcher investigating the long-term effects of a hypertension-reducing drug, suspected to have different effects depending on the sex of the patient, might follow a group of male and a group of female patients on the medication at three-monthly intervals over the course of a year. The between-groups factor is the sex of the patient, with two levels (male and female), while the within-subjects factor is expressed by the repeated measurements taken at four different times. Table 3.3 demonstrates the structure of this example. We have not shown totals.

⦿ Finally, the most complex of the mixed designs would involve a combination of all these elements – equal and unequal groups, between-groups and repeated measures. Extending our medical example, if there were two new drugs, the male and female patients might be assigned randomly to one or other of the two medications, and again measures taken at three-month intervals. Table 3.4 illustrates this.

It should be apparent from the above discussion that factorial designs allow a high level of sophistication in research, with the opportunity to combine different types of variable in ways which enable studies to be carried out on almost any topic. And this is only a part of what is possible. There is, for instance, no (theoretical) limit on the number of

Table 3.3 Measures of diastolic blood pressure (dbp) of male and female patients taken at three-month intervals.

Dbp	Time 1	Time 2	Time 3	Time 4
Male	100	98	90	85
Female	100	102	95	95

Table 3.4 Measures of diastolic blood pressure (dbp) of male and female patients on two different hypertension-reducing drugs, taken at three-month intervals.

	Time 1		Time 2		Time 3		Time 4	
	Drug A	Drug B	Drug A	Drug B	Drug A	Drug B	Drug A	Drug B
Male	100	100	98	98	90	95	85	96
Female	100	100	102	95	95	85	95	80

independent variables which can be included in this design, or the number of repetitions over which measurements can be taken. It is also possible to design factorial studies in which other factors can be treated as extraneous variables and controlled for, although consideration of such complex designs go beyond the introductory scope of this book.

3.9 Some reservations on factorial designs

Factorial designs allow for more complex studies than is possible with the basic experiment in which two or more groups are compared on a single independent variable. However, being able to measure simultaneously the effects of several factors on some dependent variable (as opposed to carrying out several studies, each of which looks at the relationship between a single independent variable and a dependent variable) is not the only advantage of the factorial approach. The key here is that interactions among variables can be explored and this is a huge development in research terms. It has to be said that the analysis of such interactions is complex and 10 to 15 years ago would not have been possible in the average undergraduate programme – students would certainly have been advised against such designs and directed towards something less statistically demanding. Nowadays, though, there are many computer packages available which make the required analyses accessible to undergraduates and there is no reason why such designs should not be attempted. Some words of caution are required, though, concerning factorial designs: just because it is now possible to carry out quite complex studies (complex in terms of the number of independent variables considered) it is not always desirable to do so. There are many experimental studies in which the basic two-group, single independent variable design is the most appropriate. The point is that merely because we can carry out complicated research does not mean we should. The complexity of our design must always be a matter of judgement, judgement based on the number of factors we believe will influence a dependent variable, and whether or not we wish to view all of these factors as potentially causal, or extraneous.

A final note here is a practical one: factorial designs, whatever their merit, are heavy on sample sizes. If we were to take a minimum sample size of 30 as being sufficient for most comparison purposes, then in a typical two-group design we would need 60 participants in our study (30 in each condition). Were we to consider a factorial design with two independent variables, each with two groups, or conditions, then to maintain our minimal 30 participants per group we would require 120 participants. (Imagine trying to persuade 120 people to participate in your study.) Quite simply, the more variables we wish to include in our study, the more participants we will require, and for most undergraduates this will be a major problem. Factorial designs may be desirable in some circumstances, but they are costly in numbers. We conclude with a statistical point: the more interacting factors we include in our design, the more difficult it becomes to tease out particular effects. In spite of the accessibility of sophisticated statistical analyses, it remains the case that when we are obliged to perform large numbers of comparisons, as is required in factorial studies, the likelihood of demonstrating real effects becomes reduced. This point is further discussed in Part 5.

Review

In this chapter the essential characteristics of the experiment have been introduced, with emphasis on causality. You should now be able to distinguish between true and quasi-experimentation, appreciate the differences between repeated measures and between-groups designs, and recognise how the basic experiment can be expanded into factorial and mixed designs. In the next chapter, our interest in causality is replaced with an emphasis on the demonstration of association, as a different type of research design is considered – that of correlation and regression.

Suggested further reading

Christensen, L. B. (2004). *Experimental methodology* (9th ed.). Boston: Allyn & Bacon.

An excellent guide to experimental design with accessible arguments on the advantages and disadvantages of the various procedures. Describes a number of counterbalancing models.

Shaughnessy, J. J., & Zechmeister, E. B. (1994). *Research methods in psychology* (3rd ed.). New York: McGraw-Hill.

Of special interest for those proposing complex repeated measures designs. This contains a useful section on counterbalancing procedures which is both informative and of practical value.

7 Analyses of differences between two conditions: the t-test

Chapter overview

In the previous chapter, you were introduced to the idea of looking at how scores on one variable related to scores on another variable, and for this analysis you learnt about the parametric statistical test, Pearson's r. In this chapter, however, we will be looking at the differences between scores in two conditions. For instance, you could compare the memory ability of spider-phobics and non-phobics to see how they differ. Such a design is called a between-participants, independent or unrelated design, since one group of participants gives scores in one condition and a different group of people gives scores in a different condition. On the other hand, one group of participants may perform in both conditions, for instance one group of participants learn both high frequency words and low frequency words. They are then measured by the amount of recalled words. This is called a within-participants, repeated measures or related design, because the same people perform in both conditions. In this chapter we are going to discuss the analyses of two conditions by using the parametric test called the t-test. We are particularly interested in the differences between the two groups: specifically, the difference between the mean of the two groups. In this chapter we are going to show you how to analyse the data from such designs. Since the t-test is a parametric test, you must remember that your data need to meet the normal assumptions for parametric tests – that is, the data have been drawn from a population that is normally distributed. We tend to assume this is the case when your sample data are normally distributed. If you have reason to think this is not the case, then you need to use the non-parametric equivalents of the t-test described in Chapter 16.

To enable you to understand the tests presented in this chapter you will need to have an understanding of the following concepts:

- the mean, standard deviation and standard error (Chapter 3)
- z-scores and the normal distribution (Chapter 4)
- assumptions underlying the use of parametric tests (Chapter 5)
- probability distributions like the t-distribution (Chapter 5)
- one- and two-tailed hypotheses (Chapter 5)
- statistical significance (Chapter 5)
- confidence intervals (Chapter 4).

7.1 Analysis of two conditions

The analysis of two conditions includes the following:

1. *Descriptive statistics*, such as means or medians, standard deviations; confidence intervals around the mean of both groups separately, where this is appropriate; graphical illustrations such as box and whisker plots and error bars.
2. *Effect size* – this is a measure of the degree to which differences in a dependent variable are attributed to the independent variable.
3. *Confidence limits* around the difference between the means.
4. *Inferential tests* – t-tests discover how likely it is that the difference between the conditions could be attributable to sampling error, assuming the null hypothesis to be true.

7.1.1 Analysis of differences between two independent groups

Twenty-four people were involved in an experiment to determine whether background noise (music, slamming of doors, people making coffee, etc.) affects short-term memory (recall of words). Half of the sample were randomly allocated to the NOISE condition, and half to the NO NOISE condition. The participants in the NOISE condition tried to memorise a list of 20 words in two minutes, while listening to pre-recorded noise through earphones. The other participants wore earphones but heard no noise as they attempted to memorise the words. Immediately after this, they were tested to see how many words they recalled. The numbers of words recalled by each person in each condition are as shown in Table 7.1.

Table 7.1   Raw data for NOISE/NO NOISE conditions

NOISE	NO NOISE
5.00	15.00
10.00	9.00
6.00	16.00
6.00	15.00
7.00	16.00
3.00	18.00
6.00	17.00
9.00	13.00
5.00	11.00
10.00	12.00
11.00	13.00
9.00	11.00
$\sum = 87$[a]	$\sum = 166$
$\bar{X} = 7.3$[b]	$\bar{X} = 13.8$
SD = 2.5	SD = 2.8

[a] $\sum$ represents the total of the column
[b] $\bar{X}$ represents the mean (average)

Table 7.2   Mean, standard deviation and 95% confidence limits for NOISE/NO NOISE conditions

	NOISE			NO NOISE	
$\bar{X}$	SD	95% CI	$\bar{X}$	SD	95% CI
7.3	2.5	5.7–8.8	13.8	2.8	12.1–15.6

7.1.2   Descriptive statistics for two-group design

The first thing to do is to obtain descriptive statistics through the *Explore* procedure in SPSSFW (see page 51). You can then gain insight into the data by looking at graphical illustrations, such as box and whisker plots and/or histograms. Summary statistics such as the means, standard deviations and confidence intervals are available through SPSSFW, which gives you the results in the form of tables. (These statistics are also given as part of the output when you analyse the data by using the t-test procedure.)

You can see in Table 7.2 that the means differ, in the expected direction. Participants in the NO NOISE condition recalled a mean of 13.8 words, while those in the NOISE condition recalled a mean of 7.3. People in the NO NOISE condition showed slightly more variability, as indicated by the *standard deviations*.

7.1.3   Confidence limits around the mean

The means you have obtained, for your sample, are *point estimates*. These sample means are the best estimates of the population means. If, however, we repeated the experiment many times, we would find that the mean varied from experiment to experiment. For example, the sample mean for the NO NOISE condition is 13.8. If we repeat the experiment we might find that the sample mean is 13.3. If you repeated the experiment many times, the best estimate of the population mean would then be the mean of all the sample means. It should be obvious, however, that our estimate could be slightly different from the real population mean difference: thus it would be better, instead of giving a point estimate, to give a *range*. This is more realistic than giving a point estimate.

The interval is bounded by a lower limit (12.1 in this case) and an upper limit (15.6 in the above example). These are called *confidence limits*, and the interval that the limits enclose is called the *confidence interval*. You came across these in Chapter 4. The confidence limits let you know how confident you are that the *population mean* is within a certain interval, that is, it is an interval estimate for the population (not just your sample).

Why are confidence limits important? When we carry out experiments or studies, we want to be able to generalise from our particular sample to the population. We also want to let our readers have a full and accurate picture of our results. Although our *sample* mean of the NOISE condition is 7.3, telling the reader that 'we are 95% confident that the *population mean* falls between 5.7 and 8.8' gives more information, and is more realistic, than simply reporting our sample mean. Confidence intervals are being reported more and more in journal articles, and so it is important for you to be able to understand them.

Figure 7.1   95% confidence limits for NOISE and NO NOISE conditions

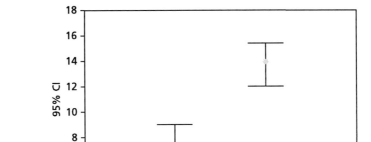

7.1.4   Confidence intervals between NOISE and NO NOISE conditions

For the noise condition, we estimate (with 95% confidence) that the population mean is within the range (interval) of 5.7 and 8.8. This can be represented graphically, as shown in Figure 7.1.

7.1.5   Measure of effect

We can also take one (sample) mean from the other, to see how much they differ:

7.3 – 13.8 = –6.5

This score on its own, however, tells us very little. If we converted this score to a *standardised score*, however, it would be much more useful. The raw score (the original score) is converted into a z-score. The z-score is a standardised score, giving a measure of effect which everyone can easily understand. This measure of effect is called *d*; *d* measures the extent to which the two means differ, in terms of standard deviations. This is how we calculate it:

$$d = \frac{x_1 - x_2}{\text{mean SD}}$$

This means that we take one mean away from the other (it does not matter which is which – ignore the sign) and divide it by the mean standard deviation.

Step 1: find mean sample SD

$$\frac{\text{SD of condition 1 + SD of condition 2}}{2} = \frac{2.5 + 2.8}{2} = 2.65$$

Step 2: find *d*

$$\frac{x_1 - x_2}{\text{mean SD}} = \frac{7.3 - 13.8}{2.65} = \frac{6.5}{2.65} = 2.45$$

In this case, our means differ by 2.45 standard deviations. This is a very large effect size, an effect size not often found in psychological research.

7.1.6 The size of the effect

The effect size here, d, is expressed in standard deviations. Think of the normal curve of distribution:

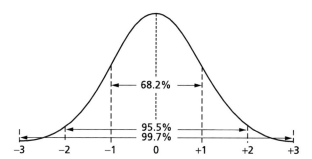

Z-scores are standardised so that the mean is zero and the standard deviation is 1. You can see that, if the means differed by 0.1, they would differ by only a tenth of a standard deviation. That is quite small, on our scale of 0 to 3. If the means differed by 3 standard deviations, that is a lot, using the scale of 0 to 3. There is no hard and fast rule about what constitutes small and large effects. Cohen (1988) gave the following guidelines:

Effect size	d	Percentage of overlap (%)
Small	0.2	85
Medium	0.5	67
Large	0.8	53

When there is little difference between our groups, the scores will overlap substantially. The scores for the groups can be plotted separately; for instance, scores for the NOISE condition can be plotted and will tend to be normally distributed. Scores for the NO NOISE condition can also be plotted, and will tend to be normally distributed. If there is little difference between them, the distributions will overlap:

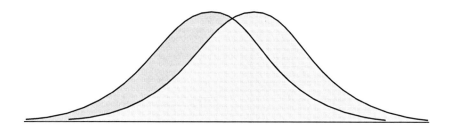

If there is a large difference between the two groups, then the distributions will be further apart:

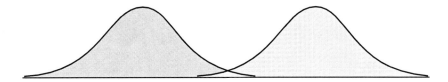

This is what is meant by the percentage of overlap. This measure of effect enables us to interpret our findings in a meaningful way. The exact extent of the overlap is given in the table below:

D	Percentage of overlap (%)
0.1	92
0.2	85
0.3	79
0.4	73
0.5	67
0.6	62
0.7	57
0.8	53
0.9	48
1.0	45
1.1	42
1.2	37
1.3	35
1.4	32
1.5	29

Effect sizes are discussed further in Chapter 8.

Activity 7.1

Calculate the effect size of a two-group test using the following figures:

- Group 1: mean = 50, SD = 10
- Group 2: mean = 70, SD = 5

7.1.7 Inferential statistics: the t-test

The t-test is used when we have two conditions. The t-test assesses whether there is a statistically significant difference between the means of the two conditions.

Table 7.3   Raw data for NOISE/NO NOISE conditions

NOISE	NO NOISE
5.00	15.00
10.00	9.00
6.00	16.00
6.00	15.00
7.00	16.00
3.00	18.00
6.00	17.00
9.00	13.00
5.00	11.00
10.00	12.00
11.00	13.00
9.00	11.00
$\sum = 87$	$\sum = 166$
$\bar{X} = 7.3$	$\bar{X} = 13.8$
SD = 2.5	SD = 2.8

The *independent t-test* is used when the participants perform in only *one* of two conditions, i.e. an independent, between-participants or unrelated design. The *related* or *paired t-test* is used when the participants perform in *both* conditions, i.e. a related, within-participants or repeated measures design.

The t-test was devised by William Gossett in 1908. Gossett worked for Guinness, whose scientists were not allowed to publish results of their scientific work, and so Gossett published results using his new test under the name of Student, which is why, of course, you will see it referred to in statistical books as Student's t.

Look again at our raw data for the NOISE/NO NOISE condition (Table 7.3). The first thing you should note is that participants vary *within* conditions. In the NOISE condition, the scores range from 3 through to 11. In the NO NOISE condition, the scores range from 9 to 18 (this within-participants variance can be thought of as variance *within* each column). You should recall from Chapter 3 that the standard deviation is a measure of variance – the larger the standard deviation, the greater the scores vary, within the condition. The participants differ *between* the conditions too. You can see that scores of the NO NOISE condition, in general, are higher than those in the NOISE condition – the means confirm our visual experience of the data. This is the *between-participants variance*, and can be thought of as the variance *between* the columns.

We want to know whether the differences between the means of our groups are large enough for us to be able to conclude that the differences are due to our independent variable – that is, our NOISE/NO NOISE manipulation. This is accomplished by performing mathematical calculations on our data. The formula for the t-test (not given here) results in a test statistic, which we call 't'. The t-test is basically a ratio between a measure of the between-groups variance and the within-groups variance. The larger the variance *between* the groups (columns), compared with the variance *within* the groups (rows), the larger the t-value.

Once we have calculated the t-value we (or rather the computer) can find the probability of obtaining such a t-value by chance (sampling error) if the null hypothesis were true.

Figure 7.2   Sampling distribution

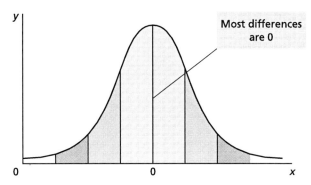

That is, if there were no differences between the NOISE condition and the NO NOISE condition, how likely is it that our value of *t* would be found?

If there were no real differences between the NOISE and the NO NOISE conditions, and we took repeated samples, most of the differences would fall around the zero mark (mean of NOISE condition and mean of NO NOISE condition would be almost the same). Sometimes, however, we would find a value larger than zero (maybe, for instance, participants in the NOISE condition would actually do *better* than participants in the NO NOISE condition). Sometimes we would find a very large difference. These differences are often chance differences, which arise just because we have used different samples each time – we say that these differences arise due to *sampling error*. The differences that we might find if we took repeated samples can be plotted as shown in Figure 7.2 (this is another example of a sampling distribution).

If there were no difference between the means of our particular experiment, it would be more likely that our *t* would fall in the middle region than in one of the 'tails' of the sampling distribution. This is because we know, through the Central Limit Theorem, that most of our obtained values will fall in the middle range (see pages 98–9). It would be rare (but possible) for our *t* to be found in the extreme edges of the tail as shown above. That is, if we perform 100 repeated NOISE/NO NOISE experiments, using different samples, in a small percentage of experiments we would find a *t* that falls in the extreme edges of the distribution. If, in practice, we obtain a *t* that is found in one of these tails, then we conclude that it is unlikely to have arisen purely by *sampling error*. We can put a figure on this 'unlikeliness' as well. Each obtained t-value comes with an exact associated probability level. If, for instance, our obtained *t* has an associated probability level of 0.03,[1] we can say that, assuming the null hypothesis to be true, a t-value such as the one we obtained in our experiment would be likely to have arisen in only 3 occasions out of 100. Therefore we conclude that there is a difference between conditions that cannot be explained by *sampling error*. As you have seen in Chapter 5, this is what is meant by 'statistical significance'. This does not necessarily mean that our finding is *psychologically* important, or that we have found a *large effect size*. We have to take into consideration our descriptive statistics and any measure of effect sizes, confidence intervals, etc., that we have also computed.

---

[1] Often psychologists call this achieved significance level (ASL), and we use these terms interchangeably in this book.

Activity 7.2

What does the independent t-test examine?

(a) The difference between the median values for each condition
(b) The differences between the variances for each condition
(c) The differences between the mean scores for each condition

7.1.8 Output for independent t-test

In our experiment, the dependent variable is the number of words correctly recalled, and the independent variable is NOISE (either NOISE condition, or NO NOISE condition). All good computer packages, such as SPSSFW, will give the following information:

■ *Means of the two conditions* and the difference between them. What you want to know is whether the difference between the two means is large enough to be important (not only 'statistically significant', which tells you the likelihood of your test statistic being obtained, given that the null hypothesis is true).

■ *Confidence intervals*: SPSSFW, using the t-test procedure, gives you confidence limits for the *difference* between the means.[2] The difference between means, for your sample, is a *point estimate*. This sample mean difference is the best estimate of the population mean difference. If, however, we repeated the experiment many times, we would find that the mean difference varied from experiment to experiment. The best estimate of the population mean would then be the mean of all these mean differences. It is obviously better to give an interval estimate, as explained before. Confidence limits let you know how confident you are that the *population mean difference* is within a certain interval. That is, it is an *interval estimate* for the population (not just for your sample).

■ *t-value*: the higher the t-value, the more likely it is that the difference between groups is *not* the result of sampling error. A negative value is just as important as a positive value. The positive/negative direction depends on how you've coded the groups. For instance, we have called condition 1 NOISE and condition 2 NO NOISE. This was obviously an arbitrary decision; we could just as well have called condition 1 NO NOISE and condition 2 NOISE – this would result in exactly the same t-value, but it would have a different sign (plus or minus).

■ *p-value*: this is the probability of your obtained t-value having arisen by sampling variation, or error, given that the null hypothesis is true. This means that your obtained *t* is under an area of the curve that is uncommon – by chance, you would not expect your obtained t-value to fall in this area. The p-value shows you the likelihood of this arising by sampling error. For instance, $p = 0.001$ means that there is only one chance in a thousand of this result arising from sampling error, given that the null hypothesis is true.

---

[2] It is more important that you report the confidence interval for the difference between the means than it is for you to report the confidence interval for both means separately.

■ *Degrees of freedom (DF)*: for most purposes and tests (but not all) degrees of freedom roughly equate to sample size. For a related t-test, DF are always one less than the number of participants. For an independent t-test, DF are $(n - 1) + (n - 1)$,[3] so for a sample size of 20 (10 participants in each group) DF = 18 (i.e. 9 + 9). For a within-participants design with sample size of 20, DF = 19. DF should always be reported in your laboratory reports or projects, along with the t-value, p-value and confidence limits for the difference between means. Degrees of freedom are usually reported in brackets, as follows: $t(87) = 0.78$. This means that the t-value was 0.78, and the degrees of freedom 87.

■ *Standard deviations*: this gives you the standard deviation for your sample (see page 74).

■ *Standard error of the mean (SEM)*: this is used in the construction of confidence intervals (see page 112).

Degrees of freedom

This is a mathematical term that is often used in formulae for our statistical tests. There are mathematical definitions that are not useful for most psychologists, and there are working definitions, e.g. DF refers to the number of individual scores that can vary without changing the sample mean. Examples can help illustrate the concept. For instance, if we ask you to choose two numbers at random, with no constraints, then you have two degrees of freedom. If we ask you to choose two numbers that must add up to 10, however, then once you have chosen the first number, e.g. 7, the other is fixed: it is 3, and you have no choice in the matter! Thus the degrees of freedom are reduced to 1.

Let's take a non-mathematical example. Imagine you are hosting an important dinner party, and you need to seat ten people; a knowledge of where the first nine sit will determine where the tenth person sits – you would be free to decide where the first nine sits, and the tenth would be known, by a knowledge of the first nine (DF, then, is 10 − 1 = 9). Imagine now that you are hosting a very old-fashioned formal dinner party, where you have five women and five men, and you need to sit each woman next to a man. In this case a knowledge of where the first four pairs sit (eight people) leads to the last pair (a man and a woman) being determined (DF, then, is 10 − 2 = 8).

This is because, as can be seen in our dinner party example, we are free to vary all the numbers but one, in order to estimate the mean. The last number is determined by a knowledge of the others. The formulae we use in calculations often incorporate this restriction.

Of course psychologists are usually busy doing psychology, not going to dinner parties. So a more useful way of thinking about degrees of freedom is to say that DF are the number of observations made, minus the number of parameters which are estimated. When calculating statistical tests, we often have to 'estimate' figures Once we have to estimate a mean, we lose one degree of freedom. (This is why you often have to divide by $n − 1$ rather than n.) The more measures you have to estimate, the more you reduce your degrees of freedom. DF is a result of both the number of participants in the analysis, and the number of variables. It's not easy to find a statistical textbook that explains DF well, or shows you the relevance of DF. Dr Chong Ho Yu gives one of the best explanations of DF that we have seen, but much of the explanation is based on concepts which you will learn in Chapter 12, so we will be talking more about DF there. If you wish to hear and see Dr Chong Ho Yu's Degrees of Freedom tutorial on the web, the site address is given at the end of this chapter (Yu, 2003).

---

[3] n is the number of participants in each group.

Activity 7.3

It is easy to become confused sometimes when psychologists use several different names for the same thing! What are the alternative names for within-participants designs? What are the alternative names for between-participants designs?

7.1.9   Assumptions to be met in using t-tests

The t-test is a *parametric* test, which means that certain conditions about the distribution of the data need to be in force, i.e. data should be drawn from a normally distributed population of scores. We assume this is the case if our sample scores are normally distributed. You can tell whether your data are skewed by looking at histograms. In the past, in order to be able to use a t-test you would have been instructed to use interval data only. However, for many years now psychologists have used t-tests for the analysis of data from Likert-type scales (where variables have been rated on a scale of, say, 1 to 7).

The t-test is based on the normal curve of distribution. Thus, we assume that the scores of our groups, or conditions, are each normally distributed. The larger the sample size, the more likely you are to have a normal distribution. As long as your data are reasonably normally distributed, you do not need to worry, but if they are severely skewed, you need to use a non-parametric test (see Chapter 16).

At this stage, we recommend a simple eyeballing of the histograms for each variable (these can be obtained from the SPSSFW *Frequencies* program). You should do this for each group separately. Figures 7.3 to 7.6 are guidelines.

Remember that in using the t-test we compare a difference in *means*, and if our data are skewed, the mean may not be the best measure of central tendency.

In the past, psychologists were advised to perform a t-test only when the variances between the two groups were similar. This is because, in calculating part of the formula (for the t-test), the variances for the two groups are added together and averaged. If the variances are very unequal, the 'average' obtained will not be representative of either of the conditions. SPSSFW, however, uses a slightly different method of calculating a t-value when the variances are unequal, allowing you therefore to use the t-test under these conditions.

Figure 7.3   Slight positive skew

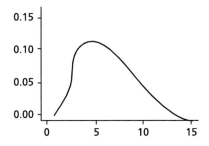

Figure 7.4   Slight negative skew

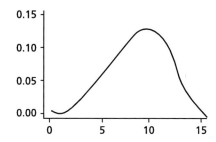

Figure 7.5   Strong positive skew

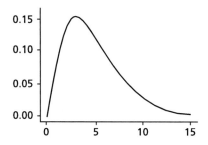

Figure 7.6   Strong negative skew

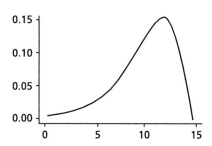

When we have different numbers of participants in the two groups, taking a simple average of the two variances might be misleading, because the formula would give the two groups equal weighting, when in fact one group might consist of more participants. In this case we would use a weighted average. The weighted average for the sample (called the pooled variance estimate) is used in order to obtain a more accurate estimate of the population variance.

If your data are extremely skewed and you have very small participant numbers, you will need to consider a non-parametric test (see Chapter 16). This is because non-parametric tests do not make assumptions about normality.

7.1.10   t-test for independent samples

Let's use our example of the NOISE/NO NOISE experiment to go through the SPSS instructions and output for a t-test for independent samples.

SPSSFW: for an independent t-test

Open your datafile. First you should set up a file suitable for independent designs. You have been shown how to do this in the SPSSFW section in Chapter 1, so please refer back to this.

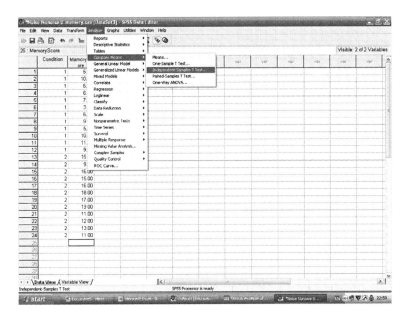

This opens the *Independent-Samples T Test* dialogue box, as follows:

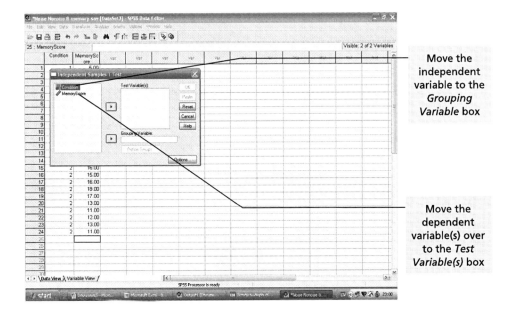

Move the independent variable to the *Grouping Variable* box

Move the dependent variable(s) over to the *Test Variable(s)* box

This gives the *Define Groups* dialogue box:

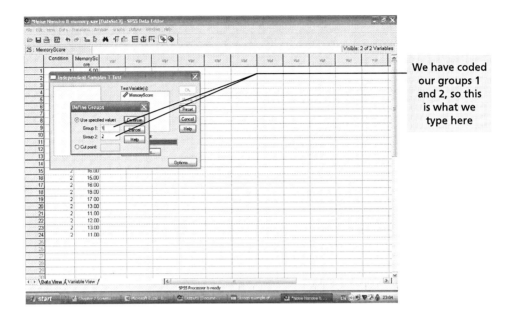

You then have to give the value you have assigned to the groups, i.e. if you have coded women as 0 and men as 1, then sex (0,1) is the correct format. In our example, however, our groups are coded as 1 and 2.

Click on *Continue*. This brings you back to the previous dialogue box; you can then click on *Options*. This gives you the following options box. It is here that you can change your confidence level, from 95% to 90%, for instance.

Click on *Continue*, and then *OK*.

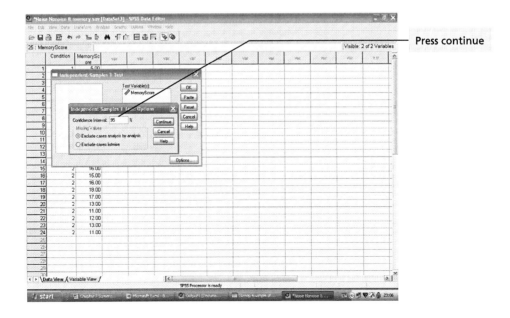

The results will appear in the output window. Most outputs give you far more information than you need; at first glance, it might look just like a jumble of numbers. However, you'll soon learn to pick out what really matters for your particular experiment or study. Some of the output will simply tell you what you already know! For instance, in the first section of the output below we are given the following:

- the name of the two conditions
- the number of cases in each condition
- the mean of each condition
- the standard deviation and standard error of the mean of the two conditions.

The above information can be scanned quite quickly; this information is already known to us. Once we know what to disregard, our output is fairly easy to read. These are the group statistics that appear first in the output:

Group Statistics

	noise and no noise	N	Mean	Std. Deviation	Std. Error Mean
SCORE	noise	12	7.2500	2.4909	.7191
	no noise	12	13.8333	2.7579	.7961

The next section of the output is what really interests us:

Independent Samples Test

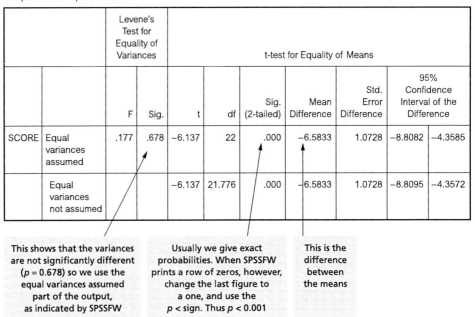

		Levene's Test for Equality of Variances		t-test for Equality of Means						
		F	Sig.	t	df	Sig. (2-tailed)	Mean Difference	Std. Error Difference	95% Confidence Interval of the Difference	
SCORE	Equal variances assumed	.177	.678	−6.137	22	.000	−6.5833	1.0728	−8.8082	−4.3585
	Equal variances not assumed			−6.137	21.776	.000	−6.5833	1.0728	−8.8095	−4.3572

This shows that the variances are not significantly different ($p = 0.678$) so we use the equal variances assumed part of the output, as indicated by SPSSFW

Usually we give exact probabilities. When SPSSFW prints a row of zeros, however, change the last figure to a one, and use the $p <$ sign. Thus $p < 0.001$

This is the difference between the means

One of the things you will notice is that SPSSFW uses a test called Levene's Test for Inequality. This is used to test whether the conditions have equal variances. Equal variances across conditions is called 'homogeneity of variance'. Some statistical tests such as the t-test assume that variances are equal across groups or samples. Levene's Test can be used to verify that assumption. The t-test gives two sets of results – one to use when we have met the assumption (i.e. variances are similar) and one to use when we have failed to meet this assumption (i.e. variances are different). Levene's Test provides us with an F-value, which you have not come across yet, but it is a test statistic just like t – in fact when DF = 1, $t^2 = F$ or $t = \sqrt{F}$. So if $t = 3$, then you know that this is equal to an F-value of 9. You will come across the F-test statistic later, in Chapter 10.

Levene's Test is a test of homogeneity of variances that does not rely on the assumption of normality. In making our decision as to whether we have met the assumption of equal variances, we need to look at the p-value given alongside the F-value. Consistent with the traditional convention, we should conclude that our variances are different (unequal) if this p-value is less than 0.05. If the p-value is greater than 0.05 then we assume that our variances are roughly equal. SPSSFW uses a criterion value of $p < 0.05$ to decide whether the variances are equal. Obviously this decision is subject to the same constraints outlined for hypothesis testing in Chapter 5. For simplicity, however, we will adhere to the SPSSFW criterion, as explained above.

The textual part of the results might be reported as follows:

Participants in the NOISE condition recalled fewer words ($\bar{X}$ = 7.3, SD = 2.5) than in the NO NOISE condition ($\bar{X}$ = 13.8, SD = 2.8). The mean difference between conditions was 6.58, which is a large effect size (d = 2.45); the 95% confidence interval for the estimated population mean difference is between 4.36 and 8.81. An independent t-test revealed that, if the null hypothesis were true, such a result would be highly unlikely to have arisen ($t(22)$ = 6.14; $p < 0.001$). It was therefore concluded that noise affects short-term memory, at least in respect of recall of words.

Example: need for cognition

Some people spend a lot of time actively engaged in problem-solving. Others do not. There are large individual differences in people's tendency to engage in and enjoy this 'cognitive activity'. This individual difference dimension is called need for cognition (NEEDCOG). In the following section of the output, men and women were compared on this dimension. There were far more men in the study. The means look similar, as do the standard deviation and the standard error of the mean.

Group Statistics

	Men and women	N	Mean	Std. Deviation	Std. Error Mean
NEEDCOG	Men	440	62.4886	9.942	.474
	Women	290	63.1586	8.484	.498

Here is the next section of the output:

Independent Samples Test

		Levene's Test for Equality of Variances		t-test for equality of means					95% Confidence Interval of the Difference	
		F	Sig.	t	df	Sig. (2-tailed)	Mean Difference	Std. Error Difference		
NEEDCOG	Equal variances assumed			−.94	728	.346	−.6700	.710	−2.064	.724
	Equal variances not assumed	14.577	.000	−.97	631.39	.330	−.6700	.688	−2.020	.680

The variances here are significantly different, i.e. not equal, so we use the 'equal variances not assumed' row

$p = 0.33$ – thus there is a 33% chance of these results being obtained by sampling error alone, assuming the null hypothesis to be true

You can see that the mean difference between conditions is 0.67. The variances between the two groups differ significantly, and so we use the 'equal variances not assumed' row. This shows a t-value of −0.97. The confidence interval shows that we are 95% confident that the population mean difference is between −2.02 and 0.68 – in other words, a very large range. The confidence interval includes zero – which means, if we repeat the study with a different sample, the women might score higher than the men (as in this case, where the mean difference is −0.67), the men might score higher than the women, or there might be absolutely no difference at all (zero). This is obviously not good enough for us, and we have to conclude that the groups do not differ on NEEDCOG. This is borne out by the small t-value (0.97) and the associated significance level of $p = 0.33$. This means that, assuming the null hypothesis to be true, we have a 33% chance of finding the t-value of 0.97.

CAUTION!

Remember that the minus sign when obtaining a t is equivalent to a plus sign. In other words, a t of, say, −5 is equivalent to a value of +5.

Example from the literature: differences between men and women in music experience

Werner *et al.* (2006) designed the Music Experience Questionnaire (MEQ). The MEQ contained six subscales, listed below in the first column of Table 7.4. As part of their study, they wished to see whether women and men differed on the six scales of the MEQ. Note that although they didn't give exact probability levels, they have given Cohen's *d*, the measure of effect between two conditions (see page 215).

Table 7.4   Descriptive statistics on Music Experience Questionnaire (MEQ) variables, by gender

MEQ variable	Women		Men		*t*	Cohen's *d*
	M	SD	M	SD		
Scales:						
Commitment to music	2.41	0.79	2.71	0.83	−3.07*	0.37
Innovative musical aptitude	2.65	0.84	2.84	0.86	−1.77	0.22
Social uplift	2.98	0.89	3.03	0.87	−0.45	0.05
Affective reactions	4.05	0.63	3.80	0.73	3.12*	0.38
Positive psychotropic effects	3.33	0.75	3.37	0.75	−0.03	0.00
Reactive musical behaviour	3.80	0.86	3.60	0.80	1.19	0.23

* $p < 0.001$

Activity 7.4

On which scale do women and men differ the most? On which do they hardly differ at all?

Example from the literature: insomnia: behavioural experiment versus verbal feedback

People who suffer from insomnia tend to overestimate the time they take to get to sleep and underestimate the time they have slept. Tang and Harvey (2006) investigated whether a behvioural experiment or verbal feedback reduced some misperceptions. Forty-eight people kept a sleep diary; their sleep time was also recorded on an actigraph. The discrepancy between the two were either shown via a behavioural experiment or verbally. As part of their analysis, they took post-experimental ratings as to whether participation in the study was (a) enjoyable, (b) beneficial, (c) acceptable to self and (d) acceptable to others. These results (together with many others) were presented as a table. Their (partial) table is reproduced in Table 7.5.

Table 7.5   Mean values, standard deviations and confidence intervals for postexperiment ratings

	Behavioural experiment group			Verbal feedback group		
	M	SD	CI	M	SD	CI
Enjoyable[c]	7.5	1.5	7.2–7.9	6.5	2.1	6.1–7.0
Beneficial[d]	7.4	1.9	7.0–7.8	5.3	2.8	4.7–5.9
Acceptable to self[e]	7.6	1.6	7.1–7.9	6.5	3.0	5.8–7.1
Acceptable to others[e]	7.8	1.6	7.5–8.2	6.3	3.0	5.6–6.9

[c] Response scale: 0 = not at all enjoyable, 10 = very enjoyable
[d] Response scale: 0 = benefitted nothing at all, 10 = benefitted a lot
[e] Response scale: 0 = not at all acceptable, 10 = very acceptable

The authors state 'Although the behavioral experiment group gave higher ratings on each of these scales, independent-sample t tests indicated that there were significant between-groups differences for the "beneficial", $t(40) = 2.8$, $p < .01$, and "acceptable to others," $t(30) = 2.1$, $p < .05$ ratings. The differences for the "enjoyable," $t(40) = 1.8$, $p = .08$, and "acceptable to self," $t(31) = 1.5$, $p = .14$, ratings did not reach statistical significance.'

7.1.11 Related t-test

The related t-test is also known as the paired t-test; these terms are interchangeable. As explained on page 212, the related t-test is used when the *same* participants perform under both conditions. The formula for this test is similar, not surprisingly, to the independent t-test. However, the related t-test is more sensitive than the independent t-test. This is because each participant performs in both conditions, and so each participant can be tested against him- or herself. If we have 20 people in a related design (20 people taking part in both conditions), we would need 40 in an unrelated design (20 in each condition). So the formula for the related t-test takes into account the fact that we are using the same participants. If you compare an independent and related t-test using the same dataset, you will find that the related t-test gives a result with a higher associated probability value – this is because the comparison of participants with themselves gives rise to a reduced within-participants variance, leading to a larger value of *t*.

Imagine that we want to find out whether different types of visualisation help pain control. To make it simple, assume there are two types of visualisation:

- imagine performing an exciting t-test (statistics condition)
- imagine lying on a sunny beach, drinking cocktails (beach condition).

Participants sit down, and are taken through the visualisation as they plunge their hands into ice-cold water. Although we have not tried this, we are assured it is very painful. The dependent variable is the number of seconds that our participants are able to keep their hands in the iced water. Now, as we are running this as a within-participants design (because it is more sensitive), we cannot simply have the participants doing one condition, then the other (this might lead to order effects, or it might be that no one returns for the second condition!). Therefore half the participants do condition A, then condition B, and

Table 7.6   Time (seconds) hands kept in water for each condition

Participant	Statistics condition	Beach condition
1	5	7
2	7	15
3	3	6
4	6	7
5	10	12
6	4	12
7	7	10
8	8	14
9	8	13
10	15	7

half do condition B, then A (see counter-balancing, Chapter 1). Now some people might think that our hypothesis is one-tailed, because they might think visualising lying on a sunny beach would help with pain control more than thinking about statistics. However, we advise you to determine whether your hypothesis is one- or two-tailed on the basis of previous research, not just a hunch you have! Since there is no research on this topic (as far as we know), we are going to have a two-tailed hypothesis. The data are shown in Table 7.6.

SPSSFW: two samples repeated-measures design – paired t-test

Open your datafile. Choose the *Paired-Samples T Test* from the *Compare Means* menu:

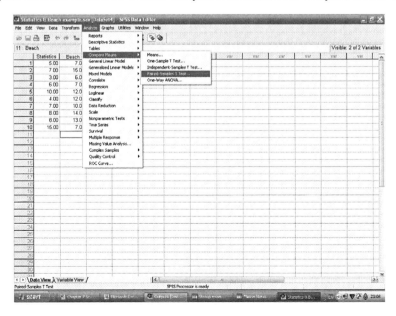

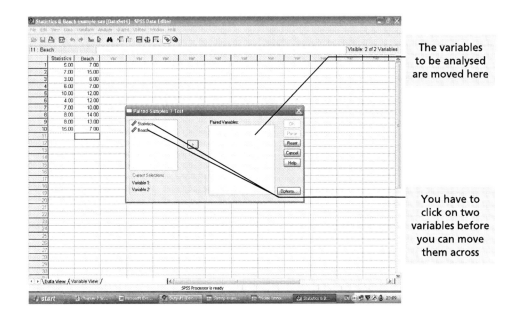

The variables to be analysed are moved here

You have to click on two variables before you can move them across

To select a pair of variables:

1. Click on the first variable.
2. Click on the second variable.
3. Click on ▶ to move the pair over.

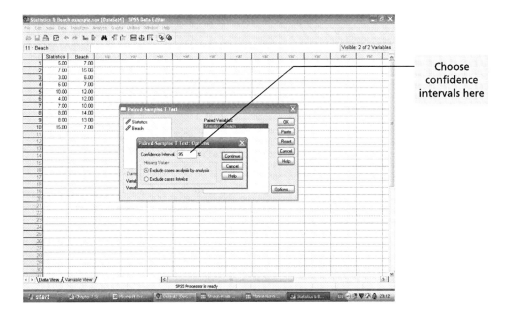

Choose confidence intervals here

Click on *Options*, if wanted (see above), then click on *Continue* within that dialogue box. Then click on *OK*. Your results will appear in the output window.

First of all, we obtain the group statistics. This gives the usual descriptive statistics: the mean, number of participants, standard deviation and standard error of the mean.

Paired Samples Statistics

		Mean	N	Std. Deviation	Std. Error Mean
Pair 1	STATISTI	7.3000	10	3.4010	1.0755
	BEACH	10.3000	10	3.3350	1.0546

The next section of the output provides us with a correlation between the two conditions:

Paired Samples Correlations

		N	Correlation	Sig.
Pair 1	STATISTI & BEACH	10	.070	.849

This shows that there is no relationship between scores in the BEACH condition and scores in the STATISTICS condition ($r = 0.07$, which is very weak indeed).

Then we come to the paired sample statistics:

Paired Samples Test

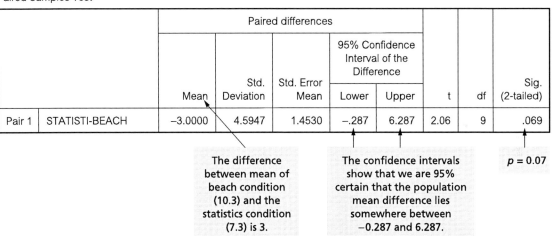

		Paired differences							
					95% Confidence Interval of the Difference				
		Mean	Std. Deviation	Std. Error Mean	Lower	Upper	t	df	Sig. (2-tailed)
Pair 1	STATISTI-BEACH	−3.0000	4.5947	1.4530	−.287	6.287	2.06	9	.069

The difference between mean of beach condition (10.3) and the statistics condition (7.3) is 3.

The confidence intervals show that we are 95% certain that the population mean difference lies somewhere between −0.287 and 6.287.

$p = 0.07$

Although we can see, oddly enough, that participants in the BEACH condition did keep their hands in the iced water longer (mean = 10.3 seconds, as opposed to the mean of the statistics condition, 7.3 seconds), the analysis gave us a t-value of 2.06, with an associated probability level of 0.069. The confidence interval is wide – we can say, with 95% confidence, that the true population mean difference is somewhere within the interval −0.287 and 6.827. This means that we cannot really be sure, if we repeated the study, that the beach visualisation would have given the better result. Therefore we have to conclude that there is no evidence to suggest that this type of visualisation affects pain control.

Part of your textual analysis might read:

Although it can be seen that participants in the BEACH condition held their hands in ice-cold water for a mean of 10.3 seconds, as opposed to the mean of 7.3 in the STATISTICS condition, the 95% confidence limits show us that, if we repeated the experiment, the population mean difference between the conditions would lie somewhere between −0.287 and 6.287. Thus we cannot be sure that, in the population, the beach visualisation would give the better result ($t(9) = 2.06$; $p = 0.07$)

Example: the verbal and performance IQ of people with chronic illness

A study was carried out comparing the verbal IQ (VIQ) and the performance IQ (PIQ) of people with chronic illness. In a normal population you would expect the two IQ measures to be similar. The population mean IQ is 100.

SPSSFW provides us with a correlation between the two conditions:

Paired Samples Correlations

		N	Correlation	Sig.
Pair 1	verbal iq & performance iq	40	.680	.000

As would be expected, there is a strong and positive relationship between the two IQ measures.

Remember to scan the first part of the output, which confirms how many pairs you have, and the names of the variables:

Paired Samples Statistics

		Mean	N	Std. Deviation	Std. Error Mean
Pair 1	verbal iq	94.8750	40	12.03880	1.90350
	performance iq	109.1000	40	12.86777	2.03457

It can immediately be seen that the verbal IQ of the group is lower than their performance IQ.

Paired Samples Test

		Paired differences								
					95% Confidence Interval of the Difference					
		Mean	Std. Deviation	Std. Error Mean	Lower	Upper	t	df	Sig. (2-tailed)
Pair 1	verbal iq – performance iq	−14.2250	9.98842	1.57931	−17.4195	−11.0305	−9.007	39	.000

In this case, our sample mean paired difference (between verbal and performance IQ) is 14.23. Regarding the population mean difference, we are 95% confident that the value falls between 11.03 and 17.42.

$t(39) = -9.01$ has an associated p-value of $p < 0.001$, which means that, assuming the null hypothesis to be true, such a value would have occurred less than once in 1000 times. This is so unlikely that we conclude that the differences between the verbal and performance IQ of the group are unlikely to have arisen by sampling error.

Activity 7.5

Look at the following printout, which relates to the next *two* questions:

Group Statistics

	condition	N	Mean	Std. Deviation	Std. Error Mean
Memory	Con1	10	15.6000	5.621	.1778
	Con2	10	23.9000	11.130	3.520

Paired Samples Correlations

		N	Correlation	Sig.
Pair 1	Con1 and Con2	10	.786	.007

Paired Samples Test

		Paired differences							
					95% Confidence Interval of the Difference				Sig.
		Mean	Std. Deviation	Std. Error Mean	Lower	Upper	t	df	(2-tailed)
Pair 1	Con1 and Con2	−8.3000	7.558	2.390	−13.707	−2.893	−3.47	9	.007

1. The value of the test statistic is:
    (a) 0.007
    (b) −8.30
    (c) −3.47

2. The difference between the mean of condition 1 and 2 is:
    (a) −8.3
    (b) 7.558
    (c) 2.390

Example from the literature: perceived control and distress following sexual assault

Frazier (2003) collected data from women who had suffered a serious sexual assault, at four time-points after the assault. The data provided information relating to the way in which beliefs about controllability and distress change over the time following the assault. Descriptive statistics were as follows:

Variable	2 weeks (n = 88)		2 months (n = 98)		6 months (n = 89)		12 months (n = 92)	
	$\bar{X}$	SD	$\bar{X}$	SD	$\bar{X}$	SD	$\bar{X}$	SD
Control								
Behavioural self-blame	3.54	1.18	3.37	1.07	3.07	1.14	2.88	1.10
Rapist blame	3.85	0.95	3.65	1.15	3.73	1.16	3.47	1.21
Control over recovery	3.74	0.77	3.93	0.71	3.91	0.79	4.03	0.78
Future control	4.07	0.63	4.23	0.64	4.13	0.72	4.12	0.64
Future (un)likelihood of assault	2.40	0.76	2.63	0.84	2.72	0.75	2.81	0.75
Distress								
Anxiety	2.31	0.85	1.78	0.98	1.52	1.01	1.29	0.96
Depression	2.04	0.98	1.64	1.03	1.50	1.02	1.18	0.94
Hostility	1.58	0.90	1.44	0.96	1.31	1.04	1.03	0.88
Distress	2.00	0.74	1.63	0.85	1.45	0.92	1.17	0.82

The authors state that:

Rapist blame was more common than behaviour self-blame, with small effect sizes at 2 weeks, $t(87) = -.78$, $p = .08$, $d = 0.19$, and 2 months, $t(94) = -.80$, $p = .07$, $d = 0.19$, and medium effects at 6 months, $t(84) = -4.61$, $p < .0001$, $d = 0.50$, and 12 months, $t(89) = -4.50$, $p < .0001$, $d = 0.48$, postassault. According to Cohen's (1992) conventions for effect sizes (ds) for t tests, .20 is a small effect size, .50 is medium, and .80 is large.

Note that the authors have performed four paired t-tests. That is, they have compared ratings on 'behavioural self-blame' with ratings on 'rapist blame' at four time-points. The first comparison was made two weeks after the assault. Although participants rated rapists more to blame than themselves, the difference between these two variables was small – the effect size is given as 0.19, which is, as the authors have told us, a weak effect. The difference between the two 'blame' variables at this time-point has an associated probability level of 0.08. A second t-test was performed on the same variables at two months – again the effect is weak. Six months later, however, when they perform the third t-test, the difference between the conditions becomes more marked. The two conditions here differ by half a standard deviation. At the fourth time-point, the difference is similar.

Multiple testing

If you perform several tests within one study or experiment, then some of your inferential statistical analyses will give rise to results with low associated probability levels (e.g. 0.001) by sampling error alone. To allow for this, we recommend that you interpret your results in the light of this knowledge. The easiest way to do this is to divide 0.05 (the traditional criterion variable for significance) by the number of tests you are performing (in any one study), and then interpret your ASL accordingly.

So if, in your experiment, you carry out three t-tests, then:

$$\text{ASL} = \frac{0.05}{3} = 0.0167$$

Any ASL > 0.0167 may be due to sampling error. Remember, however, that interpreting significance levels is just one piece of information contributing to the interpretation of your results. There are also effect sizes and confidence intervals.

Summary

- Confidence limits allow you to infer with a certain degree of confidence (usually 95%) that a population mean (or difference between means) falls within a certain range.

- *d*, an effect size, gives the magnitude of difference between two independent means, expressed in standard deviations.

- t-tests allow us to assess the likelihood of having obtained the observed differences between the two groups by sampling error: e.g. $p = 0.03$ means that, if we repeated our experiment 100 times using different samples, then assuming no real difference between conditions, we would expect to find our pattern of results three times, by sampling error alone.

- t-tests are suitable for data drawn from a normal population – they are parametric tests.

Discover the brand new website at **www.booksites.net/dancey** where you can test your knowledge with multiple choice questions and activities, discover more about topics using the links to relevant websites, and explore the interactive flowchart designed to help you find the right method of analysis.

SPSSFW exercise

Twenty schoolchildren (ten boys and ten girls) have been measured on number of episodes of illness in one year, performance in a test at the beginning of the year, and performance in a similar test at the end of the year. Enter the following data into SPSSFW. Code the boys as group 1, and the girls as group 2.

Group	Episodes of illness	Test at beginning of year	Test at end of year
1	24	13	16
1	20	16	20
1	8	7	18
1	12	30	35
1	5	5	5
1	24	10	15
1	0	9	10
1	8	15	24
1	20	18	30
1	24	20	27
2	7	18	17
2	30	14	10
2	2	20	20
2	10	9	10
2	18	13	9
2	9	13	16
2	20	10	1
2	10	16	14
2	15	5	6
2	8	7	14

Assume that data are drawn from a normally distributed population.

1. Perform an independent t-test between boys and girls on 'episodes of illness', and on the end of year test.

2. Calculate the effect size, d, where appropriate.

3. Imagine that your friend does not understand the output you have obtained, nor does the friend know about effect sizes or confidence intervals. Write a few paragraphs explaining the meaning of the results to your friend.

4. Perform a repeated-measures t-test on performance on the test at the beginning of the year and the end of the year. Give a written explanation of the meaning of your results to your friend. The prediction is that the group will perform better at the end of the year.

MULTIPLE CHOICE QUESTIONS

1. The DF for an independent t-test analysis with 20 participants in each condition is:
   (a) 38
   (b) 20
   (c) 40
   (d) 68

2. For a paired t-test with 40 participants, the appropriate DF is:

    (a) 20
    (b) 39
    (c) 38
    (d) none of these

3. For an independent t-test with 15 participants in each condition, the appropriate DF is:

    (a) 28
    (b) 14
    (c) 30
    (d) 15

4. One hundred students were tested on their anxiety before and after an anxiety coun-selling session. Scores are drawn from a normally distributed population. Which statistical test is the most appropriate?

    (a) Independent groups t-test
    (b) Related measures t-test
    (c) Levene's Test
    (d) None of these

5. The most important assumption to meet when using a t-test is:

    (a) The variation in scores should be minimal
    (b) Scores should be drawn from a normally distributed population
    (c) Conditions should have equal means
    (d) All of the above

6. The higher the t-value, the more likely it is that the differences between groups are:

    (a) A result of sampling error
    (b) Not a result of sampling error
    (c) Similar to each other
    (d) None of the above

7. A t-value of –5 is:

    (a) Less important than a value of +5
    (b) More important than a value of +5
    (c) Equivalent to a value of +5
    (d) Less significant than a value of +5

Questions 8 to 10 relate to the following table of results:

Group Statistics

	SEX	N	Mean	Std. Deviation	Std. Error Mean
Total of stigma	1.00	62	33.8710	12.1149	1.5386
	2.00	53	34.8302	13.0586	1.7937

Independent Samples Test

		Levene's Test for Equality of Variances		t-test for Equality of Means						
									95% Confidence Interval of the Difference	
		F	Sig.	t	df	Sig. (2-tailed)	Mean Difference	Std. Error Difference	Lower	Upper
Total of stigma	Equal variances assumed	.755	.387	–.408	113	.684	–.9592	2.3493	–5.6136	3.6951
	Equal variances not assumed			–.406	107.199	.686	–.9592	2.3632	–5.6439	3.7255

8. The difference between the means of the groups is (correct to one decimal place):

(a) 0.41

(b) 0.69

(c) 0.96

(d) 0.76

9. The variances of the two groups are:

(a) Indeterminate

(b) Unequal

(c) Assumed to be equal

(d) Skewed

10. What can you conclude from the results?

(a) There are no statistically significant differences or important differences between the two groups

(b) There is a statistically significant difference but it is not important

(c) There is an important difference between the two groups but it is not statistically significant

(d) There are both statistically significant and important differences between the groups

11. The effect size for independent groups, d, can be calculated by:

(a) (mean 1 – mean 2) ÷ mean SD

(b) (mean 1 + mean 2) ÷ mean SD

(c) (mean 1 – mean 2) ÷ SEM

(d) (mean 1 + mean 2) ÷ SEM

12. If the 95% confidence limits around the mean difference (in a t-test) are 10.5 – 13.0, we can conclude that, if we repeat the study 100 times, then:

(a) Our results will be statistically significant 5 times

(b) Our results will be statistically significant 95 times

(c) 95% of the time the population mean difference will be between 10.5 and 13.00; 5% of the time the population mean difference will be outside this range

(d) 5% of the time the population mean difference will be between 10.5 and 13.00; 95% of the time the population mean difference will be outside this range

13. In an analysis using an unrelated t-test, you find the following result:

Levene's Test for Equality of Variances: $F = 0.15$ $p = 0.58$

This shows that the variances of the two groups are:

(a) Dissimilar
(b) Similar
(c) Exactly the same
(d) Indeterminate

14. In the SPSSFW output, if $p = 0.000$, then you should report this as:

(a) $p = 0.000$
(b) $p = 0.0001$
(c) $p < 0.001$
(d) $p < 0.0001$

15. In an independent t-test, you would use the 'equal variances not assumed' part of the output when Levene's test is:

(a) Above a criterion significance level (e.g. $p > 0.05$)
(b) Below a criterion significance level (e.g. $p < 0.05$)
(c) When numbers of participants are unequal in the two conditions
(d) When you have skewed data

16. For a within-participants design using 20 people, the degrees of freedom are:

(a) 20
(b) 38
(c) 19
(d) 40

17. Levene's test is:

(a) A test of heterogeneity that relies on the assumption of normality
(b) A test of homogeneity that relies on the assumption of normality
(c) A test of heterogeneity that does not rely on the assumption of normality
(d) A test of homogeneity of variances that does not rely on the assumption of normality

Read the following excerpt from a results section of a journal article (Ratcliff et al., 2003) then answer question 18:

The changes in mean scores on all tests between Wave 4 and Wave 5 were statistically significant based on the paired t-test (all of the p *values < .001, except MMSE,* p *= .012; Word List Learning, Delayed Recall,* p *= .009; Boston Naming,* p *= .019).*

18. Why are 'all of the p values' reported as $p < 0.001$, when the other named variables have been reported with the exact probability values?

    (a) The researchers could not work out the exact probability values
    (b) The significance level in their statistical program calculated $p = 0.000$
    (c) The unnamed variables are not as significant
    (d) All of the above

Questions 19 and 20 relate to the following table:

Independent Samples Test

		Levene's Test for Equality of Variances		t-test for Equality of Means						
									95% Confidence Interval of the Difference	
		F	Sig.	t	df	Sig. (2-tailed)	Mean Difference	Std. Error Difference	Lower	Upper
Serious economic consequences	Equal variances assumed	.113	.738	.923	106	.358	.5258	.56951	−.60327	1.65494
	Equal variances not assumed			.882	16.607	.391	.5258	.59644	−.73481	1.78649

19. Which row would the researcher use to interpret the independent t-test results?

    (a) The equal variances row
    (b) The unequal variances row

20. Generalising to the population, what sign would the expected t-value take?

    (a) Positive
    (b) Negative
    (c) It could be either positive or negative

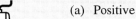

Cohen, J. (1988) *Statistical Power for Behavioral Sciences*, 2nd edn. New York: Academic Press.
Cohen, J. (1992) 'A power primer', *Psychological Bulletin*, **112**: 155–9.
Frazier, P.A. (2003) 'Perceived control and distress following sexual assault: a longitudinal test of a new model', *Journal of Personality and Social Psychology*, **84**(6): 1257–69.
Ratcliff, G., Dodge, H., Birzescu, M. and Ganguli, M. (2003) 'Tracking cognitive functioning over time: ten-year longitudinal data from a community-based study', *Applied Neuropsychology*, **10**(2): 89–95.

Tang, N.K.Y. and Harvey, A.G. (2006) 'Altering misperception of sleep in insomnia: behavioral experiment versus verbal feedback', *Journal of Consulting and Clinical Psychology*, **74**(4): 767–76.

Werner, P.D., Swope, A.J. and Heide, F.J. (2006) 'The Music Experience Questionnaire: development and correlates', *Journal of Psychology*, **140**(4): 329–45.

Yu, C.H. (2003) 'Illustrating degrees of freedom in multimedia', available at www.creativewisdom.com/pub/df/default.htm [accessed 14 November 2006].

Answers to multiple choice questions

1. a, 2. b, 3. a, 4. b, 5. b, 6. b, 7. c, 8. c, 9. c, 10. a, 11. a, 12. c, 13. b, 14. c, 15. b, 16. c, 17. d, 18. b, 19. a, 20. c

10 Analysis of differences between three or more conditions

Chapter overview

In previous chapters you learned how to compare two conditions, and how to analyse relationships between two variables. As part of these analyses you learned how to report effect sizes, confidence intervals and achieved significance levels (ASLs). You now have all the tools you need to go on to a more complicated analysis – the analysis of three or more conditions. You are used to the idea of comparing two conditions (see Chapter 7), and the analysis of three or more conditions is just an extension of this. Instead of the t-tests, for two conditions, we now have ANOVA (for three or more conditions). ANOVA is the parametric equivalent of the t-test, for more than two groups. ANOVA is an acronym for Analysis of Variance. As in the t-test, you need to meet certain assumptions in order to be able to perform ANOVA. You will recognise these from your work on the t-test:

- Scores must be drawn from a normally distributed population. We assume this is the case if our sample data show a normal distribution: the more participants we have in the study, the more likely it is that the distribution will be normal (see Chapter 3, page 73).

- Homogeneity of variance. This means that the variances are similar for the different groups. SPSSFW will test for this. In the case of the independent ANOVA, the test is called Levene's Test. In the case of the repeated-measures ANOVA, it is F Max.

- In a repeated-measures analysis, there is an additional assumption – that of sphericity. However, there is an adjustment used in repeated-measures ANOVA when this assumption has been violated. The adjustment is called the Greenhouse–Geisser Epsilon, and is given routinely in SPSSFW.

ANOVA is relatively robust in respect of these assumptions, so that small violations (e.g. you have normally distributed data, equal number of scores in the conditions but variances are not equal) mean that you can still go ahead. (Within-participants ANOVA is not robust to violations of sphericity, however, which is why the F must be routinely adjusted to take account of this.) If you have small numbers of participants, your data are skewed, and if you have unequal numbers of scores in the different conditions, you must consider performing a non-parametric equivalent of ANOVA, which is covered in Chapter 16.

In this chapter you will:

- gain a conceptual understanding of what is meant by the analysis of variance
- learn how to analyse data by the use of parametric ANOVAs
- learn about an overall measure of effect (partial eta^2)
- learn how to present your results graphically.

The analysis of three or more conditions includes the following:

- descriptive statistics, such as means, confidence intervals where appropriate, medians, standard deviations; graphical illustrations such as box and whisker plots
- effect size – the magnitude of the difference between the conditions, called *d*, and an overall measure of effect, partial eta^2 (η^2)
- inferential tests: a statistical test called Analysis of Variance (ANOVA) evaluates how likely it is that any differences between the conditions are due to sampling error.

10.1 Visualising the design

It is easy to visualise an analysis of the differences between three or more groups by representing it as shown in Table 10.1.

This is called a *one-way* design, because we have one factor – Factor A. This has three levels – A1, A2, A3. We can tell this is a between-groups design because each participant appears under only one level, e.g. Participant 1 (P1) appears only under the A1 condition.

Table 10.2 is also a one-way design,[1] because there is only *one* factor (called A). Factor A has three levels, or conditions (A1, A2, A3). You can tell that the design is repeated-measures, because each participant is shown to give a score under each level, e.g. P1 appears under A1, A2 and A3, as do Participants 2 to 10.

Three levels (or conditions) of one factor (Factor A)

Table 10.1   Independent participants (between-groups)

A1	A2	A3
P1	P11	P21
P2	P12	P22
.	.	.
.	.	.
.	.	.
.	.	.
.	.	.
.	.	.
P10	P20	P30

[1] Although sometimes a repeated-measures one-way design such as this is, confusingly, known as a two-way. This is because the repetition of participants over all conditions is itself called a factor.

Table 10.2   Repeated measures (within-participants)

A1	A2	A3
P1	P1	P1
P2	P2	P2
.	.	.
.	.	.
.	.	.
.	.	.
.	.	.
.	.	.
P10	P10	P10

ANOVA looks to see whether there are differences in the means of the groups. It does this by determining the grand mean[2] and seeing how different each of the individual means is from the grand mean.

There are two types of ANOVA:

1. Independent ANOVA (used when the participants perform in only *one* condition of several, i.e. an independent or between-participants design).
2. Related ANOVA (used when the participants perform in *all* conditions, i.e. a related or within-participants design).

Related and independent ANOVAs test whether there is a significant difference between some or all of the means of the conditions by comparing them with the grand mean.

ANOVA is the t-test, generalised to more than two groups, and because of this, there is a direct relationship between them; in fact, if you use ANOVA on two conditions, the results will be equivalent to those obtained using a t-test.

10.2   Meaning of analysis of variance

Analysis of variance (ANOVA), as the name suggests, analyses the different sources from which variation in the scores arises. Look at the scores in Table 10.3.

You will note that scores do not vary at all in the first condition. The variance is greater in the second condition, and even greater in the third.

10.2.1   Between-groups variance

ANOVA looks for differences between the means of the groups. When the means are very different, we say that there is a greater degree of variation *between* the conditions. If there were no differences between the *means* of the groups, then there would be no variation. This sort of variation is called *between-groups variation*, e.g. you can see from Table 10.3 that the means vary from 9 to 22.2.

---

[2] The grand mean is the mean of the means, e.g. (M1 + M2 + M3)/3.

Table 10.3 Scores for participants in three conditions

A1	A2	A3
9	15	21
9	15	25
9	16	17
9	15	22
9	16	26
$\bar{X} = 9$	$\bar{X} = 15.4$	$\bar{X} = 22.2$

Variation within the third group (from 17 through to 26)

Variation between the groups (9 to 22.2)

Between-groups variation arises from:

■ *Treatment effects*: When we perform an experiment, or study, we are looking to see that the differences between means are big enough to be important to us, *and* that the differences reflect our experimental manipulation. The differences that reflect the experimental manipulation are called the treatment effects.

■ *Individual differences*: Each participant is different, therefore participants will respond differently, even when faced with the same task. Although we might allot participants randomly to different conditions, sometimes we might find, say, that there are more motivated participants in one condition, or they are more practised at that particular task. So sometimes groups vary because of the unequal distribution of participants.

■ *Experimental error*: Most experiments are not perfect. Sometimes experimenters fail to give all participants the same instructions; sometimes the conditions under which the tasks are performed are different, for each condition. At other times equipment used in the experiment might fail, etc. Differences due to errors such as these contribute to the variability.

The between-groups variance can be thought of as variation *between the columns*. In the scores above, there *is* variation *between* the columns.

10.2.2 Within-groups variance

Another source of variance is the differences or variation *within* a group. This can be thought of as variation *within* the columns. You can see from the scores above that condition 1, A1, has *no variation* within it; all the participants have scored the same: 9. Condition 2, A2, has little variation. Condition 3, A3, has much more variation. We have given these scores in order to illustrate variation – we might not want to perform ANOVA on data like these, because one of the assumptions of ANOVA (see later) is that the variances in each group are similar. This is because the formula for ANOVA takes the variances of each group and calculates an average. It only makes sense to use such an average if the groups are similar.

Within-groups variation arises from:

■ *Individual differences*: In each condition, even though participants have been given the same task, they will still differ in scores. This is because participants differ among themselves – they have different abilities, knowledge, IQ, personality and so on. Each group, or condition, is bound to show variability – thus the scores in condition 1, A1, above are unrealistic.

■ *Experimental error*: This has been explained above.

10.2.3   Partitioning the variance

As you know, the purpose of ANOVA is to discover whether there are differences in the means of the groups, and it does this by first calculating a grand mean, and then looking to see how different each of the individual means is from the grand mean. It does this by what is known as *partitioning the variance*, as explained below. The variability in scores both across the groups and within the groups represents the total variance, and there are two sources that will determine this total variability – between-groups influences and within-groups influences. What ANOVA does is to partition this total variability into these two components. In order to do this ANOVA has to estimate how much variability is contributed by each of these components:

1.   First, ANOVA calculates the *mean* for each of the three groups.
2.   Then it calculates the *grand mean* (the three means are added together, then divided by 3).
3.   For each group separately, the total deviation of each individual's score from the mean of the group is calculated. This is the *within-groups variation*.
4.   Then the deviation of each group mean from the grand mean is calculated. This is the *between-groups variation*.

As you can see, these calculations involve the grand mean. For instance, the total variance of a group describes the distance between the grand mean and the furthest score (see Figure 10.1). The total variance can then be partitioned into that due to differences between the means of the groups (between-groups variance) and that due to random error, that is, they are not manipulated by the experimenter (within-participants variance).

This is done for each of the groups. Approximately speaking, the final calculations involve finding an average of the three groups' between-groups variance, the within-groups variance, and the total variance. The test statistic, F, is a ratio between the between-groups variance and the within-groups variance.

Between-groups variance ÷ within-groups variance = F ratio

As we said earlier, the F test has a direct relationship to the t-test. In fact when we have only two conditions,

$t^2 = F$

When we conduct our experiment, we hope that the within-groups variance is minimal – because this way, our F ratio will be larger. When the between-groups variance is very much larger than the within-groups variance, the F-value is large and the likelihood of such a result occurring by sampling error decreases.

Figure 10.1   Three-group design showing partition of variance and distances from grand mean

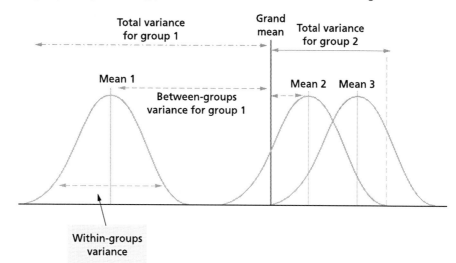

In Figure 10.1 you can see that there is a lot of overlap between groups 2 and 3 suggesting that they do not differ from each other. Group 1, however, shows no overlap with groups 2 and 3. The grey vertical line is the grand mean (simply the three means added up and divided by 3). The distribution of scores on the left is for group 1. The total variance for group 1 starts at the edge of the distribution and finishes at the grand mean. This can be broken down into between-groups variance (from the mean of group 1 to the grand mean) and within-groups variance (from the edge of the distribution to the group mean).

You should be able to see that the total variance for both groups 2 and 3 is far smaller. The distance from the individual means of group 2 and group 3 to the grand mean (the between-groups variance) is much smaller than the distance from group 1's mean to the grand mean.

In Figure 10.2 you can see that there is a lot of overlap between the three groups, and that none of the individual group means will be far from the grand mean. The effect is small.

Figure 10.2   Schematic representation of a small one-way effect

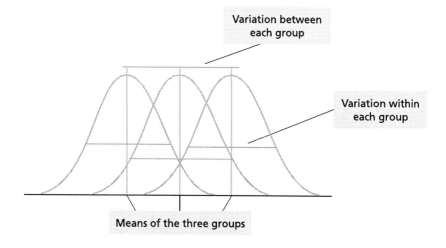

Figure 10.3   Schematic representation of a large one-way effect

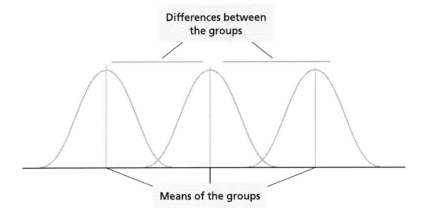

In Figure 10.3, you can see that there is a much smaller area of overlap, and that the individual group means will be much further from the grand mean. The effect will be larger.

The larger the (average) between-groups variance is in relation to the (average) within-groups variance, the larger the F ratio. This shows us that one (or more) of the individual group means is significantly different from the grand mean. It does not tell us which means are significantly different: this will require a further test.

Activity 10.1

Consider a design that has four independent conditions. Think of some reasons why scores in the different conditions might be different from each other. Then consider some of the reasons why participants might vary *within* each group.

Example: alcohol and driving ability

Thirty-six people took part in an experiment to discover the effects of alcohol on driving ability. They were randomly assigned to three conditions: placebo (no alcohol), low alcohol and high alcohol. The non-alcoholic drink looked and tasted exactly the same as the other drinks(!). Participants were weighed and given the appropriate amount of drink. Thus the design is an independent one (between-participants). After half an hour of drinking, participants drove in a simulator for ten minutes, and the number of errors made was automatically registered by the computer. Data were as shown in Table 10.4.

Table 10.4   Data in three alcohol conditions

Placebo	Low alcohol	High alcohol
5	5	8
10	7	10
7	9	8
3	8	9
5	2	11
7	5	15
11	6	7
2	6	11
3	4	8
5	4	8
6	8	17
6	10	11
$\sum = 70^a$	$\sum = 70$	$\sum = 123.00$
$\bar{X} = 5.83^b$	$\bar{X} = 6.17$	$\bar{X} = 10.25$
SD = 2.69	SD = 2.33	SD = 3.05

[a] $\sum$ = total
[b] $\bar{X}$ = mean

SPSSFW: performing a one-way ANOVA

Enter data in the usual way: save datafile. Select *Analyze*, *Compare Means* and *One-Way ANOVA*.

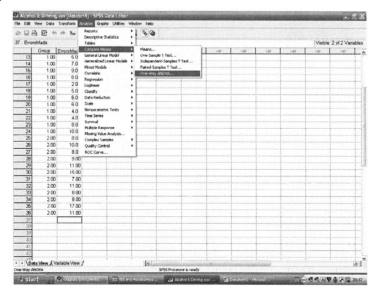

This brings you to the following dialogue box:

DV (*ErrorsMade*) is moved to the *Dependent List* box

IV (grouping variable) is moved to the *Factor* box

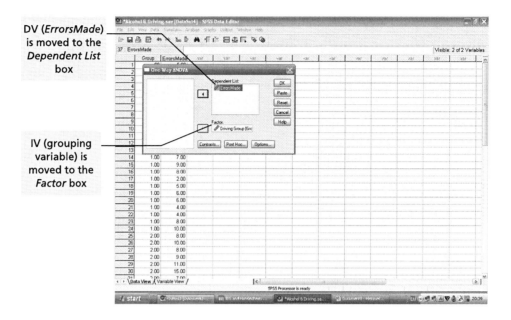

If you want post-hoc tests, click on the *Post Hoc* box (post-hoc tests are explained on page 309):

Select the test(s) that you want

Check the test you require, then click on *Continue*. Click on *Options* if you require descriptive statistics for each condition.

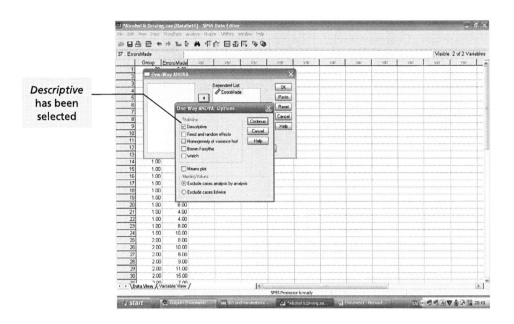

Descriptive has been selected

Then click on *Continue*, then *OK*. Your results will appear in the output window.

10.3 Descriptive statistics

The descriptive statistics option gives standard deviations, and confidence limits around the means. Look at Table 10.5.

The means appear to be different; the variances are similar. Let's look at the means plotted on a graph, with the confidence intervals around the means – see Figure 10.4.

Although the means of the placebo group (5.83) and the low alcohol group (6.17) are slightly different, the confidence intervals overlap substantially. Thus any difference we see between the means could be due to sampling error. After all, the confidence limits for the placebo tell us that we are 95% confident that the population mean is between 4.12 and 7.54; the confidence limits for the low alcohol group tell us that we are 95% confident that the population mean for this group is 4.69–7.65. Thus, if we ran the experiment again on a different sample, we might find that the means were exactly the same!

The mean of the high alcohol group is much higher than the other two means, but, more importantly, the confidence interval of this group does not overlap at all with groups 1

Table 10.5   Descriptive statistics and confidence limits for three alcohol conditions

	Placebo	Low alcohol	High alcohol
$\bar{X}$	5.83	6.17	10.25
SD	2.69	2.33	3.05
CI	4.12–7.54	4.69–7.65	8.31–12.19

Figure 10.4   95% confidence limits around the means

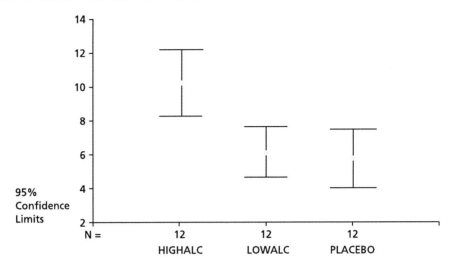

and 2. Thus we can already see that any effect is between the high alcohol group and the other two groups.

The test statistics for a one-way independent ANOVA are as follows:

ONEWAY

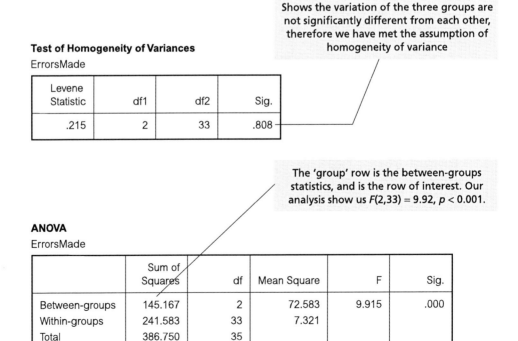

Shows the variation of the three groups are not significantly different from each other, therefore we have met the assumption of homogeneity of variance

Test of Homogeneity of Variances

ErrorsMade

Levene Statistic	df1	df2	Sig.
.215	2	33	.808

The 'group' row is the between-groups statistics, and is the row of interest. Our analysis show us $F(2,33) = 9.92$, $p < 0.001$.

ANOVA

ErrorsMade

	Sum of Squares	df	Mean Square	F	Sig.
Between-groups	145.167	2	72.583	9.915	.000
Within-groups	241.583	33	7.321		
Total	386.750	35			

In journal articles, you will see that the F-value (9.9), the degrees of freedom (2,33) and the associated probability (here $p < 0.001$) are always reported in the text. It is useful to report the overall size of the differences between the groups; however, SPSSFW does not have an option for this using the procedure described above (*Analysis, Compare Means, Oneway*). If you follow the procedure for ANOVA described in Chapter 11 you will get the same results as presented above but SPSSFW will also compute partial η^2 (eta^2) automatically under the ANOVA procedure. Partial eta^2 for the above example is 0.375. Thus 37.5% of the variation in the scores on driving ability is accounted for by the amount of alcohol consumed.

We now have a fair bit of information about the effect of alcohol on driving errors. Although it looks as if the differences between the groups are between the high alcohol condition and the other groups (rather than between placebo and low alcohol), ANOVA does not test for such comparisons. ANOVA lets us know whether there is a difference between some (or all) of the conditions, but that is as far as it goes. We can, however, obtain a further statistical test in order to confirm our belief that the differences that exist are between the high alcohol group and the others.

Multiple comparison procedures are used to assess which group means differ from means in the other groups.

10.4 Planned comparisons

Researchers can usually predict which means will differ from other means, and often such comparisons are planned in advance. These comparisons are usually carried out after the overall *F* ratio has shown that there are significant differences between two or more of the means. Although there are several tests for making such comparisons, we recommend you make your planned comparisons by using the t-test, since you are already familiar with this.

10.5 Controlling for multiple testing

Often researchers want to make several comparisons after running a one-way ANOVA. If you carry out multiple comparisons, then, as stated on page 237, you increase the likelihood of a Type I error. In order to take into consideration multiple testing you need to be more strict about the criterion used for declaring a result statistically significant. One way to control for multiple testing is to divide an acceptable probability value (e.g. 0.05) by the number of comparisons you wish to make. Thus, if you decide to make three pairwise comparisons, you divide 0.05 by 3. This gives you a value of 0.016. You then accept as statistically significant a probability level of less than 0.016. This avoids a Type I error.

10.6 Post-hoc tests

Sometimes researchers explore differences between the various sets of means without having specified these on the basis of theory. There are many post-hoc tests available to use, and these vary according to their power and ability to produce a Type I error – that is, they differ according to the extent to which they are liberal or conservative (these terms were explained in Chapter 5, page 149). When we perform post-hoc tests using SPSSFW, we do not have to correct for a Type I error (as explained in the paragraph above) because the tests available have been corrected to account for multiple testing. When you are making a large number of comparisons, you should choose a post-hoc test that is more conservative. Such a test is called the Tukey honestly significant difference (HSD) test. A test that tends to be more liberal is called the least significant difference test (LSD). Full discussion of these tests is not within the scope of this book; interested students are referred to Howell (2006) – or a search on the Internet.

If we (or rather our statistical package) perform a Tukey HSD on our alcohol data, we obtain the following:

Multiple Comparisons
Dependent Variable: SCORE
Tukey HSD

(I) condition	(J) condition	Mean Difference (I–J)	Std. Error	Sig.	95% Confidence Interval Lower Bound	Upper Bound
placebo	low alcohol	−.3333	1.1046	.951	−3.0438	2.3771
	high alcohol	**−4.4167***	**1.1046**	**.001**	**−7.1271**	**−1.7062**
low alcohol	placebo	.3333	1.1046	.951	−2.3771	3.0438
	high alcohol	**−4.0833***	**1.1046**	**.002**	**−6.7938**	**−1.3729**
high alcohol	placebo	4.4167*	1.1046	.001	1.7062	7.1271
	low alcohol	4.0833*	1.1046	.002	1.3729	6.7938

* The mean difference is significant at the .05 level.

This shows that there is a statistically significant difference between the placebo and high alcohol group, and between the low and high alcohol groups (emboldened). There is obviously no difference between the placebo and low alcohol group. You can now calculate the effect size, d, for the differences between the two conditions, in exactly the same way as you did for the t-test (see page 215). Just to remind you, the formula is as follows:

$$\frac{\text{Mean of condition 1} - \text{Mean of condition 3}}{\text{Mean SD}} = \frac{5.83 - 10.25}{\text{Mean SD}} = \frac{-4.42}{\text{Mean SD}}$$

So for conditions 1 and 3, the effect size is

$$\text{Mean SD} = \frac{2.69 + 3.05}{2} = 2.87$$

$$\text{Effect size} = \frac{-4.42}{2.87} = 1.54 \quad \longleftarrow \text{Ignore the sign}$$

Therefore the means of the placebo and high alcohol condition differ by 1.54 of a standard deviation; and this is statistically significant. If you calculate the effect size for the low and high alcohol conditions, you will find that they also differ by 1.54 SD. Calculation of the effect size for the placebo and low alcohol condition leads to a figure of 0.135. Thus these conditions differ by approximately one-seventh of a standard deviation. Such a difference could be due to sampling error. We now have plenty of information to write our report. The textual part of the analysis might be written as follows:

> Descriptive statistics (Table x)[3] show that there were more errors made in the high alcohol condition than in the other two conditions. A one-way analysis of variance showed that any differences between conditions were unlikely to have arisen by sampling error, assuming the null hypothesis to be true. $F(2,33) = 9.92$, $p < 0.001$ represented an effect size (partial eta^2) of 0.375, showing that nearly 38% of the variation in driving errors can be accounted for by differing levels of alcohol. A post-hoc test (Newman–Keuls) confirmed that the differences between conditions 1 and 3, and 2 and 3 (both effect sizes $(d) = 1.54$) were unlikely to have arisen by sampling error. There was no significant difference between the placebo and low alcohol conditions (effect size $(d) = 0.14$).

Activity 10.2

In calculating an effect size between two conditions in a one-way ANOVA, you obtain an effect size (d) of 0.490. The conclusion is that the means differ by:

(a) About half a standard deviation
(b) About a quarter of a standard deviation
(c) 4.9 standard deviations
(d) None of the above

Example from the literature: eating attitudes and irritable bowel syndrome

The following is a study on eating attitudes and the irritable bowel syndrome (IBS). Some people think there might be a link between eating disorders (such as bulimia or anorexia) and IBS. There is some research showing a coexistence of eating disorders and inflammatory bowel disease (similar symptoms to IBS but with a known cause for such symptoms). One questionnaire measuring the extent to which a person has an eating disorder is called the Eating Attitudes Test (EAT). Sullivan

---

[3] You should refer your readers to the table where you give your descriptive statistics.

Table 10.6   Table of results by Sullivan *et al.* (1997)

Group	Count	Mean score	95% CI for the mean
IBS	48	16.67	13.6–19.7
Eating disorder	32	56.7	48.7–64.8
Bowel disease	31	10.4	8.0–12.9
Controls	28	9.6	7.2–12.0

et al. (1997) gave the EAT to four groups of people: IBS sufferers, people with an eating disorder, people with inflammatory bowel disease and people without any disorder. Table 10.6 shows the results.

It can be seen immediately that, as expected, people with an eating disorder score higher than all other groups on the EAT. Indeed, if this were not the case, the EAT would not be a valid test. The confidence intervals show that the inflammatory bowel disease group and the control group overlap, showing that there are no important differences between these two groups on the EAT. The IBS group, however, not only has a higher sample mean than these two groups, but the confidence interval for the mean does not overlap with them, suggesting that any differences (discounting the eating disorders group) will be between the IBS group and the bowel disease/control groups. The confidence interval for the eating disorder group does not overlap with any of the other groups.

Sullivan *et al.* report as follows: 'When all four groups were compared using ANOVA (F = 93.7217) and multiple range testing using the Least Significant Difference test (LSD) with a significance level of 0.05, both the eating disorder group and the IBS group achieved a significantly higher EAT score than the IBD and the control group.'

Example from the literature: psychological symptoms and ecstasy use

Soar *et al.* (2006) carried out a study looking at Ecstasy use. Their study had four separate groups of people: problem Ecstasy users (n = 53); non-problem Ecstasy users (n = 62); polydrug controls (n = 62) and illegal drug-naïve controls (n = 111). The participants completed questionnaires on recreational drug use, personal and family details, and a brief symptom inventory. As part of the study, they looked at whether these four groups differed on the Brief Symptoms Inventory. The table they presented is reproduced as Table 10.7.

The authors summarise these results as text also, e.g. 'Problematic Ecstasy users reported significantly higher levels of somatization ($F(3,284)$ = 4.35, p = .005) compared to non-problematic Ecstasy users, illegal drug-naïve and polydrug controls.'

Note that Soar *et al.* have given exact probability levels, and that the last column shows the direction of the differences.

Table 10.7 Mean scores (SDs) across all dimensions of the BSI for illegal drug-naïve

Symptom dimension	Illegal drug-naïve (N)	Polydrug controls (C)	Non-problematic Ecstasy users (E)	Problematic Ecstasy users (P)	Group effect	Post hoc comparisons
Somatization	0.46+/−0.53	0.48+/−0.56	0.45+/−0.49	0.77+/−0.64	0.005	N, C, E < P
Obsessive-compulsive	1.05+/−0.77	1.41+/−0.92	1.21+/−0.74	1.47+/−0.76	0.003	N < C, P
Interpersonal sensitivity	0.98+/−0.89	1.14+/−0.96	1.04+/−0.88	1.38+/−0.92	0.062	
Depression	0.69+/−0.78	0.83+/−0.82	0.74+/−0.69	1.11+/−0.89	0.014	N, E < P
Anxiety	0.63+/−0.65	0.83+/−0.87	0.63+/−0.65	1.11+/−0.82	0.001	N, E < P
Anger/hostility	0.65+/−0.69	0.95+/−0.89	0.81+/−0.83	0.97+/−0.91	0.046	
Phobic anxiety	0.37+/−0.56	0.47+/−0.71	0.36+/−0.55	0.54+/−0.69	0.285	
Paranoid ideation	0.88+/−0.78	1.03+/−0.86	0.85+/−0.75	1.06+/−0.75	0.306	
Psychoticism	0.58+/−0.68	0.6+/−0.74	0.6+/−0.70	0.8+/−0.77	0.216	

10.7 Repeated-measures ANOVA

The repeated-measures ANOVA consists of one group of participants performing under all the conditions. You will remember that, for the independent design, we partitioned the variance into two parts:

■ between-groups variance
■ within-groups variance.

When we carry out a repeated-measures design, we can further partition the within-groups variance as follows:

1. The variability in scores due to individual differences.
2. The variability due to random error.

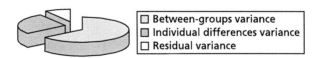

□ Between-groups variance
▨ Individual differences variance
□ Residual variance

We can measure (1) above because, in the repeated-measures design, each participant is tested under all conditions. Thus we can compare each participant's overall score (scores on all conditions added up) with the other participants' overall scores.

You will probably remember that the *F* ratio for our independent groups design was a ratio:

$$F = \frac{\text{Between-groups variance}}{\text{Within-groups variance}}$$

The between-groups variance was made up of variation due to treatment effects, individual differences and experimental error. In a repeated-measures design, there is no between-groups variation due to individual differences, as the participants in each group are one and the same. The formula for calculating F in repeated-measures designs takes into account the fact that the participants are the same in each condition. Variation due to individual differences (which we can measure; see above) are removed from both the top and bottom of the equation; this tends to give rise to a more sensitive and powerful statistical test:

$$F = \frac{\text{Between-groups variance}}{\text{Within-groups variance (with individual differences removed)}}$$

Let's now imagine a situation where we re-run our alcohol experiment as a repeated-measures design. This means that each person will perform the task in all three conditions (placebo, low and high alcohol). It would not make sense for each person to perform all the conditions in one day, so the participants will have to be tested, say, every Monday for three weeks. In order to offset practice and order effects, the conditions will have to be counterbalanced. This is a more powerful design than the between-participants experiment, as each participant acts as their own control. We will assume that the scores, however, are the same (see Table 10.8).

The analysis starts in the same way as the between-participants design, with descriptive statistics and graphical illustrations.

Table 10.8   Data from participants in three alcohol groups

Participant	Placebo	Low alcohol	High alcohol
1	5	5	8
2	10	7	10
3	7	9	8
4	3	8	9
5	5	2	11
6	7	5	15
7	11	6	7
8	2	6	11
9	3	4	8
10	5	4	8
11	6	8	17
12	6	10	11
Σ	70	74	123

SPSSFW: instructions for repeated-measures ANOVA

From the menus, choose *Analyze*, *General Linear Model* and *Repeated Measures*:

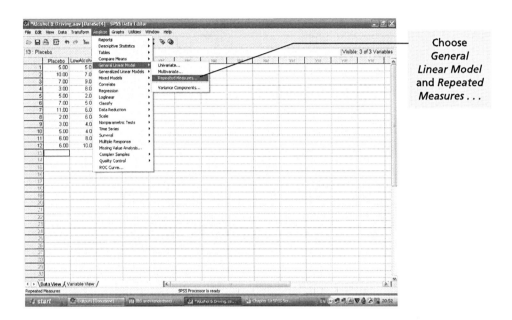

Choose *General Linear Model* and *Repeated Measures . . .*

This brings you to the following dialogue box:

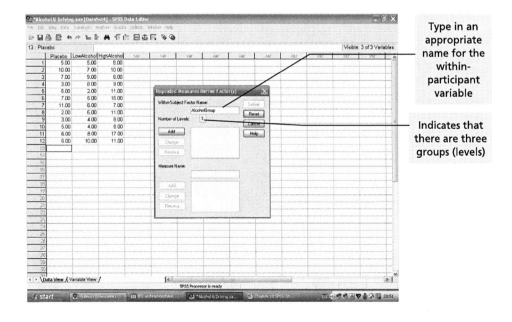

Type in an appropriate name for the within-participant variable

Indicates that there are three groups (levels)

Change 'Factor 1' to a sensible name – in this case we have called the factor *AlcoholGroup* – and insert the number of levels. Since we have PLACEBO, LOW and HIGH doses, we have three levels. Then press the *Add* button. Then click on *Define*.

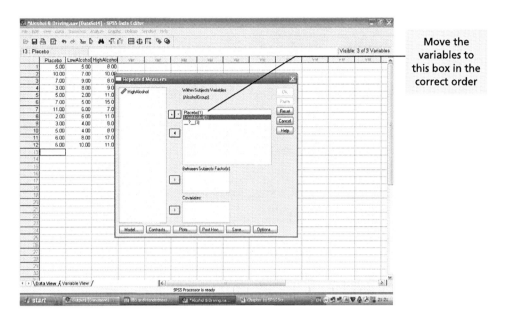

Move the variables on the left, one at a time, into the *Within-Subjects Variables* box on the right. In the example, *Placebo* is moved first, into the number one position, *LowAlcohol* is moved into the second position, and *HighAlcohol* the third. This represents our three levels. Then press *Options*. (Ignore the *Between-Subjects Factor(s)* and the *Covariates* buttons, as we are not interested in these for our analysis.)

This gives you the following dialogue box:

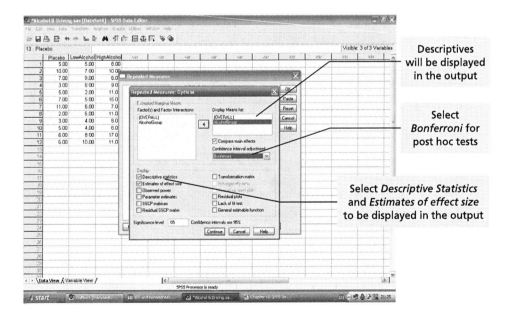

Make sure that you check *Compare main effects*. You are then given a choice of three tests: *LSD*, *Bonferroni* or *Sidak*. We suggest you use *Bonferroni*, which corrects for the number of pairwise tests that you are carrying out (see Multiple testing on page 237).

You can then check the options you require. Here we have asked for descriptives, effect size, means and power. The confidence intervals are given routinely. Then press *Continue*. This brings you back to the *Repeated Measures ANOVA* dialogue box. Press *OK*. Your results will appear in the output window.

10.7.1   Sphericity

In ANOVA we start from the assumption that the conditions are independent. In repeated measures designs, however, we use the same participants in each condition, which means there is likely to be some correlation between the conditions. If you have three conditions, then there are three bivariate correlations: condition 1 vs condition 2, condition 2 vs condition 3, and condition 1 vs condition 3. We make the assumption that these correlations are similar. Thus we assume that all of the covariances are similar. The assumption of sphericity holds when the variance of the difference between the estimated means for any pair of groups is the same as for any other pair. Since this assumption is unlikely to be met, and violations of sphericity are deterimental to the accuracy of ANOVA, we recommend that you routinely interpret the 'Greenhouse–Geiser' row of the output. In other words, it's better to assume that we *have* broken the assumption. The Greenhouse–Geiser works (as you can see from the output overleaf) by adjusting the degrees of freedom. This correction formula makes our test more stringent, so that, even if we have broken the assumption of sphericity, we are less likely to make a Type I error.

10.7.2   Output for ANOVA

We have emboldened the row of interest. The degrees of freedom look odd in the SPSSFW output, because they are given to several decimal places. The degrees of freedom, instead of being given as 2, 22 (for the sphericity assumed rows) are given as 1.833 and 20.164. Don't use such precision when reporting your degrees of freedom when using the Greenhouse–Geiser rows – just round them to whole numbers – in this case, 2,20. Here you will see that $F = 10.83$, and $p = 0.001$. The effect size, rounded up, is 50%. Therefore 50% of the variation in scores measuring driving ability is accountable by the different amounts of alcohol consumed.

Tests of Within-Subjects Effects
Measure: MEASURE_1

Use the Greenhouse–Geisser row

Source		Type III Sum of Squares	df	Mean Square	F	Sig.	Eta Squared
ALCOHOL	Sphericity Assumed	145.167	2	72.583	10.826	.001	.496
	Greenhouse– Geisser	**145.167**	**1.833**	**79.194**	**10.826**	**.001**	**.496**
	Huynh-Feldt	145.167	2.000	72.583	10.826	.001	.496
	Lower-bound	145.167	1.000	145.167	10.826	.007	.496
Error (ALCOHOL)	Sphericity Assumed	147.500	22	6.705			
	Greenhouse– Geisser	147.500	20.164	7.135			
	Huynh-Feldt	147.500	22.000	6.705			
	Lower-bound	147.500	11.000	13.409			

Note that $F_{(2,20)} = 10.83$, $p = 0.001$

10.7.3 Post-hoc tests/planned

This is the output obtained under the *Compare main effects* option, using Bonferroni:

Estimates
Measure: MEASURE_1

FACTOR1	Mean	Std. Error	95% Confidence Interval	
			Lower Bound	Upper Bound
1	5.833	.777	4.123	7.543
2	6.167	.672	4.687	7.646
3	10.250	.880	8.313	12.187

The table above shows the mean score for each of the conditions, plus the 95% confidence limits.

Pairwise Comparisons
Measure: MEASURE_1

(I) FACTOR1	(J) FACTOR1	Mean Difference (I–J)	Std. Error	Sig.[a]	95% Confidence Interval for Difference[a]	
					Lower Bound	Upper Bound
1	2	−.333	.924	1.000	−2.939	2.272
	3	−4.417*	1.196	.011	−7.790	−1.043
2	1	.333	.924	1.000	−2.272	2.939
	3	−4.083*	1.033	.007	−6.997	−1.170
3	1	4.417*	1.196	.011	1.043	7.790
	2	4.083*	1.033	.007	1.170	6.997

Based on estimated marginal means
* The mean difference is significant at the .05 level.
a. Adjustment for multiple comparisons: Bonferroni.

The table above compares each condition with every other condition, giving the mean difference between every pair, the standard error, the probability value, and the 95% confidence limits around the mean difference.

The first row compares 1 (placebo) with 2 (low alcohol). The mean difference is 0.333. This is not statistically significant at any acceptable criterion value. This row also compares level 1 (placebo) with level 3 (high alcohol). The difference here is 4.417, and the associated probability level is 0.011. Have a go at interpreting the rest of the table yourself.

Activity 10.3

Think about what the confidence limits are telling us. How would you explain the meaning of the confidence interval of the mean difference to a friend who did not understand the output?

The write-up is similar to the independent groups ANOVA. This time, however, we can say:

A repeated-measures ANOVA was carried out on the driving data. Assumptions of normality and homogeneity of variance were met. Using the Greenhouse–Geisser correction, results showed that there was a significant overall difference between conditions ($F(2,20) = 10.83$, $p = 0.001$); an overall effect size of 0.496 (partial η^2) showed that 50% of the variation in error scores can be accounted for by differing levels of alcohol. Pairwise comparisons showed that the difference between the placebo and the low alcohol condition was minimal (mean difference .13, $p = 1.00$) whereas the difference between the placebo and the high alcohol condition was large (mean difference = 4.42, $p = .011$), CI(95%)1.04–7.79). There was also a significant difference between the low and the high alcohol conditions (mean difference = 4.08, $p = .007$, CI(95%)1.17–7.00). It can therefore be concluded that the more alcohol consumed, the greater the number of driver errors.

Example from the literature: randomised double-
blind placebo controlled trial of neutroceutical
supplement (IntestAidIB) in people with irritable
bowel syndrome

Dancey *et al.* (2006) carried out a clinical trial to determine whether a neutroceutical product (nutritional supplement) improved symptoms of irritable bowel syndrome. Thirty-seven people with diagnosed IBS rated symptoms daily for 24 weeks. Conditions were baseline (4 weeks when no treatment was given) the experimental condition (8 weeks when participants took IntestAidIB capsules) and a placebo condition (8 weeks when participants took the placebo, which were identical to the IntestAid capsules but without the active ingredients). There was a four-week 'washout' period between the placebo and experimental condition, during which participants took no capsules. A repeated measures ANOVA was carried out on each of the seven symptoms. The authors presented the mean severity ratings under each of the conditions, with 95% confidence intervals and Eta^2 as a measure of effect. The graph and text from the article is reproduced below (see Figure 10.5):

Figure 10.5   Mean symptom severity ratings with 95% confidence intervals

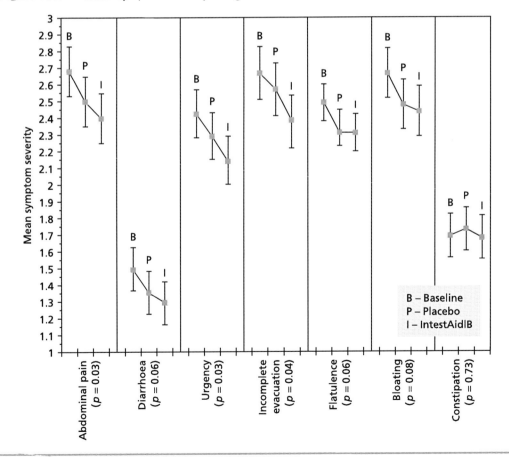

A repeated measures ANOVA on each of the symptoms was carried out. Sphericity was not assumed and therefore the Greenhouse–Geisser correction for degrees of freedom was used. The difference between conditions for abdominal pain ($F_{2,67} = 3.71$; $Eta^2 = .10$), urgency to have a bowel movement ($F_{2,64} = 3.82$; $Eta^2 = .10$) and a feeling of incomplete evacuation ($F_{2,67} = 3.52$; $Eta^2 = .09$) were significant at $p < .05$. Diarrhoea ($F_{2,58} = 3.08$; $Eta^2 = .08$), Flatulence ($F_{2,70} = 2.89$; $Eta^2 = .07$), Bloating ($F_{2,68} = 2.61$; $Eta^2 = .07$) and Constipation ($F_{2,49} = .31$; $Eta^2 = .01$) were not statistically significant at $p < .05$.

Symptom severity for all symptoms (except constipation) are in the expected direction of baseline > placebo > IntestAidIB.

Summary

- ANOVAs allow us to test for differences between three or more conditions.

- ANOVAs are suitable for data drawn from a normal population – they are parametric tests.

- ANOVAs allow us to assess the likelihood of having obtained an observed difference between some or all of the conditions by sampling error.

- Planned or post-hoc tests show us which conditions differ significantly from any of the other conditions.

- Partial eta^2 is a correlation coefficient that can be used as a measure of effect in ANOVA. It lets us know, in percentage terms, how much variance in the scores of the dependent variable can be accounted for by the independent variable.

Discover the brand new website at **www.booksites.net/dancey** where you can test your knowledge with multiple choice questions and activities, discover more about topics using the links to relevant websites, and explore the interactive flowchart designed to help you find the right method of analysis.

SPSSFW exercises

Exercise 1

Enter the data from Table 10.9 into SPSS, analyse it by the use of *ONEWAY* (which is in the Compare Means menu), and obtain the results. Perform a post-hoc test. Copy down the important parts of the printout. Interpret your results in terms of the experiment.

At the local university, students are randomly allocated to one of three groups for their laboratory work – a morning group, an afternoon group and an evening group. At the end of the session they were given 20 questions to determine how much they remembered from the session. Were there differences between the groups, and, if so, in which direction?

Table 10.9   Data from morning, afternoon and evening laboratory groups

Morning		Afternoon		Evening	
P1	15	P11	14	P21	13
P2	10	P12	13	P22	12
P3	14	P13	15	P23	11
P4	15	P14	14	P24	11
P5	17	P15	16	P25	14
P6	13	P16	15	P26	11
P7	13	P17	15	P27	10
P8	19	P18	18	P28	9
P9	16	P19	19	P29	8
P10	16	P20	13	P30	10

Exercise 2

There is some evidence to show that smoking cannabis leads to short-term memory loss and reduced ability in simple tasks. Seven students, smokers who normally did not take cannabis, were recruited to answer difficult arithmetic questions, under four different conditions. In the placebo condition they smoked a herbal mixture, which they were told was cannabis. In condition 2 they smoked a small amount of cannabis, increasing to a large amount in condition 4. Students were required to smoke cannabis alone. To avoid practice effects, there were four different arithmetic tests, all at the same level of difficulty. To avoid the effects of order and fatigue, the order in which participants took the tests was counterbalanced.

Results are as follows:

Participant number	Placebo	Low dose	Medium dose	High dose
1	19	16	8	7
2	14	8	8	11
3	18	17	6	3
4	15	16	17	5
5	11	14	16	7
6	12	10	9	8
7	11	9	5	11

Enter the data into SPSSFW, analyse with a repeated-measures ANOVA, and write up the results in the appropriate manner.

MULTIPLE CHOICE QUESTIONS

1. Parametric one-way independent ANOVA is a generalisation of:
   (a) The paired t-test
   (b) The independent t-test
   (c) χ^2
   (d) Pearson's r

Questions 2 to 4 are based on the following information:

Alice, a third-year student, noticed that she and her friends learned more statistics when they were in Madame MacAdamia's class than in Professor P. Nutt's. They could not determine whether this was due to the style of the teaching or the content of the lectures, which differed somewhat. For her third-year project, therefore, she persuaded three statistics lecturers to give the same statistics lecture, but to use their usual lecturing styles. First-year students were allotted randomly to the three different lecturers, for one hour. At the end of the lecture, they were tested on their enjoyment of the lecture (ENJOYMENT), and also on what they had learned in the lecture (KNOWLEDGE). Alice then conducted a one-way ANOVA on the results. This is the SPSSFW printout for ENJOYMENT:

ANOVA
ENJOYMENT

	Sum of Squares	df	Mean Square	F	Sig.
Between Groups	94.4308	2	47.2154	.4893	.6141
Within Groups	13798.1240	143	96.4904		
Total	13892.5548	145			

Descriptives
ENJOYMENT

	Mean
1.00	62.9063
2.00	61.2041
3.00	62.9091

2. Which is the most appropriate conclusion?
    (a) There are statistically significant differences between the three groups of students on ENJOYMENT
    (b) There are important differences between the three groups but these are not statistically significant
    (c) There are no statistical or important differences between the three groups
    (d) No conclusions can be drawn

3. The following is also given with the above printout:

Test of Homogeneity of Variances
ENJOYMENT

Levene Statistic	df1	df2	Sig.
1.3343	2	143	.267

What can you conclude from this?
    (a) The variances of the groups are significantly different from each other
    (b) The variances of the groups are similar
    (c) The variances are heterogeneous
    (d) None of the above

4. Here are the results for the KNOWLEDGE questionnaire, which the students completed after their one-hour lecture:

ANOVA
KNOWLEDGE

	Sum of Squares	df	Mean Square	F	Sig.
Between Groups	110.3100	2	55.1550	5.3557	.0057
Within Groups	1482.9689	144	10.2984		
Total	1593.2789	146			

Descriptives
KNOWLEDGE

		Mean
1.00	P.Nutt	10.5781
2.00	MacAdamia	10.0408
3.00	Cashew	12.3235

Which is the most sensible conclusion?

(a) There are significant differences between the groups on KNOWLEDGE; specifically, Colin Cashew's group retained more of the lecture than the other two groups

(b) There are significant differences between the groups on KNOWLEDGE; specifically, Madame MacAdamia's group retained more of the lecture than Professor P. Nutt's group

(c) There are significant differences between all of the groups on KNOWLEDGE; specifically, Professor P. Nutt's group retained more of the lecture than the other two groups

(d) There are no significant differences between the groups on KNOWLEGE

5. The *F*-ratio is a result of:

(a) Within-groups variance/between-groups variance

(b) Between-groups variance/within-groups variance

(c) Between-groups variance × within-groups variance

(d) Between-groups variance + within-groups variance

6. The relationship between the *F*-ratio and t-value is explained by:

(a) $t^3 = F$

(b) $F^2 = t$

(c) $t^2 = F$

(d) $f^3 = t$

7. Professor P. Nutt is examining the differences between the scores of three groups of participants. If the groups show homogeneity of variance, this means that the variances for the groups:

(a) Are similar

(b) Are dissimilar

(c) Are exactly the same

(d) Are enormously different

8. Differences between groups, which result from our experimental manipulation, are called:

(a) Individual differences

(b) Treatment effects

(c) Experiment error

(d) Within-participants effects

9. Herr Hazelnuss is thinking about whether he should use a related or unrelated design for one of his studies. As usual, there are advantages and disadvantages to both. He has four conditions. If, in a related design, he uses 10 participants, how many would he need for an unrelated design?

(a) 40

(b) 20

(c) 10

(d) 100

10. Individual differences within each group of participants are called:

    (a) Treatment effects
    (b) Between-participants error
    (c) Within-participants error
    (d) Individual biases

11. Dr Colin Cashew allots each of 96 participants randomly to one of four conditions. As Colin Cashew is very conscientious, he meticulously inspects his histograms and other descriptive statistics, and finds that his data are perfectly normally distributed. In order to analyse the differences between the four conditions, the most appropriate test to use is:

    (a) One-way between groups ANOVA
    (b) t-test
    (c) Pearson's r
    (d) Repeated-measures ANOVA

12. The assumption of sphericity means that:

    (a) The variances of all the sample groups should be similar
    (b) The variances of the population difference scores should be the same for any two conditions
    (c) The variances of all the population difference scores should be similar
    (d) The variances of all the sample groups should be dissimilar

13. If, in an analysis of variance, you obtain a partial eta^2 of 0.52, then how much of the variance in scores on the dependent variable can be accounted for by the independent variable?

    (a) 9%
    (b) 52%
    (c) 25%
    (d) 27%

14. Calculating how much of the total variance is due to error and the experimental manipulation is called:

    (a) Calculating the variance
    (b) Partitioning the variance
    (c) Producing the variance
    (d) Summarising the variance

15. The following is output relating to a post-hoc test, after a one-way ANOVA:

Multiple Comparisons
Dependent Variable: Current Salary
Tukey HSD

(I) Employment Category	(J) Employment Category	Mean Difference (I–J)	Std. Error	Sig.	95% Confidence Interval	
					Lower Bound	Upper Bound
Clerical	Custodial	−$3,100.35	$2,023.76	.276	−$7,843.44	$1,642.74
	Manager	−$36,139.26*	$1,228.35	.000	−$39,018.15	−$33,260.37
Custodial	Clerical	$3,100.35	$2,023.76	.276	−$1,642.74	$7,843.44
	Manager	−$33,038.91*	$2,244.41	.000	−$38,299.13	−$27,778.69
Manager	Clerical	$36,139.26*	$1,228.35	.000	$33,260.37	$39,018.15
	Custodial	$33,038.91*	$2,244.41	.000	$27,778.69	$38,299.13

* The mean difference is significant at the .05 level.

Which groups differ significantly from each other?

(a) Clerical and custodial occupations only
(b) Custodial and manager occupations only
(c) Manager and clerical occupations only
(d) Manager and clerical plus manager and custodial

16. Look at the following output, which relates to a repeated measures ANOVA with three conditions. Assume sphericity has been violated.

Tests of Within-Subjects Effects
Measure: MEASURE_1

Source		Type III Sum of Squares	df	Mean Square	F	Sig.	Partial Eta Squared
FACTOR1	Sphericity Assumed	542.857	2	271.429	7.821	.007	.566
	Greenhouse–Geisser	542.857	1.024	529.947	7.821	.030	.566
	Huynh-Feldt	542.857	1.039	522.395	7.821	.029	.566
	Lower-bound	542.857	1.000	542.857	7.821	.031	.566
Error	Sphericity Assumed	416.476	12	34.706			
(FACTOR1)	Greenhouse–Geisser	416.476	6.146	67.762			
	Huynh-Feldt	416.476	6.235	66.796			
	Lower-bound	416.476	6.000	69.413			

Which is the most appropriate statement?

The difference between the conditions represented by:

(a) $F(2,12) = 7.82, p = 0.007$
(b) $F(1,6) = 7.82, p = 0.030$
(c) $F(2,12) = 7.82, p = 0.030$
(d) $F = (1.6) = 7.82, p = 0.031$

17. Which is the most appropriate answer? The effect size is:

(a) 5.7%
(b) 57%
(c) 0.57%
(d) 5%

Questions 18 to 20 relate to the output below, which shows a repeated measures ANOVA with three levels. Assume sphericity has been violated.

Tests of Within-Subjects Effects
Measure: MEASURE_1

Source		Type III Sum of Squares	df	Mean Square	F	Sig.
COND	Sphericity Assumed	521.238	2	260.619	5.624	.019
	Greenhouse–Geisser	521.238	1.073	485.940	5.624	.051
	Huynh-Feldt	521.238	1.118	466.251	5.624	.049
	Lower-bound	521.238	1.000	521.238	5.624	.055
Error (COND)	Sphericity Assumed	556.095	12	46.341		
	Greenhouse–Geisser	556.095	6.436	86.406		
	Huynh-Feldt	556.095	6.708	82.905		
	Lower-bound	556.095	6.000	92.683		

Pairwise Comparisons
Measure: MEASURE_1

(I)COND	(J)COND	Mean Difference (I–J)	Std. Error	Sig.[a]	95% Confidence Interval for Difference[a]	
					Lower Bound	Upper Bound
1	2	−11.857	3.738	.058	−24.146	.431
	3	−3.429	1.494	.184	−8.339	1.482
2	1	11.857	3.738	.058	−.431	24.146
	3	8.429	4.849	.339	−7.514	24.371
3	1	3.429	1.494	.184	−1.482	8.339
	2	−8.429	4.849	.399	−24.371	7.514

Based on estimated marginal means
a. Adjustment for multiple comparisons: Bonferroni.

18. Which is the most appropriate statement?

    (a) $F(2,12) = 5.62, p = 0.020$
    (b) $F(1,6) = 5.62, p = 0.050$
    (c) $F(2,12) = 5.62, p = 0.049$
    (d) $F(1,6) = 5.62, p = 0.055$

19. Which two conditions show the largest difference?

    (a) 1 and 2
    (b) 2 and 3
    (c) 1 and 4
    (d) They are identical

20. Assuming that the null hypothesis is true, the difference between conditions 1 and 2 has a:

    (a) 5% chance of arising by sampling error
    (b) 6% chance of arising by sampling error
    (c) 19% chance of arising by sampling error
    (d) 20% chance of arising by sampling error

References

Dancey, C.P. Attree, E.A. and Brown, K.F. (2006) 'Nucleotide supplementation: a randomised double-blind placebo controlled trial of IntestAidIB in people with Irritable Bowel Syndrome', *Nutrition Journal*, **5**: 16.

Howell, D.C. (2006) *Statistical Methods for Psychology*, 6th edn. Boston: PWS-Kent.

Soar, K., Turner, J.J.D. and Parrott, A.C. (2006) 'Problematic versus non-problematic ecstasy/MDMA use: the influence of drug usage patterns and pre-existing psychiatric factors', *Journal of Psychopharmacology*, **20**(3): 417–24.

Sullivan, G., Blewett, A.E., Jenkins, P.L. and Allison, M.C. (1997) 'Eating attitudes and the Irritable Bowel Syndrome', *General Hospital Psychiatry*, **19**: 62–4.

Answers to multiple choice questions

17. b, 18. b, 19. a, 20. b

1. b, 2. c, 3. b, 4. a, 5. b, 6. c, 7. a, 8. b, 9. a, 10. c, 11. a, 12. b, 13. b, 14. b, 15. d, 16. b,